Memoir of a Wildman

by Timber Cleghorn

ISBN: 979-8-9917999-0-4

Created with the helpful input of Jacob Dufour
Edited by Laura-Lee Alford

For Levi, Elliot, and Brooke

Foreword

As I read Timber's thoughts about how his *Alone* journey unfolded, I was amazed by the depth of his writing, tying together the struggles of survival in the Arctic with the struggles of his past.

I was blessed to meet Timber in the Arctic as we simultaneously launched the most exciting journeys of our lives, in some of the harshest land imaginable. During our short times together, we created an unbreakable bond of friendship that will last forever. Never in my life have I met someone with a more interesting backstory, more creative thoughts, and more raw determination. You'll be impressed by the challenges you see and the practical wisdom you learn throughout this book.

Whether you are a seasoned survivalist, a complete amateur, or even uninterested in wilderness survival at all, this book will teach you valuable lessons for every aspect of your life. Timber's tale is a masterclass on how to compete with your own mind, conquer your worst fears, and overcome unimaginable struggles. You are certain to learn survival tactics that you have never seen before. Further, you'll love the amazing stories dotted throughout the book showcasing Timber's adventurous life that forged him into what he is today.

By the time you reach the end of this story, you will likely experience your own transformation, by just getting a glimpse into the mind of one of the finest, strongest, and kindest people I've ever met.

— Dub Paetz, fellow contestant on *Alone: Arctic Circle.*

Table of Contents

Train to Nowhere..1

The Cut...9

The Truth...21

The Lay of the Land...35

Opportunity..63

A Time to Kill...91

Work..110

Shift...130

Wild at Last..148

The Loose Ends...167

Tremors..185

Turmoil..203

Life..218

Peace..233

Freeze-up...266

Winter..277

The Mental Game..291

Silence...313

Darkness...346

The Deadly Cold..367

Choosing a Path...380

Epilogue..388

Chapter 1

Train to Nowhere

*   *   *

If I give all my goods to feed the poor,
if I give my very body to be burned,
and do it all without love,
I am nothing.
- 1 Corinthians 13:3

The rocking and jolting of iron wheels is the first thing I'm aware of. Gusts of cold air blow down my neck. Slowly I open my eyes, trying to claw through layers of sleep. The long night has been endless, and I'm exhausted. The half-hour or so of sleep I've just tasted has put me under so deeply that my memory feels temporarily erased.

"Where am I?"

A train. I'm on a train. I look around, seeing the weary, tear-stained eyes of the people packed in around me and it all comes back in a flood of reality. I'm riding with people who have just lost everything. They're leaving their homes, their lives, everything they've known, putting it all behind them in the smoking ruin of war.

There are thousands of people riding with me, hundreds in this car, dozens crammed into the aisle where I'm drowsily waking up. We're so packed in that many people have had to stand up all throughout the interminable night. Most of them haven't slept for days, carrying their belongings and their children, moving west from car to bus to train, fleeing the Russian onslaught against Ukrainian cities like Kharkiv, Sumy, Irpin, Bucha, Mariupol, and Kherson. This is the most restful moment they've had since the missiles started falling.

My brain still foggy; I close my eyes again and try to savor the delicious remnants of sleep. It's cold. I must have slept a bit. When I open my eyes again, an early morning glow of frost-chilled sunshine streams through the big picture windows all along the train.

Struggling to reach the window without upsetting anyone's carefully balanced luggage and the sleeping people sandwiched among it, I get my first glimpse of a breathtaking vista.

The countryside of Poland sweeps by. I didn't know there were forests in Poland; I thought Europe was one continuous city. But here before me is a pristine forest landscape, swathed in ice and sparkling in the silver dawn sunlight. Here and there, meadows push the trees back from the railroad, and in those meadows stand small herds of deer feeding silently.

The frost steams gently as the sun heats it. The resulting fog frames the deer in mist that changes from silver to gold as the light grows stronger. They look like a painting. It's too peaceful, too good to be real.

Back inside the train, I consider what brought me here to this moment. I think about my mission and wonder whether I accomplished it. I came to Ukraine on the first day of the invasion, and I've been working with my buddies, all combat medics. We came to bring medical aid, strong hands, and a good word—to help people, any people. We've done everything we could do: setting up casualty collection points, evacuating people from areas near the front. We've brought truckloads of medical supplies, bandages and tourniquets. Most of us have spent everything in our bank accounts. But have we made a real difference? The question plagues me.

My buddies are still there doing the work, but I'm leaving. It hurts to leave them there. But looking around me on the train, my woes seem small. These families have all suffered for real. Nearby sits a woman whose husband was killed two days ago by a missile strike on Sumy. Beside her is a young girl, just married, who left her husband behind defending their city of Kharkiv. During the night she's tried to act brave and console the newly-made widow beside her. But I can see the fear of loss in her eyes.

Beyond them sits a grandmother who believes she won't ever see her home or any of her sons and grandsons again. Beside the grandmother is a shell-shocked woman of forty. She can't see the child she's holding because her eyes are still staring at the image of her oldest son's lifeless body lying on a snowy street in Bucha.

A little brother and sister sit beside me. They never make a peep or close their eyes. They just stare at nothing. I don't know what their little eyes see, but I can imagine. Everyone in this crowded mass of rumbling metal is a speechless statue of sadness.

Undisturbed by the clattering machine passing by, the deer go on feeding and the meadows roll on, each different but full of life. The frost steams, and the steam glows. The trees beckon, and the dawn light streaming through the train windows grows stronger.

In the face of such peace, the war is made slightly smaller. Destruction has not yet ruined everything. This land is just what it should be, the essence of tranquility, a cradle of life.
And to me, it's much more that that. It's home.

I grew up in the woods of Southern Indiana, and the woods have always been to me the welcoming voice of home. Now my soul reaches right through the window to touch this woodland. If I could just get there, sit quietly in the frozen trees, all would be well. I wish I could rush out into that gleaming frost and forget the world that is. I could lose myself out there and become one of the creatures who belong. I thirst for the woods, for the peace of solitude in a wilderness untouched by the chaos of war.

Taking a moment to glance up and down the packed isle of refugees, I see every eye fixated on the same vista. They're staring out the window just like I am, drinking in the same peace.

They all seem to rouse from a shock-induced coma, drawn into the world of freedom, beauty, and vibrant life in those woods. It's so free, so beautiful, so full of life. Each one of these people must be thinking that it looks so different from the world they know, and I have no doubt, wishing to live in such a world. They're thirsty too.

My heart hurts for these people, but I've reached the end of my service to them for this season. I'm leaving to help my family and community in another desperate situation, but at this moment, I just want to be in the wilderness. I want to be alone. The thought feels so good, so needed.

Where my wife and kids are waiting for me, another violent conflict has broken out. This time the brutality is taking the lives of our neighbors and friends. Under the cover of the Ukraine war garnering the world's attention, this other conflict has raged silently until all freedom of speech and thought has been snuffed out for an entire tribe of people. Innocent people of all ages have been killed. The fatherless homes number in the hundreds, and families are put out into the streets, their homes bulldozed to rubble.

I arrive weary from the Ukraine mission and find the town we call home wracked by grief. Our formerly peaceful community has been turned into a trauma-stricken land of silence and loss. We get to work immediately distributing aid and words of encouragement.

Months later, I'm spent. I've done what I could do, worked as hard as I can work. We've distributed groceries and aid, sat with the grieving to share their pain. But yet again it seems too small an effort to matter.

So many of my close friends have died over the past brutal year. On top of it all, I've lost my own little brother, Silas, to a drowning accident back in the States. His death hurts in a way that I've never felt before. My soul is tired now, and empty. I've lost myself somewhere along the line. Deep inside, I understand that it's time to go home and figure things out.

The trip home is a blur of conflicting interests, wanting my family to be safe and well, but knowing that we've left our friends behind in a situation they can't escape. At some point I let go, and as I stare out the plane window I remember my longing from the train. The idea of being alone in the woods hasn't left me since that train ride. It has only grown.

As I step onto American soil I'm not ready to face the rhythms of every day life. All the noise bothers me, whether it's a helicopter or just traffic. Gun shots from hunters make me want to grab my boys and hide them under a couch. Whenever a kid on the playground shouts or squeals it makes me tremble. I hate that I can't just be normal. For no good reason, I'm a bit of a wreck.

Then one evening, sitting in a quiet house, my kids turn on a TV show I haven't thought of for a long time. I can overhear the narrator from where I sit in the kitchen.

"On *Alone's* most dangerous season yet, ten survivalists must endure isolation…"

Quickly joining my kids on the couch, I see the ten contestants heading into a northern forest to disappear for three months, and somewhere in my heart I start longing for what they have. I'm back on that train, looking out the window at the frost and the deer.

"That's what I want to do right there," I say aloud, though no one hears me because my family's attention is riveted on the first episode of Season Eight.

"What if I could just get on that show?" I muse. "What's holding me back?" I think about it as I only half pay attention to a contestant trying to chase down a mountain lion.

For years I've refused to watch the show because after watching one season, I wanted to apply so badly that I was almost beside myself. But I couldn't apply because of the missions and work I was involved in. There was too much that had to be done.

That went on for years, hearing about new *Alone* seasons and having friends tell me, "Hey, there's this show you should apply for. You're perfect for it."

I know I'm cut out for the show. My whole life has pointed me at it. I've lived that life of surviving off the land for real, starting as early as my first memories. And now I realize that for the first time in my life I don't have anything stopping me. For the time being, I literally have no other plan.

"What am I going to do?" I ask myself the question a thousand times a day. There are many other conflict zones where I could work, many missions I could join. But I see how weary my whole family has become and I think back to that train where I just stared out the window and longed for the wilderness.

My family is in a quiet, safe place now. They're going to be okay. But what about the wilderness? Can I finally lose myself out there among the rivers, lakes, and trees?

After less than ten minutes of thought, I've decided to apply for the show.

"Hey Babe, I'm applying for *Alone*. What do you think?"

My wife is cooking supper in the other room, enjoying a quality American kitchen for the first time in years.

"Yeah, why not?" She replies. "You should do it. If you're lucky enough to get on, you'd really benefit from all that peace and quiet."

"I'm applying right now."

As I type up a resume that looks pretty flimsy to me, I ask God to allow it to happen. I also ask for one more thing: "God, will you bring me there and show me something? Show me again who you are, who I am, and what I should do next."

*　　　*　　　*

One Year Later

I am alone. Perfectly alone, as I have been for nearly three months now. Standing at the very top of the North American continent, where the sun disappears as the world freezes. As lost and isolated in the wilderness as a man can be, with only ten tools to help me survive, and a camera to tell the story.

For several hours I crunch through the snow, wrestling with the choice I have to make. My fish lines and snares are all buried deep in snow and I dig down to check and reset them. The arctic landscape is smothered in winter, the river frozen, the lakes a glassy sheen of windswept ice. There is no sound except for my soft footfalls and heavy breathing. No animals move out in the whiteness. No birds caw overhead. Everything has left this area to escape the deep cold. Everything, that is, except me. I'm still here: alive, well, and happy. I am alone, and against all odds, I'm getting to live out my dream from the train. But what has it all meant? Is this everything I had hoped it would be? Has it beaten me, or built me up?

I'm not beaten. I've made a real home in this wilderness. I'm not just surviving, but thriving with food to spare and a good place to live in. I have done everything I dreamed of — hunting, eating and living free. Every challenge has been faced and overcome. I have rushed out into this forest and forgot the world that was. I have lost myself and become one of the creatures who belong. Though my thirst for the wilderness isn't quenched, I've drunk as deeply as a human being can drink.

The choice I wrestle with today is a new one: "Should I stay?"

A week ago I couldn't have even imagined asking myself that question. Never did I dream that anything could take away my reason to finish this race. But something is different now. I don't need the things I thought I needed then. Something much more valuable has taken place. I'm not the same person who arrived in this wilderness months ago. My spirit is reborn.

*   *   *

This is the story of how that took place. It's told to the best of my memory. The events are sequential, just as they happened. My mind may have misplaced some things by a day or two on the timeline because I didn't keep a detailed calendar, but I've done my level best to relate everything exactly as it took place.

I chose to approach this story in the most open and transparent way possible, just like I was encouraged to do on camera during the show. It means that there are embarrassing things, harsh things, even shameful things to be revealed, but I haven't concealed anything or shied away from hard topics. I haven't made anything seem better or worse than it really was. I hope this brings the story to life, and maybe even helps someone dealing with the same types of baggage I took with me to the arctic.

Chapter 2

The Cut

*   *   *

From childhood's hour I have not been
As other were—I have not seen
As others saw...
-Edgar Allan Poe, "Alone"

"Yes!" I scream under my breath. My friend who has been walking through the hardware store beside me startles and asks what's going on.

"I just got an awesome email." That's all I can say, but inside I'm bursting with joy, reading and re-reading the words.

"We've received your application for *Alone Season Eleven*, and we're interested in hearing more about you. Please respond to schedule a call with a casting specialist."

That's where the process started. After four months of tough auditioning, I find myself on the phone once more, my spine tingling with anticipation.

"Well, the network has made their final decision, Timber."

My heart almost stops, but I have to keep driving. I'm cruising a winding highway in West Virginia, heading to meet one of my

Marine buddies and closest friends, Sky Barkley. We're camping together with our families for a few days. The silence on the other end
of the phone call spans only a couple seconds, but it seems endless.
If they haven't selected me, then a lot of effort, serious effort, has
been for nothing.

"You're in!"

"Whoooyahhh!" I yell. "You're serious?"

"Yep! Congratulations! You're going to be on Season Eleven
of *Alone*. You've got one month to get ready."

Struggling not to veer off the road and crash, I grip the
phone in disbelief. I've been holding my breath and hoping for something like this ever since that train ride out of Ukraine. This is what I
need so badly right now and what I've dreamed about all my life. I
can hardly believe it's going to be a reality.

"Well, where are we going?" I can finally ask. The location is
everything. Not knowing has been killing me.

"It's going to be particularly cold. You'll be well inside the
arctic circle, further north than the show has ever been."

"Wow, that sounds great!" I reply. But it doesn't sound very
great to me. I'm thin and have bad circulation in my feet. I've had
frostbite twice and it's no fun. "How cold?"

"Check your email. I'm sending you an introductory page on
the area."

After parking the truck I download a page with a very vague
location and a short writeup on the area.

"Wow, this is *way* up north!"

The Mackenzie River Delta will be the location. I've never
heard of it, so I'm surprised to find that it's the second largest river
delta in North America. The Mackenzie River drains almost as much
of the continent as the Mississippi, flowing northward to empty into
the arctic ocean. Most of the shows previous locations (such as Great
Slave Lake) shed their water into the Mackenzie River, and then the

water travels hundreds of miles further north until it fans out into a myriad of river channels and lakes just before it hits the Arctic Ocean. Looking at a satellite view on Google Maps, I see the immense swamp and my heart sinks a bit. This enormous, boggy delta is where my *Alone* experience will take place, much further north than I anticipated. It's going to be a hard location, but it's where I'll have to survive and build a life.

Reading and re-reading the info sheet sent by production, a few details stand out to me right away. The location will be at the northern extent of the forest, only ten miles or so from the tree line. There is an extremely high number of grizzlies. During one study, thirty-seven different grizzlies showed up on one camera trap during the span of a week. There could even be the odd polar bear, although they tend to stick more to the coastline.

My heart sinks as I read more details. There will be arctic hares, but their population is on the declining side of their cycle. Grouse numbers are really low, and fishing could be difficult. The water quality is bad, full of mud and silt, and most discouraging of all is the fact that the location scout claims he hasn't seen a single rock or stone on several scouts.

My heart jumps for joy when I read that moose are on the menu. I've been hoping to be allowed to shoot big game, so that detail pleases me greatly.

Over the course of the next two days of camping and fishing, I try to digest all the details and end up believing that this location is going to be particularly challenging. I'm excited to face any environment that they might throw me into; it's the chance of my lifetime, and I'd go no matter the location. But I have to take a moment or two just to admit that I am daunted. It's not the grizzlies or the polar bears or wolves that worry me. The weather is the scary thing. If it gets as cold as the info page warns about, that temperature could kill.

Camping with Sky is a fun way to get my head screwed on right for *Alone*. He always challenges me with his ideas, and his warrior mentality helps me steel my mind for the adventure ahead. We've been through some massive experiences together, and he's also a big fan of the show. He has forged a mind-blowing knife for me to take, anticipating that I would get cast. I guess he had more faith than I did about me getting on the show.

We fish for an afternoon and he catches several nice rainbow trout while I catch nothing but a couple of little suckers.

"You'd better get your fishing dialed in before you get to the arctic, buddy," Sky tells me with a grin.

"I know. I'm really not much of a fisherman, bro, but hopefully I'll get it together."

That afternoon fishing and sitting around the fire turns out to be the last peaceful hours I get to enjoy for the next five chaotic weeks. As I drive home, Sky's parting words ring in my ears. We had sat by the fire late one evening while cooking trout and talking about what my time on *Alone* might look like. My kids were poking sticks into the dwindling fire and my wife, Cara, had just gotten out the chocolate to make some s'mores.

"Look," Sky began seriously. "I hope you intend to tell your story while you're out there."

I pause, pondering his words.

I have a strange life story. It's filled with chaos and weird happenstances. Growing up in total isolation, being often mistaken for Amish people, secretly training on all kinds of weapons and survival tactics - my childhood wasn't dull. In my adult life, I've stayed on board the crazy train, doing very different things, but equally bizarre, from cutting timber and working construction, to ducking bullets and missiles in war zones on the other side of the world. I've met the Taliban in one village and been mistaken for the Taliban in the next, climbed mountains that had never been summited, escaped from ambushes, had antitank missiles pointed at me, explored un-mapped caves, and published text books. It's a weird life. But through all these experiences, I've found meaning and hope that has brought me out from deep darkness.

I don't really want to discuss any of those things once I'm filming the Alone show, however. I'm a private person. I've been thinking I could focus strictly on survival and who I am now, instead of digging into the past very much.

I look up at Sky. "I haven't decided how much to tell."

"Tell everything," Sky said with conviction. "Don't hold it back. You never know. It might help somebody. Do you think there's no one else out there facing a life of fear and looking for the answer?"

Sky is one of the very few people who know my story. When two guys go through deep experiences together, like war, you tend to trust those people with your deep truths. So he knows how I grew up in a militia training camp from the time I was five years old, training to survive a collapse of society and conduct insurgency warfare. It made me tough and resilient, but there was darkness too. I've told him how I almost took my own life and that I found hope instead.

Later, driving the seven hours toward home, I think about what he recommended and I wonder if I can do it. Can I talk freely about my life, unashamed to have all the details out there where people can see?

It's easy to relate how my life has brought me to *Alone* and made me a survivalist and a wilderness man. There's no difficulty in saying that I grew up completely isolated and off-grid. My family of eleven kids lived without electricity, running water, and the associated conveniences that define modern life. It was an odd blend of pioneer life mixed with Marine Corps boot camp.

Living that way can be healthy and good. It's also easy to talk about how we lived off the land, growing and killing almost everything we ate. Life was all about survival, and we worked hard to make ends meet. Because of that, I'm no stranger to living hand-to-mouth.

I can also say that we were extremely poor. There's no shame in that. But it's the dark parts of the story that I don't want to discuss, and that's not just because ignoring it would be easier.

Darkness and fear - those are the primary memories of my childhood. They shaped me in ways that I appreciate, but it wasn't fun. Nothing peaceful or good comes from a culture of constant fear and overwhelming punishment. But I never dwell on the hurt I may have absorbed, and I don't want anyone to bear the blame for the darkness and fear I thought was normal as a kid.

For me, escaping deeper into the woods every time I had a chance was what kept me alive. Alone in the woods and creeks is where God always met me and promised me I'd find hope and life. I did find it, and that's what I want my life to be about. My preference would be to ignore everything that's led to this point in my life and think of nothing, talk of nothing but the wilderness.

"Bro, seriously," Sky had insisted. "Do you want whatever story you live out there in the arctic to mean anything? Then give it some context. Tell the whole truth. Let people see what God can do."

I know that Sky is right, so I decide to take what he said seriously.

"Ok," I had replied. "I'll do it." But I still don't know how I will.

After some struggle, I finally decide that I will just let life happen naturally. I won't hide anything when it's time to talk about it. I'll let my story play out however it does, and that's what I'll film and preserve for the show.

Preparing for *Alone* is no small task, but it's easy compared to the other stuff I have to accomplish before heading to the arctic. I long for a chance to focus on just survival prep, but that's not going to happen.

When I applied for the show my schedule looked pretty simple. I was in limbo professionally, not really knowing what to do next. It seemed like the perfect time to go into the wilderness for an extended period. But now that the audition process is over and the network has made their cast decisions, so much has changed. I find myself buried beneath several huge projects.

I'm building a massive barndominium, having won the bid together with my two close friends, Adam and Jacob Dufour, just weeks ago. My aid work also demands that I make several overseas trips to tie up the loose ends of projects and meet with people. And I've just moved my family into an old farmhouse that needs lots of work to make it comfortable. Cutting a winter's worth of firewood for my wife to burn while I'm gone is also a must-do. All of this turns the preparation phase into a nightmare. Each morning I'm at work early, my two partners and I working like mad men to get the building project done. I work almost up to dark on the construction job, come home and try to practice with my bow before it gets really dark.

Each day after the sun sets, I end up being on the phone translating for refugees who are arriving in New York from places I have worked over the previous few years. That sometimes takes hours. Getting off the phone, I'm so stressed out from translating that I can barely think. Then I try to spend some time with the kids and after putting them to bed, dig into study and bushcraft experiments.

Trying to pack on weight and build up some fat reserves is a good strategy, but it's not working for me. I eat and drink as much protein and fat as I can, but every day I sweat the weight right back off as I work.

Researching and ordering gear takes a load of time. Making the handmade gear I'll need takes even longer. With only five weeks to prepare, I stay up late into the night every day.

Weekends occasionally bring a few free hours, but my home needs a ton of work. I have to fix water pipes and a leaky roof. And even more often I end up driving to some distant city to meet with new arrivals among the refugee community.

The efforts push me toward physical exhaustion. With any downtime I get, I study the Mackenzie Delta area and try to come up with a survival plan that I feel good about. During hours of nocturnal research I ask the questions, "How will I approach this land? What will the challenges be? How did native tribes subsist here?"

Some of my early plans turn out to be of no use, given that it's a river delta I'll be living on rather than a lake. Over the summer I've developed a lot of strategies for lake survival, including a bushcraft sailing catamaran, with which I had hoped to harness the power of wind to reach deep water and fish. But that will be useless. I can see that making good snowshoes will be a much more useful skill to work on.

Above all looms the question of which ten items will be the best selection for helping me live and thrive in the arctic.

Selecting ten things to survive with shouldn't be that difficult, but it gets more complicated as I narrow the choices down. My only chance of procuring big game is by taking a bow. But if I select a bow and there's no big game, I've wasted my choice and really hurt myself. Considering how rare it is for a contestant to kill big game, the odds of such a disappointment are staggering. There is about one chance in a hundred that I'll get to kill a moose.

Other options present complications as well. If I select fishing hooks and the fishing is no good where I end up, I've hurt my chances. And what if I get to the land and realize I have no need for my saw? I could choose a block of salt instead.

My mental gymnastics go on and on. The decision is only complicated because I have no control over what piece of land I'll be facing. Usually in a survival situation, I would have the freedom to move some distance to get to a place where I could utilize the tools I bring. But not on *Alone*. Without doubt, one of the most difficult facets of this competition is that a contestant can't know exactly what he's up against until it's too late to adjust anything. When I step off the helicopter, then I'll know if I've chosen well. Until then, everything is just a wild guess.

I end up with the following list of gear, hoping I've made the best choices:

1. Sleeping bag
2. Bow and arrows
3. Knife
4. Saw
5. Ferro rod
6. Cooking pot
7. Paracord
8. Fishing hooks and line
9. Snare wire
10. Leatherman multitool

I decide to gamble on taking the bow, knowing that if I see a moose and can't kill it, I'd never forgive myself. But I carry with me a realistic sense that I may never get a chance at big game.

Everyone wants to kill a large animal, like a moose or bear. The benefits of such a windfall of red meat and fat are clear. But there is a reason that big game has only been killed two or three times on the show. It's because hunting big game isn't as simple as it may seem.

The main problem with hunting big game is the enormous range that large animals need. They roam so far that no little patch of land given to a contestant will "contain" a moose. It can simply be crossed by a moose as the animal wanders for miles each day. It may be there for mere minutes, and that may happen only once or twice per year, depending on the place. If a hunter isn't free to roam miles upon miles with the animals, then his chances of making a big kill are slim indeed.

After researching the moose population in the Mackenzie Delta, I'm not encouraged. A government report published a few years ago claims that the moose population is not very dense. And so after talking with my wife one evening about the low chances of killing moose, she says,

"Well, I'm going to pray that God will be at work bringing animals to the spot you'll land."

The idea seems ambitious, but I like it. So together we pray.

"God, please arrange for a moose to make its way to whatever land Timber will end up on, and keep it there till he kills it."

"Amen," I say, and somehow I'm at peace with taking my bow.

The five weeks pass so quickly that I feel woefully underprepared as I load up my gear and prepare to launch into one of the biggest adventures of my lifetime. While my family and I drive toward the airport, my oldest son Levi pipes up with a question from the back seat: "Dad, if you could take one person as one of your ten survival items, who would you pick?"

There's an unconcealed gleam in his eyes, and I know he believes that he and I would make the strongest pair of survivalists the world has ever seen. He just wants to hear the words, "Levi, I'd pick you buddy." My heart swells with emotion. As a dad, that gleam of happiness radiating from my son's eyes at the thought of doing something together with me, that's the best thing the world has to offer. And so I say, "Levi, I'd pick you buddy." And I really mean it. Then I add, "As long as you promise not to eat all the food I catch!"

Saying goodbye at the airport is harder than it's supposed to be. My kids are both crying as I get out of the truck, and I can tell that my wife's eyes are dry only because she's trying to be strong for the boys. She's barely holding it together.

"Dad, promise you won't tap out because you miss me," Levi says, all the while sobbing big tears that almost rip my heart out. He's building me up and tearing me down all at the same time, but he doesn't know it. This is just how he gets through. The number of times he's had to say goodbye in his young life can't even be counted.

Because of my work, my family has moved thirty-eight times in twelve years. There are a lot of goodbyes hidden in that, and they never get any easier. My kids are so used to making friends and biding them farewell forever, as well as seeing me off to some foreign country or another not knowing when I'll be back. You'd think it would make us stronger, better at the goodbyes, but it doesn't work like that. We seem to get worse at it every time.

So Levi and Elliot cry, and I don't try to stop them. They deserve to show what they're feeling.

It's time for me to say goodbye to Cara. She's the love of my life, and we can usually read each other's thoughts. But suddenly I find myself completely without any idea of what to say. So many times we've said goodbye, with me assuring her that things will be ok and I'll be home again soon. But this adventure is different somehow. She and I won't be able to communicate at all. We won't be able to lift one another up on bad days, or compare notes about the thoughts and plans we have. We won't be able to know how the other's day went or what challenges we've faced. And we have no idea how long this will take or when we will see each other again.

Standing beside the truck mute and silent, I wish I could think of some strong-hearted words. But I can't think of anything at all. The only thought in my mind is wondering whether I've showed her the kind of love that will stand by her while I'm gone.

Cara breaks the silence, and I'm glad for her initiative.

"I believe in you," she tells me. "You're the toughest man out there. Plus you really need this. You'll feel so much better in the woods." And then she looks at me with that shiny glimmer of advancing tears. I'll never forget her parting admonition: "Be a wildman. Go get drunk on the wilderness!"

The faith my wife and kids place in me is an honor and a heavy responsibility. They're my whole life. I wonder how I will cope without experiencing all three of them, their days, joys and challenges as the next few months roll by.

Shutting those thoughts down quickly, I head into the airport.

At the ticket desk I have to explain my baggage to the agent.

"Do you have any weapons?" She asks as her eyes land on the big rifle case I'm carrying my bow in.

"Yes," I reply without thinking and realize that it was a mistake as soon as the words come out of my mouth. The ticket agent's eyebrows shoot straight up through the roof of her head, and she's opening her mouth to yell for security. I have to quickly explain that I have no guns. "There's just an axe, a bow, and a knife. Survival tools."

"Oh, ok!" she breathes a sigh of relief.

Getting my bags checked in is the last challenge I face, and as I board the plane I can rest. Finally there is nothing to do. Whether I'm ready or not, nothing can be changed or added now. I'm destined for one of the greatest adventures of my life with just ten items, for better or for worse.

Chapter 3

The Truth

*　　*　　*

*"It does not require many words to speak
the truth." -Native American Proverb.*

Feeling the plane start to descend, I crane my neck to get a glimpse of the landscape slipping by beneath us. The low, gray clouds obscure all but quick glimpses of the delta, until I land and exit the little airport that services the remote town of Inuvik.

My first glimpse of the terrain I'll be surviving in feels inauspicious and gloomy. The sky is a leaden gray; as I drag my luggage outside, the damp air feels chilly and unwelcoming. A fine mist is falling. Digging through my pack, I pull out my rain jacket and shrug into it. It already feels like fall.

"Throw your gear into that truck and we'll head to the boats." A production assistant points out a 4x4 pickup, and I stuff my gear into the back.

It's a short ride to the jetty where the boats wait. I grab a bag to load, but the production folks stop me.

"We've got it from here—you just get in that other boat and ride!" They yell.

I'm uncomfortable with someone else handling my gear, but they won't let me touch it. So I board a boat, and soon we're rocketing upriver, closing in on the spot I've been dreaming about, studying and stressing over. I can't wait to see it.

Mud. Mud and willows. That's my first thought as I watch the terrain slip by along the river shore. The boat speeds on, churning the already chocolate brown waters, but my eyes are searching for survival resources. No hills, no high ground. Rotten banks caving away into soupy waters. No forests, not much usable driftwood. Lots of willow brush.

"This could suck," I tell myself silently. I won't voice any of my concerns aloud. But this terrain doesn't look promising to me. Swampy, muddy willows.

We motor around a sweeping bend and the basecamp comes into view. There's a row of white canvas tents with a larger tent positioned at one end. People are already there milling around, watching us pull closer.

One group of contestants arrived the day before, and as we jump ashore they greet us like old friends. They're shaking hands, slapping us on the back and shouting "Welcome to camp!" Everyone acts like they've known each other all their lives. Each one of them has open, honest faces and down-to-earth attitudes. It's easy to feel that holistic, leathery energy that wilderness folks all have. I already like these people.

It takes me just minutes to get settled into basecamp. I'm pleased that I have my own tent. I had expected to bunk with several people, but it will be great to have privacy. I'll be able to think, plan, and draw up my final strategy in solitude and silence.

The next morning I'm outside early to get the feel of the land. The river is drifting by tranquilly, its constantly muddy waters hiding whatever fish or food it might contain. The beach alongside our tents is covered with grizzly tracks, and a crew member stands by with a shotgun at all times in case the bear decides to come back and stroll through camp.

The weather is drizzly and cold; I'm worried that decent weather is already completely finished for the season. But though the sky is dreary, there is a fantastic energy in camp. Each of us is happy to be here and excited to get started. Several of us begin the day by taking practice shots with our bows at a target the crew set up. Most of them shoot far better than I do.

The next few days are a blur of activity and preparation. Each morning we're all up early and eating breakfast in the main tent. The cooks go all in to make sure we're well fed. The meals are healthy and substantial.

After eating, we start training on various aspects of filming the show. The most important part of basecamp is the camera training. The crew does everything they can to ensure that we know our way around the electronics that we'll use to capture the experience. We set up mock hunting scenes and discuss the ways to frame shots, learn different types of storytelling and work through solving technical problems with the gear.

$$* \qquad * \qquad *$$

All my life, I've been intrigued with filming. But when I try doing it, bad things happen. I tried my hand at making movies once, working with a production company founded by my brother Daniel and the Dufours. It was great fun working with those guys. But when I'm around cameras, nothing ever works out like I saw it happening in my brain. I imagine a scene being safe and quick, then something inevitably goes off the rails. If I continue with that track record on Alone, the filming will surely kill me.

Once, we made a film about a European girl who joined ISIS in Syria. I'll never forget the lengths we went to for that project. One night I was ramming a truck into a dirt bank over and over again to get a crash scene "just right." The next day we were igniting canisters of gasoline with black powder and shooting exploding targets to simulate grenades. I broke a rib, and we almost gave several crew members heat stroke while filming in 120°F desert heat. Another crew member nearly asphyxiated on the pyrotechnical effects we used. Then we needed a mirror to be shattered by a bullet for a particular scene, I grabbed my actual rifle and threw a live shell in, handing it to Adam. "I trust you, just shoot the dang mirror." The bullet had to go right past my head and strike the mirror. When my wife found out about that stunt, she was livid. "You're never filming anything again!"

All of those stunts were supposed to be safe and easy, but somehow things went off the rails. So I hope my luck with cameras changes here. I can just imagine myself slipping through a hole in the ice while trying to film myself fishing or something.

It's not just filming that presents hazards, though. I can be really hard on electronic gear too. Once, on an adventure in Western China I set out with a brand new drone, eager to film the world's highest natural arch. Shipton's Arch is a true marvel that few people know about. The Empire State Building could fit beneath its stone bridge.

I was really excited about flying through and over the arch with that drone. I had never flown a drone before, but I figured it couldn't be too difficult.

Reaching the remote canyon where the arch was supposed to be found, I took out the drone and launched it. Immediately I lost connection because of the tight canyon walls, and it flew directly into the ground at top speed, shattering into fragments - its first and only flight. There was nothing left but my GoPro to film with, and it felt pointless as I climbed the rest of the route, marveled at the arch, took a few shots and went home carrying the bits of broken drone.

*   *   *

And so I'm glad they're providing this training and sending me into *Alone* with some GoPros, knowing that if I break everything else, these hardy little cameras will still work. The crew says that I'll learn to love the camera, but I really doubt it.

During camera training it becomes clear what the Alone challenge is about. We thought we were here just to catch fish and chop sticks and kill squirrels. But that's not the case at all. We're also here to film. The real question is not just whether we can survive this wilderness, but whether we can do it while also filming every step of the way. The filming dramatically changes every aspect of the challenge.

Right away I can tell that the camera work is going to make an already hard job into an almost impossible one. It exponentially multiplies the work that must be done.

I like to move around light and fast. Especially when setting up a survival camp, I tend to sprint around like a caffeinated chipmunk, poking my head into holes and snatching resources to use wherever I see them. Being burdened down with not only the gear required to film, but with the responsibility of setting up multiple shots of everything, resetting up shots when I move to another spot, staying aware of linear story-telling and keeping up with batteries and media cards, I feel completely hobbled. The song "Don't Fence Me In" comes to mind, and I chafe and chafe at the restraint. The filming also takes a ton of time and burns a lot more calories.

But I constantly remind myself that one of the main things I want is for my boys to see my journey, and the only way to make that possible is to film everything. The cameras will hurt my survival effort, but it's the only way to tell the story.

Late one night the wolves make a big ruckus behind our camp. They're hunting and we can hear some prey animal bellowing or crying. Comparing notes the next morning we all conclude that a moose was killed not far from the basecamp. This makes the wild aspect of the land feel very real.

Every contestant feels a constant urge to evaluate the others' skill and strengths. Each one is gauging how good the others are, which is nearly impossible because we're all hiding some parts of our strategy. But learning who is strong and mature is easy, and those qualities make more difference to me.

Only once do I sense a slightly hostile edge amongst the group. One evening we're all talking about the risks and dangers. I comment about the annoyance of the "y-bones" in the pike. A contestant I like a lot throws a challenge at me and says, "Well, you could just go home now and save yourself the trouble."

I grin back, but say nothing. I know he's trying to see if I have a weak psyche, a crack in my resolve. Later, when he's alone and wondering who is left in the competition, it would comfort him to know that I lacked conviction. However, this is not the first time I've ever faced pressure to abandon my path and go home.

*   *   *

There was once a taxi driver who tried to scare me away during a humanitarian project. The Middle Eastern area I worked in was fairly hostile, and some of the people hated westerners. The driver scowled for most of the trip, breaking the silence once to say, "You know, we had a foreigner around here before. He died and his body was cut up into little pieces." He looked at me for a reaction, obviously hoping that I'd be frightened. But instead I smiled and said, "Great! Let's go see the body!"

There was also a time that I was apprehended by police while passing through a small village in the middle of nowhere.

"Don't you know that no foreigner is allowed here?" The commanding officer screamed at me.

"I'm sorry if I've broken a law," I said. "But I'm just a visitor passing through."

The officer yelled at me for another half hour, then demanded I give him my new boots as payment for letting me go.

In Central Asia, people have tried to stab me and hit me with cars. Once a man tried to stab me right in front of my family. After I caught his arm and yelled at him for minute, the assailant humbly asked forgiveness. "But brother," he pleaded. "Can I have some money anyway?"

*   *   *

Now, I don't scare away easily, but in this competition the mature contestants give me pause. I know that with maturity comes an indifference to suffering. Immature people feel the sting of isolation and suffering much more keenly. A fact of life is that once you've faced enough difficulties you come to a point where you say "Eh, sure it hurts. This is life. I didn't expect anything different." So I watch the more mature contestants with the feeling of dread that they can't be discouraged by discomfort.

One of the last processes of basecamp is a series of interviews where we sit down one-on-one with the producers and talk about our lives, who we are and what brought us to this point. This turns out to be the hardest part of camp for me.

I really like the producers, but they are relentless when it comes to probing into my life. They seem to possess an uncanny knack for knowing where the sensitive material is and asking questions that lead straight to it. They'd make excellent interrogators. But I'm resolved to be as open as possible anyways.

After an hour of questions I find myself getting emotional about the things that brought me to apply for *Alone*. We discuss my brother Silas's recent death and how it affected me, and we talk about aid missions in Afghanistan, Ukraine, and a couple of other countries. All summed up, it's a lot of death and failure.

"Wow," the producer says. "You've got a lot to think over out there." Then he mercifully turns the questions toward the topic of survival. "What's your strategy? How do you think you'll handle insolation, starvation and possible death? Do you think you're the best contestant here?"

This is the part where I could make inflammatory and over-confident claims. Clearly, they're looking for that person who will say "I'm the best that's ever been. I'll kill a grizzly with my bare hands. Survival in the arctic is like baby food to me." We all admit that those statements make great TV, especially when they play while the person taps out. So I try to avoid any fantastic claims.

"My strategy is to be proactive." I believe very much in the philosophy of taking initiative. Good things don't just happen. Instead, we make tomorrow though today's actions. I have no extra fat to burn, so I'll die if I sit around. I'm going to work harder, explore further, and try not to miss any opportunities. But I believe that God will create opportunities for me and instinct will guide me to them.

"What's your number one advantage over the others?" the producer prods.

I have to think about that for a moment. I know I'm not the greatest shot with my bow. I don't practice every day of my life like some of these folks. It's impossible to carry a recurve and some practice arrows when you're hopping from country to country, so my marksmanship has suffered. All of the others can snare, trap, and fish just like I can, maybe better. Some have been professional guides for years. I definitely don't have the weight advantage. I'm the smallest and lightest man here. But I don't see that as a handicap. Instead, it might be my one saving grace.

"I'm the size and build of ancient man," I reply. "I see that as my advantage. The land is going to see me coming and breathe a sigh of relief. My metabolism can be supported by an average wilderness biome."

I sound bold and certain, but inwardly I have no idea if I'll benefit from being smaller like I claim I will. It makes sense though. And there's one other thing that could set me apart.

"I'm used to suffering. It doesn't surprise me."

There will be suffering for sure. All of us will taste it. But who will drink that cup and keep asking for more? That person will win. Could it be me? Maybe.

Launch day is approaching, and a fever-like intensity rises among the contestants. We want to get out to the land and begin. Each person deals with the anticipation in their own way. The atmosphere in camp feels very much like when you're in a war zone waiting on something to happen. There's a period of stagnation that's bearable at first, but eventually the anticipation reaches a pitch that's almost worse than the real thing. It builds until you end up secretly wanting whatever is coming to just get on with it, like "just go ahead and shoot at us already!"

One more process remains for us to go through before launch: gear check. It's all about making sure no one smuggles items like sugar, salt, or antibiotics into the competition. The crew goes through our gear with a fine tooth comb, then sets it aside to be given back to us at the time of launch.

There are stories circulating from previous years about arrows full of sugar or buttons made of salt. Whoever thought of those genius solutions has my full respect. Smuggling is going to be one of the most important survival skills in the day when the world's order comes crashing down. But for this adventure, I've decided to go one-hundred percent above board. I'm not sneaking any items at all. I want this process to be fair and equal, the contestants separated only by skill and fate.

Going through gear checks is old hat for me. Pulling out my tightly folded clothing items, the crew shake them all out and feel down the seams. In one pocket they find a face mask that I forgot, leftover from some flight. Another problem arises when they look at my hand-forged knife from my buddy Sky. There's a divot in the handle created for using as a bow drill socket. That divot is evidently considered an extra item, so I switch the weapon out for my axe, sad that Sky won't get to see his awesome creation at work in the arctic.

My axe presents a problem when they spot a staple in the butt of its handle. I'd just replaced the handle and apparently forgot to pull the staple out of its end. I guess staples could be used as fish hooks, so they pull it out before giving my gear the final thumbs up.

Everything is set now. There are only a few hours of darkness to endure before I'll fly out into the delta and find my plot of land. The preparation is over. Nothing can be changed or altered. The only thing I can do is make my mind rest until the morning.

Rest doesn't come easily on the eve of something so momentous. So many thoughts fill my head. How will this play out? Will I get sick or injured? Only God knows. I trust that he can keep me from those things.

A hundred things could happen which would keep me from winning. But I have to win. I *need* to win. So many of my efforts the last few years have led to disappointment and failure. I've failed to complete major goals, failed to make a meaningful difference in conflict zones, failed to rescue people who were then killed. And recently, I failed to be there when my brother needed me the most, the day he passed away.

After so much loss, so much failure, I can't even contemplate losing. Even just the thought of losing *again* is too much to bear.

"I am nothing and I have nothing but this," I say. "If I lose again, I'll die."

There is no plan inside me for how I'll be okay if I come up short. Statistically, there is a 90 percent chance I'll lose, and I have no idea what happens then.

I'm also suddenly very uncomfortable with being judged by people on their couches as they watch my story unfold on the show. The thought of it gets under my skin. Lying in bed, I consider whether I even want this at all.

It's inevitable that thousands of naysayers and armchair critics will watch the things I do and there will be drama about what I should have done instead. I'll make mistakes that people will laugh at. I'll experience accidents that make me look foolish. Can I film those voluntarily? I've thought about it for months, and now, all of the sudden, it's a big deal. It feels like I'm shooting myself in the foot.

Every viewer looks at their screen and correctly thinks, "I could do that." Whatever the survivalist is doing at that given time, you could do. He might be casting a fishing lure and pulling it in. That's pretty easy. He might be cutting up some wood. Also not difficult. But viewers are only seeing 5 minutes out of a 24-hour day. What they're watching is a quiet moment of fishing after the man in the arena has worked like a beast for ten hours to cut trees, carry stones, or stalk food. Each thing he does that day is a critical decision, and the decisions add up into the thousands. There will be lots of mistakes, and those mistakes make great TV. They'll be presented, while the quiet things the man does right will be left on a hard drive of forgotten footage. A multitude of actions and decisions surround that 5-minute glimpse of casting and reeling a fishing line or carving a spoon, and those are the hours that are harder to get through, especially when those hours are complete darkness.

After much thought, I decide that I will film my mistakes anyways and not be ashamed of them. If my sons see me fall and get back up again, perhaps they will take courage as they grow to be men who will do the same.

Tonight I get one last opportunity to talk to my family, and then the crew will take my phone and store it with my other belongings.

Dialing my phone, I'm happy to see that the camp's connection is strong enough for a video call. My wife answers and I see my beautiful family there in my house, playing a game on the living room floor. They're smiling, and my heart swells watching their faces. They're mine—the three people that make up my world. I'm blessed to have such a world. The picture of them laughing and enjoying life etches itself into my brain. It's a sight I won't get to behold for a long time.

The camp supper is delicious, but I struggle to decide whether I should stuff myself or eat lightly to help my stomach. I swallow as much food as I can and head to my tent where I light up a fire against the cold wind.

It hits me that this is the last time for a while that I'll eat a meal prepared by someone else, sleep in a tent set up by someone else, and burn firewood cut by someone else. So I savor the luxury and enjoy the overstuffed comfort of warmth and a full belly.

After tossing some wood into the fire, I crawl into the cot and play an audiobook quietly from my phone.

Turning on an audiobook seems to clash with the wilderness setting. But listening to a book or music is the only way I've been able to get to sleep for the past few years. My brain doesn't shut down easily.

My thoughts drift to the other contestants as I try to sleep. I like all of them and in any other situation, I'd root for them to win their half-million dollars. But in this event they are my competitors. I like them but I need to beat them.

It's been tough to judge their skills and their mental strengths. I've studied them all for days and while I've noticed a lot of things, I completely give up guessing which ones will push this competition to the end. There's only one thing I know for sure: none of them want it as badly as I do.

The winner really could be anyone. The toughest people are sometimes the ones you don't suspect. As I've witnessed time and again in dire situations, strength rises from anywhere. I can't evaluate or judge these people any more than I can fly. But the wilderness will judge us all tomorrow. And the wilderness always tells the truth.

*   *   *

If you've been lucky enough, you've had that one friend who always says things exactly like they are. It's the person you go to when you want to see right through the muddy water and get back to what's simple and good. They don't dance around your feelings, trying to please you. They're not afraid to tell you the plain truth in the clearest words.

I've been lucky enough to have such a friend. When I left home as an insecure kid who didn't even know how to order food at McDonald's, I met a great guy named Wes and we became fast friends. We trained horses and did rodeos together for several years. Most days after we spent a few hours breaking a horse or trail riding, he'd suggest that we sit down at a nice Mexican restaurant. I had no money at all, but Wes wanted to do it and he never let me pay.

Eating out was really stressful because I didn't know what any of the food was on the menu, never having been to a Mexican restaurant before. Chicken tenders on the kids' menu was the only thing I recognized. So that's what I would order.

One day after watching me order the chicken tenders for about the sixth time, Wes set down his diet Coke and drawled, "If you're gonna order chicken strips every time, we ain't comin' here no more. They're a lot cheaper down at the Dairy Queen."

That directness caused me to branch out and learn what other menu items were. I loved the food, but even more I loved having a friend who would just say whatever needed to be said.

*   *   *

I've always seen the wilderness as that kind of a friend. It always tells the truth. When I wonder if I'm really a woodsman, only the wilderness can answer that question. And it will do so plainly and definitively: "Yes, you're a woodsman," or "No, you don't have the skills you thought you had."

I've been asking myself whether I've chosen my ten items well. The land will soon answer me with a simple "Yes" or "No." Have I prepared well? The wilderness will tell me.

I'm certain the wilderness will also give me answers I don't want to hear.

"Have I processed the past? Have I put things behind me? Am I a resilient person? Do I have a strong mind?" The land may answer "No," and I may not like to hear it. But at the end of the day, it's good to have the truth. The wilderness doesn't lie. It has no reason to. It doesn't need to please me or spare my feelings. It simply is. I'm eager to hear the truths that this wilderness will reveal. And tomorrow will be the day that it all starts unfolding. I'm ready.

Chapter 4

The Lay of the Land

*　　　*　　　*

*"Maybe it's not about the happy ending. Maybe it's
about the story." -Albert Camus*

I believe that the land is just as much a character in the story
of *Alone* as the human contestant is. The resources it contains, the
wildlife it attracts and sustains, the situation of the terrain, and the
weather currents—all of those factors and more determine the path
of the human survivalist. They make the difference between successful hunts or failed attempts, freezing or staying warm, and thriving
happily or just scraping by through sheer determination. Understanding the land and knowing what it offers at a glance is the highest level
of survival acumen. I hope that I can get it right.

"Will my patch of land be a good partner?" It's the biggest
question on my mind. "Will it play along? Or will it coldly offer nothing, breaking me down?"

Day 1

My eyes open early to a dark tent. The sun hasn't come up
yet. I instantly snap awake, unlike most mornings where I like to lie

around for a few minutes and ease into the day. The first thought coursing through my mind is, "It's here! It's happening!" I should feel nervous, but I don't. After being in a lot of stressful situations, I've developed a sort of mental zone based on muscle memory that helps me to do the next thing when my mind is asleep, foggy, or over-whelmed. I slip into it whenever I find myself in an experience that I can't wrap my head around. This is one of those experiences. It's going to be too huge to fully comprehend.

I felt this way last year when I entered Ukraine. The invasion was just two days old when I entered the country, and my brain was a bit overwhelmed wondering what to expect. So I relied on the muscle memory of keeping alert, keeping my gear tight, keeping fed and strong, and keeping my mind open for any event that would transpire. This morning I decide to start there. I roll out of my bag and slip into my boots, checking my gear and clothes. A chill wind is ripping at my tent, but I feel excellent. I'm ready!

My tent is almost empty. Yesterday during gear inspections, we contestants were stripped down to the gear that we will take into the field. So grabbing my bow, I step outside into Day One of *Alone*.

Outside my tent, I glance up and down the row. Some people are up and moving about. A few tents already have smoke chugging from their stovepipes. A group photo and aerial shots of us departing for the chopper are scheduled for sunrise so we've all decided to make our morning fires extra smoky so that the shot will look cool as the aircraft flies over the camp. The air is cooler than I expected and that triggers the first electrified impulse inside me which shouts, "Get moving! Winter is coming! Kill something to eat!" It will only grow louder over the coming hours and days.

My neighbor steps out of his tent and I greet him. We stand there for a few minutes holding our bows and taking in the vibe of the waking day. Neither of us say much. We just stand there.

To me it feels nice to start the journey slowly like this, being able to take the moment before sunrise to digest what's happening and try to remember what it all means to me. I think about my two boys at home and their unwavering faith in me. I remember my wife's parting words, "Go get drunk on the wilderness!" I ponder my friends' support, which takes me all the way back to my first introduction to *Alone*.

One of my best friends had seen Season One and told me about the show's premise. I felt a weird pang inside, like when you know you're missing out on something special. I watched one season that drew me in so intensely that I refused to watch any more for years. It was simply too painful to sit there and watch other people doing the stuff I love so much. I wanted to do it myself! The desire to be out there gnawed on me…and now here I am.

The sky slowly begins to brighten, but I can tell the cloud cover is going to hang around. This will be a gray day. The production team arrives at our row of tents, and suddenly the morning's events pick up pace. We line up for filming the departure sequence, one of the few moments that a professional camera crew is shooting film.

The producers guide us through a series of shots. First, they line us up in front of camp where we shoulder our packs. We have to grab our bows, turn to the left, and walk down the line of tents while looking ahead at the chopper. I focus on that line of incredible survivalists, tough and talented men and women. They look amazing. All of those leather quivers, the arrow fletching, fur-lined hoods, beards, long hair, wool sweaters, axes, and knives. It's a sight to behold; I wonder for the millionth time how I'm going to out-perform them. I don't dwell on it, but I just marvel for a minute at how capable each one looks. I think almost any of them could do a hundred days. We look like frontiersmen, masters of the wilderness. I'm one of them, and it feels awesome!

We line up for the shots several times so that they can get all the angles they want. Someone cracks a joke: "Man, at this rate of calorie burning, we'll be losing weight before we even leave base camp."

"Yeah…lousy strategy for Day One!"

A few of us chuckle nervously.

Before I know it, I'm standing in a circle with the others at the far end of camp watching the helicopter arrive, ready to launch the first contestant.

"Whomp, whomp, whomp." The prop wash blasts our faces with dust and bits of grass as the helicopter settles in. Day has fully dawned, but as promised, it's gray and chill.

The producers make sure each contestant has a camera out and rolling. From this moment forward, we're responsible for all footage that will be captured. A crew member provides a safety briefing so we can board the aircraft and stow our gear. We don't know who will be first or in what order we will launch, but I'm really hoping for an early launch. I have a mental list of objectives for the first day which I've rehearsed until it's part of my DNA. But I need all day to accomplish those goals. An anxious and eager sigh escapes my lips. "I just want to get to my land and get started."

One thing that I like about the *Alone* production system is that it's very direct. No motion is squandered, no energy wasted on fanfare and nonsense. Even something as momentous as launch day is not over-dramatized. The film crew got those sunrise shots this morning; otherwise, the team gets us on the chopper and ships us out without much ceremony. It's simply a crew of professionals trying to get ten people and their tools out onto the land.

The first name is called and that contestant is guided onto the chopper and disappears to the east. Just like that. As we wait for the helicopter to come back we check little details about our gear for the millionth time. Each contestant tries to say something that reflects their mental resolve, like "Hey, I'll see you guys next year," or "If I never come back again, just leave me be!" A few wish each other good luck or share a hug. These are good people. It strikes me that in just minutes I will leave my last footprint in the world of people, companionship, and familiarity. Launch is happening!

The chopper is back now, settling into the deep grass. My name is called and a thrill shoots through me. I'm second! Yes! I couldn't ask for anything better. I grab my gear and hand it to a crew member who stows it. I'm particularly worried about my bowstring being damaged, and I shout over the rotor's roar, "Watch out for my bow!" The guy nods back at me, and I climb on board.

The helicopter lifts, and we're veering away from basecamp. Beneath us, the weird delta landscape slips by, dotted with ponds and lakes, laced by river channels and broken by ridges of rock. It's a treat to look out over that vast river delta before I'm down in it and won't be able to see around. I try to take it all in while filming my own reactions and answering questions. A crew member queries, "What are you thinking right now? What will your strategy be when you get off this chopper?"

Those questions are easy to answer. I don't even have to think about it. My strategy is the same for almost any context.

Step 1: Secure the gear by setting up a temporary camp.

Step 2: Secure water.

Step 3: Scout to understand the landscape.

Only one thing has changed for me since basecamp: seeing that pike can be caught with fresh bait, I plan to immediately get some organic bait and start up my fishing lines. I desperately need that first bit of guts or meat to start catching fish with, and I take a second to ask God about that.

The helicopter begins dropping toward a shallow lake in a meadow. A flock of ducks and two huge swans take off from the water right in front of the chopper. It looks like a scene from National

Geographic as the helicopter swoops past the waterfowl and begins to settle into the meadow. This is my first glimpse of the land that is to be my partner for this challenge.

I get only a quick glimpse at the lay of the land, and I see terrain in which movement will be very difficult. A large curve of river, a smattering of lakes and ponds, all choked in a suffocating mass of dense brush. There are no other features that stand out as landmarks, no apparent system to the topography.

Suddenly the horizon disappears as the chopper settles in, and I'm down in the terrain.

"Alright, make sure your camera is rolling," someone shouts to me over the noise of the helicopter. "We're here. This is your spot!"

The chopper comes to rest and someone opens the door. I climb down and drag my backpack behind me until I'm just outside the radius of the rotor blades. A crew person hands me my bow, and relief surges when I see that the string is intact. I grip the bow in one hand and the camera in the other. The rotor wash generates a cyclone around me, obscuring my vision. As bits of grass and dirt storm my face, I keep my head bent down and try to film while the helicopter spools up to depart.

I'm supposed to film every bit of the drop sequence. I remember shouting something ridiculous like, "This is it!"

I must sound just like every other contestant who has ever filmed a launch. All the normal stuff. "This is it! It's finally here! That chopper is the last piece of civilization that I'll see for three months!" All the same lines. But as the chopper fades away behind me, I feel that somehow my experience will be absolutely unique. Something about this will be unlike anything I've seen or dreamed of before.

I keep the camera pointed at myself until the helicopter vanishes over the horizon and all is quiet. It's strange how long I've looked forward to this very moment, how much time I've spent imagining what I would feel as the sound of the helicopter died away. But in the reality of this moment, I actually feel nothing—no huge sense of isolation, none of the "drop shock" that contestants talk about. I don't even have some amazing sense of happiness about starting my dream adventure. I really feel nothing at all except the compulsion to get started on my day's work. The "muscle-memory" zone that I've come to rely on has kicked in and will propel me like a machine for a while.

It's just me and my tools now on the land, but before I make my first move, I want to ask God for something. I've begun to feel strongly that I need something that He has, something that must be here waiting for me. Before heading off into the brush, I take a knee. "God, would you be with me?" That's all I say out loud, but inside I'm asking for something more. I'm asking for answers, for some connection that can shed light into the dark, dead-end tunnels I've reached inside. After this venture, I want to know what's next in life. So I pause for a moment, offer prayers spoken and silent, then I forget about it. I'm ready.

I drag my backpack through the willows and into the nearest clump of spruce trees, immediately nocking an arrow to my bowstring. But as I glance around at the brush, still swaying from the choppers roar wash, I can't imagine that I will see anything today, let alone loose an arrow at something. The trees fall silent. I sit still for ten minutes or so, giving myself time to adjust to the sounds and smells of the environment. A light dripping of water droplets from the spruce limbs is the only noise to break the stillness.

I'm immediately struck by the thought that I would never choose this area to set up a shelter for winter. The ground is low and soggy, looking like it has been submerged recently.

Damp ground can spell the difference between freezing or staying warm. The dampness also affects all of the porous materials I'll rely on, from logs and firewood to fire tinder. It makes everything harder. I may camp here today, but there is no way I want to battle this damp, swampy material for long. There has to be higher ground with better spruce cover. I'm sure that I'll find it.

A theory enters my brain that the production crew dropped me in a poor shelter location just to see whether I will be complacent and stay put, or if I would be proactive enough to find that ideal spot somewhere else. It's something I would do if I were in their shoes. Well, I'm nothing if not proactive, so tomorrow I'll begin my general scout of the territory and select a much better location. For today however, I need to bivouac here and quickly.

Getting to my feet, I make sure a GoPro is strapped to my bow and recording. A faint moose trail runs through the middle of a band of spruce trees choked with alder. Glancing down the trail, I spot what seems like a denser patch of evergreens. I'll just scout this band of trees for a place with thicker cover, drier ground, and some straight material for poles. My senses alert, I start slowly down the trail.

Twenty or thirty paces into my scout, I hear a small but un-mistakable chewing sound.

"That sounds like my first meal," I think. Growing up as I did hunting in the Indiana hickory woods, I know it's a squirrel who has gnawed through the soft material covering whatever nut or seed he's eating and is down to the hard inner shell. Those little squirrel teeth make a hard, scraping sound.

Unfortunately, my hearing is actually pretty bad. I've abused my ears for years: those soft inner ear bones can only take so much gunfire and explosions, and my hearing is about fifty percent gone. Locating the source of sounds has grown incredibly difficult. Although I can hear this squirrel, I can't tell which direction his gnawing noises are coming from. I search the trees all around and see nothing. I'm about to take another step when I catch movement out of the corner of my eye. A red squirrel sits on the ground about ten feet to my right, just chewing on a pine cone and watching me, not alarmed in the slightest. I draw my bow slowly while turning, come to full draw and let it go. The arrow *thwaps* that little guy right in the middle and he's dead.

I quickly dive onto the squirrel in case he revives and makes a break for it. Seizing it by the neck, I lift and examine it. I can hardly believe my luck! Twenty minutes into my *Alone* experience, I've killed my first food. Much more importantly, I've secured my first fish bait! I'm elated.

Thanking God is the first thing I do with any and every animal I kill. I see life as a gift from God. To honor that, I hold the squirrel up toward the sky and whisper, "Thank you for this beautiful creature. I value its life."

Then I perform another ritual that I've developed. I dip my finger in fresh blood from the squirrel's wound, lift my right shirt sleeve, and apply some blood to the middle of a tattoo that's on my right shoulder: the open teeth of a saber-tooth cat, a wolf track in the center, and two arrows through it. I feed the teeth with fresh blood every time I kill something. It's just my thing, and I tell people that it brings me good hunting medicine. Some people swear that it works for me.

Anyways, having made my first kill, I'm overwhelmingly pleased that I'll have fresh, organic bait to rig up some bank lines today. Carrying the squirrel with me, I head further down the moose path.

The path peters out after another hundred yards and leaves me in an impossible alder thicket. I haven't found a clump of trees that I like for an evening bivouac, so I turn around and head back to my starting point where I placed my gear. I turn on the big camera to shoot an update about my kill.

No sooner do I film a quick update than another squirrel climbs down the spruce tree beside me and stares at me from four feet away. With the camera still running, I grab my bow, slowly turn to my left, and loose an arrow. Even from so short a distance, I miss and my arrow zips off into some alders. I nock another and manage to stun the squirrel with my second shot. He's thrashing around in a clump of dead spruce twigs, but I grab him by the tail. Successfully avoiding his sharp little teeth, I snap the squirrel's head against the tree trunk—my second squirrel for the day, only forty-five minutes into my *Alone* journey. I can't believe my luck!

"God, thank you for this crazy blessing," I say, taking a moment to think about how incredible it is having two squirrels in the first hour. "You're looking out for me." I stroke the fine, red tails of both squirrels and marvel at the lives I've just taken so I can eat.

*   *   *

I realize that this may all seem kind of 'touchy-feely' or too sensitive to some people. But for me, regarding life so highly is a huge change that I see as good. When I was younger, I was a savage killer. I killed everything—any animal that moved or breathed. I thought it made me tough or proved that I was like the frontiersmen I admired.

There was ample opportunity to kill animals, and it was partly necessary because I grew up on a farm, living off the land. Animals always need to be butchered, hunting must be done to provide food for the family, and someone has to put down hopelessly injured and sick animals. But I took it to an extreme.

There was a lot of anger in me during those years - anger and hurt. So I killed animals until I basically got drunk on it, hoping to get God's attention, wanting Him to see how angry I was inside. I had taken the lives of thousands of creatures by the time I was fifteen.

And then one day, I woke up and realized that life is precious. That realization dawned on me the day my older brother, Jon, was shot. When he left home, he moved to the city, hoping for a life that looked very different from home. He got a job delivering pizza; one night a gang tried to rob him on a delivery and he resisted. They shot him, four bullets piercing his body and causing hemorrhage that could have been fatal. Against all odds, though, he pulled through.

As I stood on that street the next day, staring at my brother's blood splashed across the ground, I vowed to be different. My brother Jon and I were always close; we did literally everything together. And the fear of losing the one life that mattered most to me shook me to my core.

Since then, my work in war-torn countries has shown me the horrors firsthand when humans brutally and carelessly take each other's lives. Those experiences only reinforced my conviction that life is the most precious gift. That's why treasuring life is now one of my core values.

One benefit from my old days, though, is that I became pretty skilled at killing. Now, as someone who values life, I'm able to take life quickly and almost painlessly when it's necessary, based on my experience. I've seen people who aren't used to it trying to put an animal down or finish one off. It makes me cringe as the poor person inflicts unnecessary pain on the suffering creature. I just want to step in and make it end quickly. It dawned on me once how unpleasant it would feel to be killed by someone who is bad at killing. That realization made me cringe, and I actually prayed to God that if somebody kills me one day it will be someone who is good and efficient at it.

*   *   *

Anyways, I hang my two squirrels in a tree, get my temporary tarp shelter set up and set a pot of water on to boil. Apparently good fire tinder is going to be even harder to come by than I imagined. Spring flood waters have evidently washed away all the fine, flammable materials and everything left is waterlogged.

Late afternoon finds me down at the river, threading the squirrel guts onto some fish hooks. I measure out about forty feet of my 20lb. monofilament line and tie one end to an alder pole. Pushing the pole down into the mud at the water's edge, I toss the baited lines out as far as they can go. I put out four lines, not knowing how much to expect from this muddy, stagnant river channel. The current is so slow that the lines stay put right where they sink. I'm grateful for that. It would be much harder to fish with bank lines if the current was stronger.

During orientation at base camp, this throw-line fishing method proved successful. Other contestants had brought spinning rods and were testing every type of tackle imaginable, but nobody had gotten a single bite. So I snagged a piece of hotdog from lunch, put it on a hook, and threw out a slack line just for kicks. In a short time, a fat pike had found his way onto my line. Everyone came running to see it and began trying the same thing with pretty consistent results. I'm hoping that this stream will yield similar success.

After boiling some water and drinking my fill, I head back down to the river. No location has grabbed my attention as a good place to set up a cook camp, and I'm pondering that as I approach my fish lines. The first pole is jerking and bobbing around, so I set up the camera as quickly as possible before hauling the fish up onto the shore. It's a pike, about twenty-six inches long. I'm overjoyed at my luck! I glance up the shore and see another line dipping and swerving. I conk the first fish on the head and race upstream to the second pole. This time a twenty-inch pike comes up when I haul the line in.

I'm basically dancing with happiness as I hold the fish up and thank God for it. This must be the best first day ever, and I can't believe it's happening like this!

Two squirrels and these two fish are definitely more food than I can eat this evening, so I put the second fish back in the water to keep fresh overnight, taking care to loop the wire leader through its jaw.

The day is fading by the time I get my cooking fire lit on the north-facing shore where I can watch my fish lines as I eat. Absorbing the atmosphere, I let the fire build into a nice bed of coals. The sun is a mere glow on the horizon now, and the light it throws through the tips of the spruce trees is weak but colorful, pink and gold. The light gleams on the surface of my stream. Here and there, patches of insect larvae swarm on the water. They're being chased and struck at by what must be grayling. A wedge of geese honk by overhead. My fire crackles happily. I've lit it right in the middle of a big set of grizzly tracks. The evening is pleasant. The air is cool but not cold, and the sounds of life all around me add a nice layer to an already perfect evening. I sit in silence on the shore for a while, taking it all in.

As I butcher and cook my fish, two realizations strike me. First, pike is a new species of fish for me, and they're the most slimy fish I've ever touched. Second, I don't know how to cook. My boiled fish and squirrel are tough and unappetizing. The awkwardness I feel preparing it almost alarms me. I've never cooked much. Maybe this is the gaping hole in my bushcraft skill repertoire.

I shove the meat into my mouth anyways. Darkness is settling in, and I'm in a rush to wrap things up at camp before I can't see anymore. I quickly clean up my cooking mess, taking care to bury some fish guts in a high bank. I'll use them for bait tomorrow. Since grizzly bears have walked this bank so much, I take any other scraps that could attract them and toss them into the river. I don't want a bear snacking here and then hanging around my camp.

As I make my way toward my temporary shelter, I realize that today I've worked so hard, I've almost overdone it. However, I've accomplished everything I had hoped for on Day One and then some. I spread out my sleeping bag on a raised platform of poles and

47

drift off to the sound of ducks squawking on the lake. I'm glad to be alive, glad to be on *Alone*, and glad to have a full belly on the first evening.

Day 2

There is no feeling comparable to waking up in a wilderness land, waking up to a day of yet-unimagined adventure and wildness. Morning has broken with gentle sunlight and a sweet smell of late-summer vegetation. The towering spruce trees around my shelter drop gentle shadows that play across my translucent tarp roof.

A cacophony of waterfowl sounds echoing from the sur-rounding lakes is almost deafening. There must be thousands of ducks, geese, loons, and every other type of aquatic bird surrounding me, and they're all squawking. Their chaotic chorus is oddly pleasing; somehow, it sounds like a party. I don't feel alone at all with so many creatures around.

There's a red squirrel, too, *chit-chit-chitting* somewhere beyond the next spruce clump.

From where I lay, I can hear and feel the magnitude of the vast and wild land that surrounds me. I don't even need to see it to feel it's pulse.

I find myself talking out loud to no one in particular, just en-joying how free I am.

"Today is the day I become a wild animal. I'm gonna let in-stinct be the only thing that tells me what to do."

I'm responsible for nobody, and to nobody. There are no set schedules to keep. I am absolutely free to do my own thing. That thought brings a grin to my face. I've always wanted to see what life could be like if I were to live guided entirely by instincts, like the wild creatures. Here is my chance to do that. I'm going to listen to the an-cient voice inside me and just go with it. If it tells me to hunt, I'll hunt. If it tells me to fish, I'll fish. If it tells me to go down a certain trail, I'll drop everything and go.

Realizing just how free I am, I decide to lie up in my sleeping bag for a few minutes (to be honest, that's more from laziness than primordial instinct). This time of day, coffee is all I can think about…that is, until the GPS unit I'm supplied with sounds its morning alert letting me know that I have to check in and tell the crew that I'm ok. That blissful, wild feeling I've been enjoying gets stabbed right in the belly by the intrusion.

I reach over and grab the GPS, sleepily navigate to the pre-programmed text I'm supposed to send, and remember that it won't send from inside my tarp shelter. I push the send button and throw the GPS out into my camp yard. Hopefully, the text will transmit from there while I bask in the warmth of my sleeping bag. Other than this tiny reminder of the outside world, I'm absolutely immersed in the wilderness.

Alone. It's everything I could ask for.

I have only made vague plans for day two, which I rehearse as I boil and eat yesterday's leftover chunk of fish. My main idea is to use this first week to scout around. That feels like the right move: I need to have a good understanding of how the land lays and choose the best shelter location before I start any real work. I also believe that the first few days are magic for hunting. The land and animals don't really know I'm here yet, so this is when I'm going to have those incredible encounters with wild game. I should take advantage of this before I ruin my advantage of surprise by chopping trees or lighting fires.

So my next few days will be all about reading the land. It's imperative that I do this correctly from the beginning. What types of food are here? What activities will be profitable and which are a waste of time? All these factors must guide how to spend my limited time and energy where they will count the most. If I set out a whole snare line and there are no hares, I've wasted my time and I'll lose. If I spend all my time hunting moose and I don't get one, I've wasted my time and I'll lose.

There's a point in time when I'll have to just keep going the direction I've chosen. After a week or two, I'll have spent too much energy on a particular course to turn back and start over. I won't have the luxury of time to change plans, so I have to judge the situation correctly from the beginning.

Before I head out into the bush, I have to make some quick gear modifications. I take my arrows out of my leather quiver and begin filling the quiver with clean, boiled water from my cooking pot. Back at home when researching this area, I got the impression that this region lacks fresh water sources, an issue that could cause serious problems as I try to stay hydrated. Acting on this hunch, I decided to make a special arrow quiver that I could use as a canteen. I sewed it as tightly as I could and sealed it with beeswax. Now it's as waterproof as if it were plastic. It will hold five or six liters of clean water and provide cool, fresh drinking water for days at a time. At the moment, I'm drawing a huge gulp of refreshing water from it and I'm happy.

Now, in order to carry my arrows, I have another invention that takes a little time to set up. I grab my leather arm guard and cut it along pre-marked lines, making two rectangles of leather. Each one has pre-punched holes the diameter of an arrow shaft. Folding each rectangle, I make small cuts with my knife so that an arrow shaft can be snapped or slipped into the punched hole. The leather grips the shaft pretty well. Then all I need is a couple of t-shaped sticks to fix the leather mounts to my bow. I sew a stick into each of the two pieces of leather and attach them to my bow above and below the handle grip with some paracord. When I'm finished, I have a bow quiver that will hold four arrows, and my back quiver is holding five quarts of clean drinking water. I'm pretty pleased with how each of my inventions is working. I grab four arrows, snap them in place on my new bow quiver, and set out along the river shore, feeling happy and ready for anything.

My mood takes a hit when I see that a thieving eagle has taken the fish I left on a stringer yesterday. I should have known better. Now there's only a small chunk of leftover
boiled fish to eat. I kick myself mentally but keep scouting downstream, poking around in every moose trail that I come to. The willows are so thick that the moose trails provide the only way through the brush that lines the river.

Slowly, a birds-eye picture of the terrain etches itself on my mind. I see that my land mainly consists of a horse shoe bend in the river, with my territory lying inside the bend. Where the center of the horse's hoof would be lie the meadow and a couple of lakes. Well, to call them "lakes" may be generous; they're more like swamps with water about a foot or two deep. They're covered with waterfowl, but I can't get anywhere near the birds. Even if I had a rifle and shot a duck out there, I couldn't reach it because of the depth of the mud. Whenever I approach the lake, I sink so deep that I'm afraid of losing my boots forever. I can't even reach a place to fill my cooking pot with water.

The meadow surrounding the lake is vast. It's completely covered in deep horsetail grass. This hip-high grass, also called scouring rush, is a silica-rich plant, so nothing really eats it and it's of little use to me. No rabbits or birds are making their home in it, so the meadow is nearly lifeless. I struggle to walk through it and wish that not so much of my land was lost to this expanse of nothing. The meadow's only positive side is the visibility it offers: I might be able to spot a passing moose.

Overall, then, I just have a dense band of alder trees along the river bank with a few spruce sprinkled throughout the thicket here and there. The spruce trees are the useful ones. They're straight enough to use as building poles and the boughs can be used as cover material. But there is no forest of spruce like I had imagined.

Continuing downstream along the river, I explore each trail and poke around in every hole. It all seems pretty much the same so far. Just a sloped muddy bank lined with impenetrable willow and alder brush.

At last I come to the first distinct feature in the terrain. It's a slightly higher bank on the edge of what must be an inlet in the springtime. If the water were deep, it would connect the lake with the river. Right now, it just resembles a small bay about a foot deep, full of stumps and silt. A beaver lodge sits on the side of the inlet opposite me. It's a bank lodge—the kind where the beavers start by digging dens into a steep dirt bank, then finish by throwing a big pile of sticks against the bank as a roof over the entrance. This beaver lodge looks abandoned. Gaping holes in the bank reveal where bears have torn into the tunnels. I doubt the lodge has been inhabited for a few years.

Finding the inlet seems fortuitous because it grants easy access from the river to the meadow. The bank is high enough that I can see almost the whole meadow, and best of all, a small patch of plantain grows on its sunny edge. It's the only edible plant I've found. I stuff my mouth with some leaves and resolve to utilize every fiber of the few plants that are here, roots and all.

Chewing the plantain, I survey the land from the high bank. Beyond the meadow and lakes I can see a forest of tall willow and alder with spruce poking out above. None of the spruce seems dense like the forest I had imagined-just sparse, ragged trees dispersed in a sea of willow.

I set off on a huge route around the entire meadow, making forays into the willow at intervals. On a map, my circuit would look like a crudely drawn sun. The circle around the lakes lies at the center, with "rays" shooting off in perpendicular lines where my path takes me deep into the willows and straight back.

On each foray into the willow breaks, I find absolutely nothing to celebrate. No ground rises higher than a couple of feet in elevation. No dense patches of spruce offer protection for a snug shelter. I haven't seen any berries or other edibles aside from the small plantain patch on the river bank. I haven't turned up a single grouse or squirrel either.

At this point, I'm beginning to feel like my territory doesn't really offer me much. I had really tried to not expect anything, to have no mental picture of what I wanted it to be like. But I admit that by the time I get back to the lakes and head for camp, I'm discouraged. I try to shoot a squirrel near my shelter and miss, and then I find nothing on my fish lines.

I'm thinking about putting a few more fish lines out when I notice something that sinks my heart right down to my boots. My remaining fish hooks are gone. I had put out a total of thirteen lines earlier, and I took the last twelve hooks along with me, tied to my belt by a strip of leather. I had hoped to put out some lines further downstream. At some point while I was breaking a trail, those impossible willows must have snagged my hooks. Not only did my survey fail to provide the resources I hoped for, the trees pickpocketed a precious resource I'd brought with me. Though I didn't feel it's loss when they stole it, I sure feel it at this moment. I'm left with only the thirteen hooks I had already deployed.

My spirit sinks. Those hooks are so important to me, more important than I can express, and I've just lost half of them. They're not in my gear anywhere. I check five times just to make sure. But it's no use. They're gone. They're out there somewhere on my two-mile path of willow brush.

Discouraged, I decide to take action instead of bemoaning my lost hooks. Taking my axe, I start hacking a path from my temporary camp to the river, tired of struggling through the brush every time I need to get water. If I only have half of my hooks, I'll focus on my other fishing strategies. And so while I chop a path through the alders, I grab any slim willow saplings I see and toss them onto a pile. They'll supply me with materials for making a fish weir.

A three-inch tree horizontally blocks my path. I can sever it with one stroke if I hit it just right. I bring my axe down in a mighty swing. Too late, I realize that the wood beneath the bark is rotten. My axe blows through the tree as if it weren't even there and ricochets off the side of a live tree. Before my brain can process what's happening, my shin is struck full force by the axe head.

My leg feels numb, and I hardly dare to look. I had honed my axe to a razor's edge before coming out here, and I've just swung it Paul Bunyan-style straight into my shin.

Pulling up my pant leg, I examine my shin. There seems to be no blood, and now that feeling is returning I can tell that the axe hit me with its flat side. I have no idea how that happened. It's razor edge should have sliced right into me, but somehow it turned mid-flight. I just avoided a catastrophic injury. Sitting on my newly cleared trail, I pause to rub my bruised but intact leg and thank God over and over.

This incident makes me think work should be over for the day. It's almost dark, and I realize that just like yesterday, I've been working for way too many hours. I hear a voice inside me caution, "Take it easier. You can't win it all in one day."

I repeat the phrase out loud a few times to make sure it sinks in. "Slow down, boy. You can't win this thing in one day."

Day 3

This morning I wake up to find a big pike on one of my lines. Fishing with these throw-lines is turning out to be a gold mine. It's a passive fishing system in that it works by itself, not requiring me to be present. All night while I'm sleeping and all day while I'm out building or scouting, these lines will be fishing for me. The only problem is that many of the fish get away since I'm not there to haul them out as soon as they're hooked. If they swallow the bait, the hook gets them right at the opening of their stomach. In this case, they can't get away unless they break the line. However, if they get hooked in their mouth and they have time to struggle, the hook will come out. So I make my lines extra long hoping that they'll stay slack, giving the fish time to carry the bait around until they taste it and swallow it. I'm seeing a lot of bait stolen, which indicates that quite a few pike are getting hooked by the mouth at night and escaping. But I just keep a pile of fish guts handy and re-bait the lines every time I walk by them.

The pike that I do land exact painful revenge. Their teeth are razor-sharp sabres, poking and stabbing my hands when I reach down inside their mouths. They pierce right through my leather gloves, and every place they manage to stab gets infected almost immediately.

Today's pike is about thirty inches long. While I'm preparing a third of it for breakfast, I decide that cooking is most definitely the hole in my skill repertoire. I feel sure that there's a way to make even boiled fish more palatable. Hoping to get the fats and nutrients from the skin as well as the meat, I boil sections of fish whole.

I've eaten a lot of weird stuff in my travels, everything from roasted sheep heads to raw grub worms. But boiled pike skin is beyond horrible. I feel like I'm chewing a mouthful of frog spawn, and swallowing it requires an elite level of self-control. Other cooking strategies must exist that would make this less disgusting. Once I get home, I'm definitely going to study cooking.

This morning, I decide that scouting will be my focus yet again. I have to find a dry location to build my main camp. So after a quick breakfast of boiled fish, I head out into the surrounding land. I take my bow, one GoPro, and the big camera with its tripod. Rain has fallen all night, but since the sky is clearing off now, I leave the camera's rain cover in camp.

Off to the southwest, some thicker spruce treetops protrude above the alder brush. If it's a patch of thick forest, it could provide me good building materials and a sheltered camp. Plotting a mental course toward the place where I see the spruce tops on the skyline, I charge into the intervening thickets of willow and alder.

All of my life I've dreamed and longed to be in a place like this one, untouched by any human hand. There's no doubt that I've seen a lot of remote and interesting places, but never any as pristine as this land. In most of the remote places I've traveled, the purpose was to reach some village, meet some tribal leader, or a group of refugees.

*   *   *

I'll never forget a time when I passed through an Afghan village so isolated that they actually thought I and my buddies were Taliban. I guess they didn't get many visitors.

We were escorting a German lady serving as a volunteer medical worker to a far-flung valley in Badakhshan Province, and we arrived weary and hungry. In the previous villages, we had remained alert for Taliban presence. Just an hour before arriving at our destination, we had passed through a chokepoint in a canyon where an ambush had taken place not long before. The ground was littered with spent shell casings. We learned that the person ambushed had been the one carrying payroll to the school teachers out in the remote Wakhan Corridor. He had been shot so many times that his body could hardly be lifted, and then he was robbed of the money.

We arrived safely at the next village, and maybe our tired frowns alarmed the people. They lined up on the side of the street opposite us, and just stared for an hour. We were too tired to extend the usual friendly greetings.

At last they selected an old man to approach us, probably thinking that he was expendable in case we killed him. He tottered across the street and spoke to my buddy in Dari.

"What do you want with us? Are you Talib?" The old man asked.

"What? Taliban?" my friend replied. "No! We're aid workers. We brought a nurse to help the kids."

Suddenly the whole village crowded across the street and swarmed us with questions, and we tried to find enough energy to be friendly.

It was a special place, one of those far-flung regions where industrialization hasn't changed or erased culture. But it still wasn't an untouched wilderness like this one.

Sometimes I've explored places that haven't been touched for hundreds of years. One of those places was a cave high in the Pamir Mountains. I heard about this cave from locals. Their place was so small and remote that only five families inhabited the valley. On my first visit, an old man told me about the caves while he slurped down strips of boiled sheep stomach.

Sitting with him as he ate noisily, I could barely make out his words. But I picked up the facts that "ancient people" had lived in the cave and that no one had ever explored far into the caverns.

This piqued my interest, and my friend and I grabbed lights and rope and climbed high above the village. We found the caverns and went inside. It was a labyrinth of passages and chambers, each one filled with broken cooking pots, countless bones, and blacked by fires.

The cave was completely unexplored by modern man. We never reached the end, and came very close to getting lost. I mean to go back there some day.

On a trip into the Taklamakan Desert, after getting our vehicle stuck in deep sand and digging it back out, I explored a truly ancient ghost town. There were mummies buried there, so old that their nation and language are lost to time. One after another, I've seen some of the worlds most secret and forgotten places. But through all my adventures, my dream has remained: to live in some wild place, totally untouched by man. Unspoiled and unseen.

*   *   *

This arctic land, the place I call home now, is unspoiled in the purest sense. The animals I meet here have never seen man. These fish have never seen a hook. The only indication I've found that humans have ever crossed my territory is a faded axe mark on a spruce tree. The mark might be a hundred years old. And so I'm reveling in the fact that finally, I'm experiencing nature exactly as it was when the first men trod the earth. It's primal.

Two hours after I launched into the brush, brimming with the joy of exploration, I find myself engulfed in impossible thickets of alder brush. Every step is a battle, and sweat pours from the effort of struggling through while dragging along all this hunting and filming gear. The wet alder leaves drench me as I push them aside. Rain starts to fall again, but I'm already soaked and nearly losing my direction as I maneuver, hack, and struggle.

The energy that one burns while breaking through an alder thicket is hard to quantify. Literally everything that must be done pits me against on of these thickets. I call this "the alder factor," and I figure it's consuming thousands of calories from all the contestants this season. Breaking a trail through alder is like swimming uphill through a dense cobweb of wooden spikes. Add hunting gear and (heaven help me) camera gear to the mix, and you're in for a real struggle. People who've never experienced it might accuse me of exaggeration, but northern hunters who have hacked their way through willow and alder thickets in search of moose will nod in agreement. If you've been there, you understand the frustration I'm talking about.

Video recordings can't do justice to the density of these thickets, so let me just say that crossing a half mile of alder thicket can easily take an hour of struggling, tripping, chopping, falling, and getting stabbed by branches. Audio cables get ripped from the camera and mics, arrows sometimes get plucked out of my quiver, and in general it's one of the most frustrating endeavors imaginable. If you're used to scampering around the land light and fast, you're in for a nasty wake up call. And there's no such thing as "sneaking" quietly, hoping to surprise game. It's a special kind of hell.

After hours of frustrating struggle, I free myself from the brush and return the way I came. I reached the edge of my territory but found no spruce thicket better than the one where I'm currently camped. I'm totally soaked and thoroughly irritated. The big camera got wet and stopped working. I'll have to dry it out and see if it's ruined.

I arrive back at camp exhausted and even more angry than I was yesterday. In spite of all the effort I'm expending, I'm not finding a single bit of high ground or a dryer place to set up a shelter. Every square inch of land floods in the spring, leaving a thick layer of mud caked on every tree. Piles of dirt rain down on me when I break off branches for a fire. I haven't found a single grouse or even hare droppings.

What am I supposed to do here? I'm simply not seeing the resources I should see to set up for the savage winter I know is coming. As I face the slow approach of freezing weather, the whole scenario just looks bad. I would never choose this spot if I were an ancient nomad or even an animal living out here through the snow and cold.

I can see hills off in the distance, rocky hills where the sun hits the slopes and warms them during the day. There must be dry ground there and places sheltered from the wind. Along those hills is where the animals will go when winter strikes, and where instinct is telling me I should go too. But the nature of this show is that I'm not exactly one-hundred percent free to follow my instincts, despite my resolve to do so. I have been given *this* plot of land; whether I would choose to winter here or not, I have to make the best of it.

As I dry out my gear and try to get the camera working, I assess all that I've learned in my two days of scouting. Every instinct I have points me to the river as the source of sustenance here. From tomorrow on, I'll just focus on utilizing the river to its fullest. It's the only answer I have.

Day 4

I believe that it's vital to set up systems that will generate food rather than to chase off after individual animals or opportunities. Walking around looking for animals isn't the best strategy. If I can set up some system that continually catches food, I'll have spent my time much better than if I go after it piece by piece. It's another application of the popular adage, "Give a man a fish and feed him for a day. Teach a man to fish and feed him for a lifetime." Basically, I want to build a partner and teach him to fish so I can eat the fish while I do other stuff. At the same time, I need to take opportunities that present themselves. If a squirrel runs through camp, you'd better believe I'll shoot it. If I see a moose crossing my meadow, I'll drop everything to pursue it. "Intentionally opportunistic" is the way to thrive in the wild.

I have several strategies in mind for food systems. I could set up some to collect birds, channel large animals into a funnel point so I can kill them, or gather fish and hold them. Later in the season after snow falls, I'll set out a snare line for hares.

For now, with no sign of grouse, hares, beaver, or even edible plants, the river is my only ally. I'll treat it like the supply line I can count on. I know there are fish in it, and I can envision three different systems that could catch fish for me passively. I will try to harness this river's resources with my systems, making it a machine that will constantly power me to do all the building and hunting I must do.

The throw lines I've set up on the bank constitute my first system. I bait hooks with meat or guts, tie them to long lines, and throw them out into the stream where they will hopefully reach deep water. The bank end is tied to a limber pole which will keep big fish from snapping the line when they hit.

My second system is the gill net. I began tying it on day three. I've never fished with a gill net before, but I'm hoping for the best and confident I can figure it out.

The third system I envision is the one I'm most excited about: a fish weir that extends way out into the river. A fish weir is a fence made from saplings that channels fish down into a narrow neck. Once they pass through the neck, they're trapped in a holding pen. Fish weirs are extremely effective if they're set up right, even able to completely wipe out fish populations in certain streams.

A big advantage of the weir system is that it keeps the fish alive, eliminating the need to smoke the meat. I can envision it being used even under the ice as well. I might be able to leave it in place as the water freezes and just chop a hole above the holding pen to dip fish out.

So I'm really excited to get a fish weir out in the river. My plan involves making the weir in panels, so I chop hundreds of willow saplings and start weaving them into panels about six feet long. I'll work on this for a few hours each day until I have several panels ready and waiting.

The work of making these fish traps is slow but enjoyable. I cut armloads of willow saplings, each about as thick as my index finger. Then I make a frame to weave them between. The frame consists of wrist-sized poles built into a structure about like a farm gate. The structure is held together by dove-tail notches instead of tying the frame with paracord or wire. The notches hold the structure together very well, and I just weave the saplings between the frame's poles until I end up with a solid fence of saplings that I can carry and place in the river when the time comes. Water will flow through it fine, but no fish larger than four inches will escape.

Evening comes before I stop work and build up my cooking fire. While checking my fish lines, I find that two lines have been snapped. Evidently some huge fish patrol this river. The twenty-pound test monofilament just isn't strong enough. I can't afford to lose any more of the few hooks I have left, so I run to camp and get a long piece of paracord. Stripping the sheath from it, I use the inner strands to replace all of my monofilament lines. These paracord strands are thirty pound test, so they should hold up better than the monofilament line. They're harder to use though, because they float and get tangled more easily.

My spirit sinks at the loss of two more hooks to whatever Leviathans live in this river. I'm down to just eleven hooks now. But the day ends on a good note when I find a twenty-four inch pike on one of my lines. I eat half for supper and save half for breakfast, hanging it in a tree and protecting it from birds and flies inside a thick ball of grass.

Even though I'm disappointed by the land, I end day four with no feeling of hunger. I have plenty to eat.

Chapter 5

Opportunity

*   *   *

*"The biggest mistake you can make in your life is to be
always afraid of making a mistake." -Dietrich Bonhoeffer*

Day 5

    Sometimes, an uncontrollable desire to see everything on my
land seizes me. I'll be working along on my shelter or fish traps and
suddenly get the strongest sense that I'm missing out on something
going on somewhere out there. So I just drop what I'm doing and go
take a look around. Nine times out of ten, there's nothing to see, but
the urge is real and won't be ignored. At times, it just means a quick
walk to the river to check my fish poles; however, occasionally it
means a long march to every corner of my territory before the feeling is satisfied and I can again settle down to work at my camp.

    On the morning of day five, I've cooked and eaten part of a
fish when I get seized by one of those feelings. Grabbing my bow
and two GoPros, I take off in search of the unknown. After my miserable hike on day three, I decide to leave the main camera in camp. I

doubt anything worth filming will happen, and even if it did I'm still disgruntled with the territory I've been seeing. So partly out of practicality and partly from a grudge I leave the big camera behind. I can move light and fast now, and that thought cheers me up.

Reaching my fish lines, nothing seems to be stirring. Still I can't shake the feeling that there's something out there to see. So I march away downstream, not really thinking but following some urge to peer out across the meadow from a particular vantage point by the old beaver lodge.

The activity of scouting around always makes me light-hearted. I'm walking with my bow in my hand, the trees and atmosphere around me are glowing with fall colors and sounds, and game could materialize anywhere. What more could I possibly want?

The river bank has become my highway, as the only place where it's easy to get around. I'm learning to exploit the river's curve. Using it, I can move quietly and quickly to the other side of my territory in case I spot something there to hunt. I notice that everything else uses it as a highway too. A profusion of animal tracks clutter the river bank: grizzlies, wolves, and mink. Less plentiful but more exciting are the moose tracks, hock-deep in the soft mud at the water's edge.

As I walk along, I form a plan to explore the river further downstream past the old beaver lodge. If I could only find an active beaver house or slide, it would make me happy. Being pretty sure that I was dropped near the upstream extent of my land, I at least want to find out how far my territory reaches downstream. And so, hoping to find endless wonders like beaver lakes, creek inlets, and most importantly, higher ground, I quietly work my way downstream along the river shore.

I've covered about half a mile when I come to a steep bank which has caved away into the river. To get through, I have to climb high up on the bank and skirt across a narrow path over deep water.

With just my bow and a GoPro to carry, it's an easy climb and I'm across and staring at the old beaver lodge in a couple of minutes.

No animal activity is visible except for a flock of ducks out on the swampy lake. The day is beautiful, however. The bank I'm standing on is the highest point on my land, rising about ten feet above the surface of the river. It's the only location providing a vantage point to see out over the lakes and horsetail grass.

I stand on top of that bank for some time. The sun is brilliant in the clear sky, and the wind is steady but not strong enough to be annoying. It's just pleasant to stand here, so I spend about ten minutes looking out over my domain.

My domain!

The thought stirs me. It's an intoxicating feeling that I've known before, though what I considered my "domain" then was much smaller, and the stakes far less impressive.

*   *   *

Memory takes me back to my first trapline. I was about twelve, and I had just gotten my dad's permission in writing to make some small stretch of public land "my" trapping territory.

"Getting permission" for that might sound strange when you consider that I grew up way out in the boonies, completely off-grid and isolated from civilization. That life sounds pretty wild and free. But even though my childhood was wild for sure, there was nothing free about it. Every aspect of life was tightly controlled, and my dad didn't let the tiniest thing slip through the cracks.

I'm one of eleven kids, as I mentioned before, and life for a large family is tough when you're struggling to survive. Putting food on the table, keeping the farm going, keeping up with milk cows, work horses, chickens, fields, and gardens—it's all full time work. Not to mention running a sawmill, hiding from the government, and training for all-out war.

The struggle for survival, plus the pressures of unrealistic expectations, creates a lot of stress. It was normal to face a lot of anger, yelling, and punishment. Life seemed overwhelming, so I wanted badly to get further away into the woods and have my own thing.

That first winter I decided to set my trapline, I had to present Dad with a stack of documents as part of his approval process. I was required to make detailed maps showing territory boundaries and distances from home, a presentation of reasons why I should become a trapper, and a long list of guarantees that I would never let it interfere with my work on the farm. The whole thing was a massive legal process my dad made up as a way to keep saying "no" for a few months, but it gave me this insight: "Know exactly what you're doing and have a polished presentation. Be persistent and break through the walls by relentless determination." Oddly enough, that process set me up well for dealing with officials in foreign countries where I've worked.

The rules for my trapping venture were fairly rigorous. I could only go work my trapline before daylight. I had to be back to milk the cows and start work no matter what, or the trapline would be taken away. So I got up at 5:00 or 5:30 every day and ran my three miles of trapline in the dark. Before the sky lightened, I would be home and back at work. Sometimes once darkness had fallen at night, I would run out there again to tend the traps. I was pretty much nocturnal. This grueling process was only worth the struggles because of how intensely I wanted to trap and how much I loved the wilderness.

Anyways, despite the rules in place and the sleep they cost me, getting my dad's approval to run that trapline made me feel like a free man. As I surveyed my territory by moonlight, I was the king of this land now. The chief. A one-man tribe who would fight off any and all invaders. Usually the "invaders" were other fishermen or hunters, but I felt compelled to fight them all off. My methods of "fighting" them included all sorts of tricks just to make their experience on my land a real drag, so frustrating and fruitless that they would give up and leave. Shooting near them when they went to their deer stands in the dark, peeing on their hunting blinds at night to scare the deer away, and burying a bucket full of sorghum scum where a particularly persistent deer hunter would step in it were all part of my tactics. Just the basics, really.

In a few cases, my war escalated until it got out of control. My traps were stolen, then I got in a fight with their hunting dogs over some raccoons and I killed all the dogs with my hatchet. That's a war crime that I deeply regret, one that reveals the dark anger in my soul at that point. But I didn't know where to stop; I was just twelve, and people were threatening to take away the one bright spot in my life.

And it really was the one bright spot for me. I loved my trapline like nothing else in the world. The cold, unyielding land accepted me more than my home did, and so I made it my sanctuary. That patch of wilderness was the happiest part of my life. I somehow felt understood out there with the wild creatures. As time went by, I came to perceive God waiting for me there too, and I knew that the ideas I had been taught of an angry God wanting to strike me down would prove to be untrue. I sensed the heartbeat of God loving his creation out there, and it held the promise of something better.

The trapline became not only my sanctuary, but also my livelihood. For my teenage years, it was the only way I could get any money, so I protected it more and more fiercely. Once the stakes jumped a bit higher when I got invaded by marijuana growers, but that's a story for another time.

*   *   *

At this moment, surveying my arctic meadow and lake is stimulating my imagination along with those memories of the past. I'm free. Free with wild land to roam. Free to be a caveman once again. I really ought to film something about this feeling. But not knowing what to say to the camera, I just make some joke about peeing on it all to make it mine.

I'm about to turn and cross the inlet ditch when I spot a dark shape against the trees on the far side of the meadow. Having seen some big, blackened stumps and root wads over there on my trek a couple days ago, I almost ignore it. But I glance back for a moment and something seems different about this object. The longer I stare at it, the more I'm convinced that I'm seeing a moose lying in the grass.

I stare for a couple of minutes more, but it doesn't move. Surely I'm just watching a stump. Then all at once, the object turns its head, and I see sunlight glint from two huge, bony antlers. There's no doubt now. It's a bull moose!

I never shake when I hunt, but right now I'm almost trembling with excitement. This is the animal that can win *Alone* for me. And it's a bull with decent antlers to boot! But how can I play this to get close enough for a shot? The distance between me and the moose is about eight hundred yards. He's lying down in thick horsetail grass, and we're separated by two sections of swamp-lake, a willow thicket, and another expanse of horsetail. It's not a good situation to stalk the moose. The wind is all wrong—if I circle the lake to approach behind cover, I'll be directly upwind. His nose would detect my scent and send him running off into the hills before I get anywhere close. The lake and marsh between us prevents a direct approach. How can I get a chance to kill this animal?

I stand motionless for several minutes, trying to contrive a plan. Eventually I see that there is only one plausible option: I'm going to try calling this beast to me. I've never called a moose before. I've never heard anyone else call a moose. This will be a brand new game for me, and my only reference point is one memory of hearing a cow moose bawling a few years ago when I was hunting grouse in Minnesota. I rummage around in my memory, trying to remember what that very unique sound was like. I won't be able to practice—I'll have to just think about it and then let it rip.

Using the sound of the wind for cover, I slip through the willows until I'm as close to the moose as I can get. I've closed the gap by about a hundred yards, and now it will be up to the moose to cross the swamp and the lake and present a shot. As I crouch there, mentally preparing to belt out my best cow call, I give my chances of success about one-percent probability.

It's impossible to spell the noise that comes out of my mouth. Loud and long, my cow call sounds horrible, but I can see the bull's reaction as he swings his head in my direction and rises to his feet. This is the defining moment. Did I make a positive impression, or have I scared him away?

For fifteen minutes he stands there staring my way. He turns and thrashes some bushes with his antlers. Then, wonder of wonders, he takes a few tentative steps in my direction. I hold my breath and silently cheer!

For about the next hour I watch the bull close in on me. Fretfully, I alternate between calling and sneaking to different spots in the willows where the bull seems to aim his slow advance.

"Please, come to Papa," I breathe. My heart is beating hard, burning calories simply from anticipation.

The bull has stopped about twenty times to call, snort, and thrash willows with his antlers, but he's slowly heading my way. I'm awed by the whole spectacle, an amazing display of raw nature. I'm careful not to call too often. I've heard someone mention that over-calling is bad, so I do my best to wait at least ten minutes between calls.

I'm on pins and needles as the bull approaches me. I can't believe it's working! He's about one hundred yards away now, so close that I can hear his grunting exhale with each step he takes. I'm witnessing a show that only a rutting moose can display.

Only those who've seen it will know the magic that such an enormous and majestic creature can embody. Every second is charged with pure beauty. His coat is almost black across the back, but golden trim gleams on his legs and chest. As he approaches, he's tossing his head, roaring deep grunts, pawing up chunks of earth, completely destroying every willow tree that he passes. He's painting me a picture of timeless, primal drama across the backdrop of a gorgeous arctic autumn—the golden sun over yellowing willows, the lake reflecting the brilliant blue sky, the surface of the water full of ducks. Every bit of it is pure magic.

I've drawn him across both sections of lake, and now only a narrow expanse of grass separates us. I realize that all of my sneaking around to different points has been needless. It seems there is a GPS in that guy's head and he knows the exact point where my first call originated from. He's headed right for me as I crouch behind a few spindly willows, fingers curled around my bowstring, breath bated.

It only takes another minute for the moose to close the distance and as it does, I come to full draw. The moose is standing stock still, having evidently heard me shift my feet. He's staring at me and looks like he could veer away. I don't want to lose the only chance I might get. It's full broadside, and I guess the distance is thirty-five yards. So I go through my sight routine, feel the killing moment arrive, and let the arrow fly.

My brain does something unique whenever I'm hunting and I take a shot. It stretches time out and makes every second seem like five minutes. It's like I can watch the arrow in slow motion as it flies. I can see the fletching slowly spin the arrow, guess the arrow's trajectory, and slowly watch it sink into the target.

This time, as soon as the arrow leaves my bow, I know that something's wrong. It's going to drop short. I can see its path clearly as it reaches the moose and zips right under its chest, not touching a hair. I'm dumbstruck, realizing I've mis-judged the distance. I estimated the distance at thirty-five yards because I didn't realize just how big this creature is! As the bull hears the twang of my bowstring and bolts, I realize that it was closer to forty-five or even fifty yards.

My arrow skitters away into the oblivion of the horsetail grass, gone forever. But my chance at the moose may not be gone. He hasn't really spooked but just bolted a few yards; now he's trying to circle me and get downwind so that he can decide what I am. With relatively poor eyesight, he needs to smell me to see if I'm a cow or something more dangerous.

Keeping about the same distance away from me, the bull circles until he's behind me in the thick willows. I very slowly spin to match him and nock my second arrow. If he will just give me a shot through an opening in the trees, I'll redeem myself. I've got the range in my mind now—I can't miss.

Then it happens. For a second time in two minutes, I'm full draw and the moose is broadside, though quartering slightly toward me this time. I focus on the vital area until all I can see is that fist-sized patch of hair where I want my arrow to strike. I let it fly, confident this time that I won't undershoot.

The shot feels right. As the arrow leaves the bow I can trace its trajectory. This is a kill shot, true and deadly. Its path will drop it right into the heart. It's almost there already. Six feet of flight left and…a flash of white as the arrow ricochets off to the right. The bull, untouched by the arrow, snorts off into the willows and is gone. With him I see my winter's food supply and my one chance for big game slip away.

My disappointment is overwhelming. My stomach feels like I've swallowed an anchor. The arrow had nicked a tiny willow sprig I hadn't seen, seemingly insignificant but enough to divert my shot and crush my hope. Turning to walk away, I don't plan where I'm going— I just go.

"Walk it off, walk it off," I chant to myself. It's the only thing I can say. Words can't be found. Every thought that courses through my mind stings like a whip. I've possibly just lost my only chance for a moose, perhaps costing me victory as well. "Walk it off, walk it off, walk it off," I groan to myself again. Over and over, endlessly I chant those words as I numbly stumble forward, seeing but hardly caring about the new territory I cross. There is more land here, but nothing that changes the big picture. No new resources to be excited about, no big patch of berries to cheer myself up, nothing but more willow and forests of that impossible alder. Everything grows bleak and coalesces into crushing despondency. I missed my moose.

Late in the evening inside my tarp shelter, I run through the whole hunt mentally for the hundredth time. I know exactly where I messed up. I'm used to shooting at whitetail deer, and I always range them instinctively, just knowing their size and guessing the distance. I had underestimated just how big this moose was. That made me misjudge the range and shoot low. But the second shot, the one that hit a sapling and zipped off? That really bothers me. I'm mostly mad that I hadn't seen the sapling. I should have seen it. But I was hyper-focused on the moose and I just missed it. Inside, I'm burning with shame at the failure.

But I can appreciate the bright spots, lessons that I learned about moose today. His long approach had been one of the most beautiful sights I've ever witnessed. I can feel lucky to have seen something so majestic. The setting was amazing. I replay the whole scene: the bull's antlers reflecting sunlight as he swam across the lake toward me, the golden willow tops swaying as he came through the thicket between the lakes, his deep grunts as he closed in on me. I will treasure the memory of that magic as long as I live.

What surprised me most was the ease with which the moose managed the terrain. The swamps and thickets that I've been blundering through are nothing to moose. The creature's internal GPS also shocked me: he had keyed in on the precise spot my calls had come from. As he approached, I had sneaked around in the willows to stay ahead of him. He had veered right and then left over and over again, making a zigzag pattern. Each time I had thought he was changing his course and stalked to where he seemed pointed. But in the end, the bull had arrived exactly at the point where I'd stood when I called.

I decide I've learned some valuable lessons and that thinking about it any more will just discourage me. Instead, I need to only focus on the things I can control. My mind goes to the river and my big plans to harness it as a food resource. "Tomorrow I'll work on that," I tell myself as I eventually drift off to sleep.

Day 6

I'm six days into this challenge before I get the first urge to take a dump. The absence of that bodily function has worried me a little. An early morning mist drizzles as I search for some moss to serve as my wilderness wipe and suddenly realize my need to poop isn't the only thing that's been missing. As I look around, hoping my present urge doesn't go away, I note that my site has almost no moss at all.

Moss comes in handy for everything: chinking those spaces between the logs of a shelter, sealing gaps and cracks, and cleaning stuff, including my rear end. This land is just so swampy, submerged in the spring so everything dies off and a mature carpet of moss can't take hold. Hints of moss pop up here and there, but the ground is mostly just muck with willow roots through it.

Once I finally scrape up enough moss to do the job, I relieve myself and start feeling much better. This lack of moss will be annoying when I'm wiping with snowballs later in the winter, but it's going to hurt my shelter construction much more.

As I proceed into my new day, the sting of yesterday's missed moose shots harasses me from the back of my mind. I'm finding it hard to shrug this off and move on. But I know what work I need to do, and that forces me onward. I need to get my fish-catching machinery in place. I will work on my fish weir and gill net all day today while I keep my hooks baited and set.

I get my gill net project set up and start tying knots. This process will take a whole day, maybe two. While I sew, I think about today's date—my younger son Elliot's sixth birthday. I didn't realize that being absent on his birthday would be so difficult for me, but the thought of him celebrating without me is tearing me up.

Elliot is an amazing kid, quiet and smart. He's always coming up with some joke or quip that takes me off guard. He loves to impress me, but he struggles to communicate his feelings, so I'm not sure how he will take my absence on his big day. As a parent, I want to help him learn that it's ok to struggle and to express his feelings to me, but I have a hard time expressing mine as well…so I'm often not sure how I can help him.

I come from a line of men who don't talk about feelings, weakness, fear, doubt, or failure at all. My grandpa raised himself, running three farms with a team of mules by age nine. His father had died from the effects of mustard gas poisoning while fighting in France during World War I. Grandpa was the breadwinner for his family until he left to join the Marine Corps and ended up fighting the Japanese on Okinawa in World War II. After his return, he raised my dad to live by the hardest codes of manhood: "Never question. Never complain. Never fail."

My dad, in turn, raised six sons and five daughters by the same codes. He took the concept of boot camp and brought it into a farm setting. His codes were just as tough as his father's, and he

added some additional ones. Strong work ethic was taught and reinforced by the fact that we worked for survival, and behavior was reg-
ulated by the most stringent discipline.

That mentality breeds certain strengths. For example, I know
how to work hard and not complain, how to suffer and not give in.
These abilities are strengths I would not have without my dad. I'm
thankful for them; relying on them has really gotten me through
some hard things in life, including war. They're standing by me again
as I labor here in the arctic.

I want my sons to have those strengths, to be forged into
strong men by the fire of difficulty and struggle. They need the gritty
resolve to fight and win no matter the cost. But I also want them to
have something I didn't have: the freedom to deal with the fears and
failures of life. Because the reality of life is the we can't *always* win.
Sometimes we fail, and what will my sons do in those instances? My
hope is to teach them how to truly face, understand, and conquer
failure and weakness rather than just burying those things beneath
hard layers of silence and anger. I pray that this approach breeds an
even stronger manhood in my sons than what I embody.

Developing both sides of my sons is one of my deepest
struggles as a parent. How can I teach them to be stoic and tough
when necessary, but open and tender when it's the right time? Maybe,
just maybe, being on this show is providing me with the perfect opportunity to engage them about it. If I can't find the words to tell
them, maybe here I can show them. So today I make a mental commitment to open up more on camera about my inner thoughts, hoping that it will show my two boys that it's ok to feel deeply and communicate that. We are men. Men should be the toughest things on
planet earth, carrying the burdens of others. But we're also made of
malleable, breakable, shreddable human fabric, which is inherently
weak. When life reveals our weak places, when we fail, if we break or
fall, we are not rejected by God. We aren't abandoned or thrown into

the rubbish heap of forgetfulness. We're still exactly what we were: men.

I missed a moose yesterday. I failed. So I'm going to take this chance to show my boys that you can miss and still be okay. You can fail and still go on.

I work on Elliot's gill net and ponder these thoughts for hours until the edge of my thumb is bleeding where I use it to tighten the knots. I decide to focus on honoring his birthday with everything I do today, so I dedicate the gill net to him and talk to the camera about how Elliot's gill net will give me a chance to win the show. I'm hoping this will be special for him when he watches it on TV.

When evening falls, I cook a chunk of leftover fish and drink some tea. Then I go to my fish lines and see that I've gotten another fish. I haul it in, raise it to the sky in thanks, and cut it up—my daily bread from heaven.

After I've wrapped it in damp grass and stashed it in a cool place, I go to bed. The sounds of waterfowl accompany me as I lie still for a long time, trying to find sleep.

Day 7

The next few days are a blur of fishing, building my fish weir, and exploring. I'm still intent on finding a better place to spend the winter. I can't accept that the band of trees on the river's shore where I was dropped is the best place around. I get depressed just thinking about spending the winter in this damp swamp, and even more depressed about the materials that are lacking here. Each night when I go to bed I lie awake trying to contrive a shelter design that incorporates an internal fireplace. It's a struggle to come up with something that I like when the only non-flammable substance I've found is sandy silt. There are no rocks here. What kind of land doesn't even have rocks?

My mental designs devour hours of darkness when I should be sleeping. I run through scenarios where I put the fireplace in the middle of the floor like a tipi. I don't like that design: inefficient and too easy to catch my sleeping bag on fire and burn up. But I can't come up with any design for a chimney made from the river silt. It's too sandy and will crumble when it dries. Hour after hour each night, I ponder possibilities before drifting off to to the chaotic, weird world of my dreams.

I've only been here a week, but these crazy dreams come every night, getting progressively more bizarre. Last night, I dreamed that I was approached by the director of a missions agency I sometimes work with. Very somberly, he walked up to me holding a big red rooster, which was struggling to get away. "Make me a clock out of this rooster for me to hang in my living room," he requested. I promised him that I would. Why do I make such promises?

Each day I shrug off the bizarre dreams and take off again into my alder-choked land searching for a shelter site that makes me happy. I always carry my bow hoping to see a grouse or hare, but I'm beginning to be convinced that neither of those creatures exist here.

Day seven finds me upstream from my tarp shelter, pushing farther than I ever have before. I'm following a fresh set of bear tracks up the river shore when I spot a grove of trees up ahead that looks promising. I hurry toward it, scramble up the bank and a wide grin spreads across my face. Here is a thick grove of spruce trees, many of which are perfect for felling and building. What's more, this grove lies right on the shore of a beaver lake, complete with a deeply worn beaver slide going from the lake down to the river. The slide is still wet from the soaked belly of a fat beaver which must have just shot through here minutes ago. I know I can get a beaver in a snare here almost any time I want. I'm thrilled!

At that moment my GPS unit sounds its alarm call, which is an annoying electronic beep. I check it with a feeling of dread and find that, sure enough, I've crossed outside of my territory. I have to turn back. That perfect spruce grove and beaver lake are outside of my limits. With a sinking feeling in my gut and wondering how I'll find the resources to survive, I turn back toward home.

Again, I choose to focus on the good. I'm still getting fish every day on my throw lines, actually averaging more than one fish per day. Occasionally a day yields nothing more than stolen bait, but the next day I catch three.

I'm using an air-cooled method to keep my butchered fish overnight. I pick clean, green grass that happens to always be damp because it's on the north-facing river bank. I wrap up leftover fish in a big arm-full of the cool grass and place it a tree crotch where the sun can't reach it and a breeze traveling upstream will chill it. The grass keeps any flies and birds off the meat and allows drops of moisture to cool the breeze passing through. The fish keeps overnight easily this way.

Keeping meat fresh isn't the only challenge for my health. I have to employ various tactics to keep my tools and hands sterile and try to avoid water-born sicknesses. The difficulty can hardly be exaggerated in this particular environment. To start with, there is no clean water source anywhere. The lake may look blue as it reflects the sunlight, but one step into the water exposes it for just a rotten soup of stagnant weeds and duck feces. The river isn't much better, being sluggish and murky. My boots sink almost to their tops in mud at the water's edge, and I can see bones and bits of decaying mystery materials floating around in it. Each pot of water I boil produces a sludge of sand and organic residue settled at the bottom. If I wash my hands in the river or lake, they're far from sterile and carry a risk of cross contamination when I eat. Getting water in minor cuts leaves them all infected.

"Never mess around with bad water," I tell myself. "It's not worth the risk." Years of experience in aid work has taught me that boiling water is a small price to pay when the alternative might mean vomiting for days.

*   *   *

The first time I learned this was unforgettable. I was in India working as a guest teacher for a linguistics program. My accommodations were so nice that I was lulled into a false sense of security, and I drank a big glass of the tap water. That very afternoon I heard a terrible commotion on my roof, and I went up top to find a throng of people surrounding the water tank that fed my building.

"What is going on?" I asked, matching their mannerisms with my most respectful head wobble.

"Sir, Rajesh is in the water!" they replied. "Look!"

"Oh, no," I thought, "I've got a body in my water tank."

But instead of a body, I looked in to find a boy chasing a wild peacock in circles around and around the water reservoir I had been drinking from.

"How long has this bird been in there?" I shouted.

"Sir, we do not know. Maybe a long time? But it's okay, Rajesh is swimming very fast. He is catching it very soon."

Rajesh did catch it, and I went back to my work. But I spent the next three days with painful stomach cramps and diarrhea. The peacock had probably been in there for days, defecating in my water.

Later, traveling through a Muslim village farther north, I was told to drink water from a certain spring that gushed out of a high-mountain crevice.

"It is mineral water, and blessed by Bibi Fatima. You will become very strong indeed, and have many sons."

"I want to see the source of this water," I said.

As we ascended the mountain, they told me story after story of the magic spring. Evidently soldiers had fired their weapons at the spring, only to be crushed by falling off the mountainside moments later. The truth that the men had been drunk and driven their jeep off the cliff didn't change the fact that Bibi Fatima had judged them.

"It is very magical, very blessed. You will like it," they assured me.

The source of the spring had been enclosed in a small cement building that contained a pool. Poking my head inside, I gagged at the smell. There were at least fifteen men in the water, crammed into the small space completely naked, and scrubbing their private parts with handfuls of sand. They just grinned at me and kept scrubbing.

"Many sons!" one of them said.

I almost threw up just imagining drinking from the stream below. So now I don't trust any water, anywhere. You never know what is just upstream.

*   *   *

In this competition, the risk of getting sick is something I can't accept. It's worth it to boil every ounce of water that I drink, but there's the fact that I only have one pot. If I'm making water drinkable or cooking fish, I have no other vessel to sterilize my knife by boiling it. With all these factors, staying clean and healthy while I gut fish, process meat, use the toilet, mess with spoiled fish bait, cook, and manage my water supply is a long, uphill battle.

I figure that my digestive system is my weakest bodily system for this challenge. I've had giardia many, many times while overseas, an illness that combined with excessive stress to wreck my digestion. So I'm constantly praying that my stomach holds up.

I make my hands as clean as possible before each meal by smoke-washing them, rubbing them vigorously in the smoke of my fire. Smoke and heat are pretty effective at killing bacteria, and the rubbing ensures that all the bacteria gets exposed to the smoke. It's a method I read about being used by prisoners in Japanese concentration camps during WWII.

I also boil my multi-tool as often as I can. Residue of wilderness life gets caught in the crevices, and those spaces between the blades are often jammed with fish scales, blood, and mud. This multi-tool may be the weakest front in my battle against cross-contamination. So each time I boil a pot of water to clean anything, I use it afterwards to boil the tool, and then I pick out all the debris from the cracks and crevices.

Day 8

I'm working in camp when I hear a huge splash from the river. Sprinting down to the shore, I immediately see one of my fish poles bending over almost to the water. Lunging to grab the line, I haul it in hand over hand. The fish has barely reached the shore when the line breaks, and I have to dive on it to keep it from swimming away. I estimate that it's four feet long and weighs around thirty pounds. I can't believe my eyes: this might be the biggest fish I've ever caught in my life! My amazement only grows when I see that not only did the line break above the wire leader, but the wire itself broke too! It's a miracle that it didn't get away.

Elated, I head back to camp and prepare to cook a meal which will now include a huge string of fish eggs from my big catch. I stoke the fire up, and while it builds, I head down to get a pot of water from the river. These days, I have to be vigilant while I'm preparing food. A pair of devilish little birds, gray jays, have taken up residence in the trees right above my camp fire, which they perceive as their own private mess hall. Any visible scrap of food constitutes an open target, and they dive bomb my camp constantly, snatching whatever they can. At first, I didn't begrudge them a few fish guts. But now, emboldened by their successful raids, they've started snatching food right out of my cooking pot.

This morning, I'm careful to cover my breakfast meat and fish eggs with some wood while I wash at the river and get a pot of water.

I have to take a moment to explain how much I *love* fish eggs. Every time I cut a fish open, I'm eager to see if eggs lie hidden inside. I didn't grow up eating cereal with prizes buried in the box, but I can't imagine that being any more delightful than finding a huge sack of golden eggs inside a fish. Today's fish brought me a particularly lucky fish egg prize, and I'm thinking about that as I return to camp from the river carrying my pot. I can already taste the warm goodness as I chew through the tough egg sack and then each little egg pops in my mouth. It's incredible!

Wryly smiling to myself, I admit that the main reason I like the eggs is because they're something other than boiled fish meat.

As camp comes into view, the very first thing I see is a gray jay wrestling with the chunks of wood I placed on my meat. He darts out with that lovely, yellow sack of fish eggs in his mouth. I explode after him, shouting threats and throwing sticks.

The bird just wants a moment of peace to swallow the eggs, but I don't allow him. Staying on his tail, I bedevil him until he gives up and leaves the eggs on a branch. Seizing them and hurling one last insult at the bird, I head back to my fire and find that his sneaky mate has dragged my chunk of fish meat out of the pot and is attempting an escape with it.

Fortunately, the fish is too heavy for the little bird to lift, and I chase her off. I have to wash dirt from the meat again, but at least I've won the battle of the gray jays…for now, anyway. And the big string of boiled pike eggs is well worth the trouble.

Day 9

When day nine dawns, I make two decisions. The first is that I'm going to build my shelter right here where I was dropped. I can't find anywhere else with better timber, drier ground, and plentiful moss. The way forward is to just get working and make do with what I have. I could never have imagined that selecting a place to set up camp would become such a difficult decision.

*   *   *

Only once before have I stressed out about where I would live. It was a few years ago when I began a long-term humanitarian project on the edge of northeastern Afghanistan. Our project would span a year or two, constructing playgrounds for children, building benches for the elderly, and digging wells for the community.

My wife, Cara, and I had spent a whole day trying to negotiate rent terms with the leader of the tribal group we had been invited to work among. The fellow was a colorful character, a real-life warlord, and a person I would come to love dearly. He had an empty house in the middle of his territory. The house was just a shell, no windows or floors, but it was made of river stone and timber beams and it looked like a hunting lodge. I loved it.

"I want you to rent this; we must become family," the warlord said. "We must trust each other. I will be your father. Nothing bad will ever happen to you. I have defeated so many enemies, and all of my men do exactly what I say. You will be very safe."

The price he quoted for the house was exorbitant, but the "homeowners association" clearly had some awesome benefits!

After an exhausting day of negotiating unsuccessfully, my wife and I found ourselves standing on the edge of a stream that ran through the center of the village. As we surveyed the clusters of homes spread out across the opposing mountain slope, we talked about where we should set up a place that could suit our family for the next year.

"I just want a place where the sun can shine in the windows in the winter time," Cara said. The canyon walls around the village were so steep and high that in winter, the sun couldn't reach the valley floor in most places.

"Yeah," I agreed. "Sunshine is important."

Suddenly a fighter jet came screaming out of the sky, appearing from over the mountaintop behind us and streaking across the valley. The stream beside us was swollen with spring melt water, so we didn't even hear the jet until it was directly overhead.

We both jolted and looked up to see an American plane headed south, further into Afghanistan. A series of four massive explosions shook the valley as the jet dropped ordnance on somebody or something. The ground shook and echoes rang throughout the canyons for a minute.

"Did that *really* just happen?" Cara looked stunned.

"Oh, crap," I thought to myself. I thought that she would be panicked, ready to leave and not come back. "I guess this is the end of our project here."

But instead she just listened as the echoes of bombs rolled away and said, "So how about that stone house we looked at this morning? It's worth the money if you really like it."

What a woman! She has been incredible like that time and time again, so I've done my best to make our homes comfortable. In the warlord's stone house, I finished the interior and we enjoyed some of our best life for the next year. I even built a water system with a pump that brought running water into Cara's kitchen and wash room, something the neighborhood had never seen before.

I remember building that water system, and the great effort and energy it cost—almost like what I'm building here in the arctic. Digging the pit for a cement reservoir was a battle because of all the huge stones. I beat at the stones with a sledge hammer until they cracked and then tossed the pieces aside. Tool after tool broke as I dug, since only cheap stuff was available. Somewhere, I have a picture of a pile of broken picks and shovels lying beside the hole. All the while, the surrounding villagers watched and tried to guess what I was doing.

"Timber, are you digging for gold?"

"Timber, how deep will you dig?"

"Did you find a ruby yet? Or any bones?"

"No, I'm making a water system," I replied. "You'll see."

"Timber, don't you know there is a ditch where you can draw water right over there?" Never mind that someone was rinsing out a pile of goat intestines in that ditch while we talked.

When the water system was finished and pressure water came out the faucets and shower inside, they each wanted such a system for themselves.

Making a comfortable home was a joy to me, but I realized that Cara didn't want to be comfortable as much as she wanted to have love, fulfillment, and adventure. And we had those things is spades. That year, our family was so happy, and every day of that year was filled with unimaginable adventures.

My warlord-landlord and I became fast friends. I had a slingshot and one morning the landlord arrived to see me and Levi shoot a bird to eat. Upon seeing the slingshot, his eyes lit up like a child's on Christmas morning.

"Can I have that?"

"Of course!" I said, handing him the slingshot. He took it home happily and when I saw him a few days later he had shot out the glass windows of all this neighbor's houses. Window glass was in short supply, and he seemed really embarrassed about having broken them all.

"Timber, these people think that children threw stones through their windows," He told me with a sheepish grin. "It would be best if it stayed that way."

Another time he heard that Levi was sick, so he brought over some medicine.

"Timber, you must listen to me. It's my responsibility to take care of your family. And here is the medicine you must give Levi."

He handed me a small box, and what was inside? A big lump of black tar opium.

"It will help him feel much better! But you must not share this with anyone else."

I did not give Levi the opium, but I did thank him for caring for my family.

I have clearly lived in some sketchy situations, and my wife has followed me through them all. More than following me, she has been equal with me. Shoulder to shoulder, we have forged a path through danger, turmoil, and wild times.

No matter the conditions we've found ourselves in, we have created a home there together, a safe and happy place to share.

$$*\qquad*\qquad*$$

"I'm going to build this *Alone* shelter so that Cara could live happily in it, if she were here," I tell the camera. "A real frontiersman could do this with a family by his side."

I've come up with an idea for my fireplace. I'll engineer the back wall of my shelter leaned outward instead of vertically plumb. That way, gravity will hold in place the mud and silt that I plaster on it. It will be a firewall similar to a cut bank, allowing me to build the fire right up against it. I'll have to let the smoke go out a hole in the roof like a tipi. The wall should reflect heat back into my shelter, and as long as the mud doesn't crack and fall, I won't burn the house down around myself.

I suddenly have an excess of fish, so my second decision of the day is to start smoking meat. Throwing together a little smoker rig, I start preserving fish meat. Then grabbing my axe and saw, looking around to survey the timber I'll cut for my shelter.

The few spruce trees on my land are much bigger than I hoped. Logs three to six inches thick are the sweet spot for energy efficiency, meaning they're easy to cut and handle, but strong and thick enough to build well. Unfortunately, my plot only provides six or eight trees that size. The rest are ten to twenty inches through at the base.

Before I begin cutting, I have to plan in what order I should cut the trees. Each patch of trees is clumped tightly together, leaning inward toward one another. Therefore, when I cut one it will hang up in another tree instead of falling. With a small tree, that hangup isn't a problem. You just grab it by the butt and haul it off, letting it hit the ground behind you. But with trees a foot thick and fifty feet tall, it's a problem. If one gets hung up too badly, I won't be able to get it down. The tree will be lost to me, and also becomes a danger around camp. Carefully, I plan which tree to take out first. It falls and opens a path for another to follow. Tree by tree, I amass quite a pile of timber on the ground by day's end.

One tree does hang up as I cut it, lodging tightly in a bigger spruce. Getting under the tree, I lift with my shoulder and push, hoping that I can get the tree to slide backwards a bit and fall. But the stump is holding the trunk in place. Without thinking, I try to twist the tree a little to break it loose. I'm in the middle of the awkward twist when I hear a pop in my lower back and immediately my whole spine goes numb and tingly. I shake my head in disgust with myself.

Injury is a good way to go home prematurely. I should know better, having handled big logs a lot, and I chide myself.

*   *   *

When I was about fourteen years old, Dad decided to sell the timber from our farm. Without any heavy machinery, we painstakingly cut and dragged hundreds of trees. With no loader, getting them on a truck was difficult. So we yarded them on a hillside above a steep bank. With a log truck parked below the bank, we laid two poles from the bank over to the truck, and rolled the logs onto the truck by hand, with nothing more than a cant hook and a steel pry bar to move them.

As the logs piled higher, we moved the poles and rolled the logs up, stacking them until the load was high above the trucks' cabs. We loaded logs like this by the hundreds, making scores of truck-loads.

Every now and then we lost hold of a log and it fell off the ramp poles. Then it was all yelling and screaming, and boys trying to get out of the log's way. Handling huge red oak logs like this, I was always surprised that at least one of us didn't get smashed.

Later, at sixteen years old, I got my first cash job cutting timber with a local logger, Adam Dufour, who happens to still be one of my closest friends. My first day on the job, there was a pile of full-length trees that had been bull-dozed into a huge pile about ten feet high.

Being the lowest man on the job site, it became my task to "buck up" the pile of trees. That means cutting them to length with a chainsaw so that the loader can get them onto a truck.

Bucking up trees is no fun. The trees have been dragged though deep mud, coating them and making them hard to cut up. The saw chain dulls quickly from cutting through dirt and it's hard on your forearms.

I was up on top of the pile and had cut most of the accessible logs into lengths. Suddenly the pile shifted and I was thrown off, landing with the chainsaw on top of me. Still running, the chainsaw hit my leg and shredded my jeans, then bit deeply into my shin before I got free of it.

I got up thinking that I had crippled myself, but after an inspection I realized that the wounds were superficial. There was a series of nine deep cuts, and blood was everywhere, but I was ok.

I really wanted to keep the job. It was my first chance to be my own person. So I pulled the remnants of my pant leg down over it and kept working. It was only a few weeks until I had to leave the job and go help Dad at home again, but I used that money to buy my first vehicle, putting myself one step closer to freedom.

*　　　*　　　*

The scars on my leg should remind me to be more careful out here. I'm hoping that I haven't torn something badly enough that it becomes a problem for this competition, but my back continues to tighten as the day wears on. I have to get back to work anyways, so I chop a long pole to use as a lever and with it I'm barely able to knock the hanging tree down. That's the way I should have done it in the first place.

My back gives me problems all night. I can't find a way to take the pressure off it. I toss and turn for hours, eventually sleeping poorly for an hour or two.

Day 10

Sitting on my log is really painful. I can barely endure the time it takes to eat a chunk of fish for breakfast. My back feels best when I'm walking so I just keep doing what I've been doing, catching fish and cutting trees.

As I run my throw lines on the river shore each day, I haul in more and more fish. I had planned on deploying a trifecta of fish-procuring machinery. However, these throw lines alone are providing everything I need. For the moment, I actually have more fish than I know what to do with. I have live fish on lines in the water and big slabs of fish hanging to smoke. I'm wrapping half-eaten fish in damp grass and keeping the meat cool on the north-facing bank. I'm eating as much fish as I can hold two to three times a day, and I always seem to have half of a fish in my pot ready to boil for the next meal. A couple of times I lament to my camera, "I could feed a village with all this fish—I just need someone to cook it for me!"

As I build my shelter and consider my needs for winter, I'm faced with yet another decision. Should I build a food cache now as well? If I kill a moose and don't have a cache built, it could be really hard to keep and protect the meat while I build a cache. But on the other had, if I build a cache and don't kill a moose, I'll have wasted loads of precious energy and calories.

Something inside me believes that building a cache first will jinx me, and I won't get a moose then. The cache will remain empty, laughing at the wasted effort and calories I invested in it. With that in mind, I decide not to build a food cache before I make a big kill. I'll just deal with the meat the best I can if and when I get it.

Chapter 6

A Time to Kill

*   *   *

"Killing is not so easy as the innocent believe" -JK Rowling.

Day 11

Today dawns clear and still. The ducks and geese are making an unearthly ruckus, and I lie here inside my tarp for a long while, just listening. Some type of waterfowl fly in formation straight overhead. I'm surprised by how loud their wings sound. They circle around my meadow, and I can hear them all splash down on the lake. Their raucous chorus reaches a crescendo as the flock of newcomers disrupt the lake's residents. They splash and squabble and squawk until everything gets sorted out and the noise returns to normal levels.

Somewhere on a lake farther west, a pair of loons call. I love the sound that loons make. I can't spell it or even describe it, but their call is both lonely and cheery all at once. I don't know how they manage that. The loon's call is one of the sounds that define the north country to me, on par with a wolf's howl and a raven's caw.

My morning reverie lasts until I have to pee so badly that I can't lie still. When I poke my head out of my sleeping bag, a new, deep chill bites my face. A fine layer of frost covers everything on the forest floor.

I crawl out of my tent wearing a wool sweater over my t-shirt for the first time. My first move is the same every day. I dress, grab my bow, and run my fish lines. I haul in the lines one by one, check the bait and toss them back out.

This morning, another small pike waits on one of my lines. Several hooks have had their bait stolen.

The frost stirs an instinct within me, clear and distinct. It's like electricity in my spine and churning in the pit of my stomach. Some primordial sentinel is shouting in my head, "The cold is coming! Go kill something! Get meat! Prepare for winter!" I don't know how to describe it, except to say it's the hunting feeling. It's telling me that this week is the time that big game must be killed. Otherwise, it won't happen at all. So in agreement with the inner voice, I decide that from now on I'll use each day's early morning hours to hunt, returning to build my shelter in the afternoons.

As I slip away from camp with my bow, I pray and ask God to direct me to the best strategy for today. I recognize that the challenges this landscape will present are new for me and for most of the other contestants. This season will come down to who can learn and adapt the quickest. That's why tuning in to instinct seems so important to me.

To succeed here, I need more than just the book knowledge of how the arctic works. I need to feel the right moves and be making them moment by moment. If a fish run is about to happen, I want to have the right system already in place and waiting. If a moose is cruising toward my landscape, I want to be there with my bow already half-drawn when he steps out. Basically, I want to do the things an experienced local would do, but I'm not an experienced local. However, I believe that instinct can fill some of the gaps where I lack experience and knowledge, so I'm constantly asking God to guide me through instincts.

Sometimes my mind puzzles over what exactly defines instinct. It's something all creatures have, including humans, though we are less sensitive to it than the animals most of the time. Our modern lifestyle has tuned it out. But what is instinct, exactly? Is it the mythical sixth sense we talk about when we feel someone watching or sense someone coming up on our blind side? Is it a spiritual connection to nature? Is it just experience coming into play through our subconscious minds?

I would say that following instinct does not mean doing what you *feel* like. For example, I may feel tired. I've worked hard and I just want to sleep. However, I don't have any fire tinder gathered for tomorrow, and I can smell coming rain in the air. So to follow instinct, I have to tap into something more than my body's wants. My body tells me to relax, but my instinct tells me to grab some tinder while it's dry and *then* rest.

From a strictly philosophical angle, I like to think of instinct as the voice of God within every living creature telling us what is good and what we must do to survive. It is the sum of the signals that he arranged in all of us, man and beast, that move us to mate, eat, hydrate, build homes, raise offspring, and seek health. I don't pretend to understand how those signals originate and are transmitted through our nervous systems to our brains and muscles. Let's just start at the point where we recognize a voice within us that drives our actions. We follow it or die. I believe it's the same voice that drives birds to migrate on time, that guides them to lakes along their route where they'll find good food. The same voice that makes squirrels stash nuts before the snow is deep and makes bears consume ten times their normal diet right before hibernation.

Each species continues to exist by following the voice that knows everything that they need. It has always been and will always be there, keeping life awake on earth. It's spoken by the one who made and admires all living things, spoken deep inside our beings in a language both inscrutable and yet undeniable. Through ages of nature's drama, playing out unseen and unrecorded by man, God has been here loving these creatures by keeping them alive with his voice.

If God speaks to them in those ways, why not to me? I'm a creature as well, but one created to do something special. Even though I'm a wild thing prowling around the landscape and trying to survive, I'm more than that. I am the image of God, the caretaker of this earth, charged to see and hear the beauty and understand it in a way other creatures can't. If God looks on every creature and says "I love you," I'm the only kind who can look to heaven and say "I love you back." I don't have to do it, but I will. It's my choice, and I'll do that as long as he keeps me alive.

This morning, instinct sends me hunting, and I stay until I'm sure that moose will be bedded down for the day. Then I head to camp and start in on my shelter. I split the remaining daylight hours between tending the fish meat that I'm smoking, and hauling heavy loads of mud from the riverbank. I place about seventy pounds of mud on my rain jacket, then hoist it by the sleeves and hood to throw it over my shoulder.

I haul about thirty of these loads of mud, plastering it onto the rear wall of my shelter. I've built the wall leaning outward so that gravity will help the sandy mud stay in place once it dries. I don't know if it will work very well as a fire place, but it's the best thing I can come up with.

I keep going until the entire wall from bottom to top is plastered about four inches thick. I'm able to keep working hard even though the weather is warm because I have my quiver canteen. I'm immensely thankful for the luxury of taking deep drinks of cool, safe water while I work.

I work a little later than I intended, but when I finally quit for the day, I have the ridge pole of my shelter in place and many logs cut to length.

Day 12

The day's waking light finds me out early, keeping my commitment to hunt while the land is still and silent. My fish lines are untouched, lying motionless in the slack river. Frost covers the landscape, and a heavy fog has swallowed the lake and meadow. I can hear the ducks out on the lake even though they're invisible in the mist. Loons are crying again from a lake farther south.

Taking my bow, I breathe deeply and sense all the fragrances that define hunting season to me: the sweet and sour scent of dying leaf cover, the faint woody smell of newly dead branches, and the freshness that moves in with the wind as the fall air cools and settles. The oxygen feels so much richer, energizing me. Occasionally, the scent of some animal's musk or droppings is added to the mix. And on top of it all is the icy tingle the frost brings to my nose. The whole experience is one of my favorite sensations, and it always makes me want to breathe all of it that there is to breathe. I fill my lungs with this magical air, the hunting wind. Like yesterday, it feels like a time to kill.

I start out by cow-calling on the east side of my meadow. It's the place near where I spotted the bull moose a week ago. After a couple of hours the wind shifts and I move, circling the lake to keep the wind blowing from me to my camp. By mid-morning, I find myself near the old beaver lodge where the false inlet connects the meadow to the river. I give a few more call sequences, waiting ten minutes between each one.

At some point during the next two hours, I actually see a bull out in the lake. The fog clears for a moment, and I spot him calmly feeding and making his way toward the far side of my territory. The view through the fog is incredibly beautiful, but the bull ignores my calls and disappears into the thickets on the eastern edge of my land. Giving up, I head back to camp.

Somehow I'm feeling weaker in spite of eating as much fish as I can stomach. My back isn't feeling any better either. The pain is especially bad when I'm sitting down. As I hunch by my fire boiling food and eating, my back screams and I shift around constantly trying to ease the pressure. I've tried everything to find a place to sit that feels good. I have a pretty nice chunk of log by my fire. It's split open and the rotten center of the log is like a small easy chair. Under normal circumstances it would be tremendous. But now I can barely sit through a meal. I must have messed my back up pretty badly.

My axe feels heavy as I pick it up and select a tree to begin felling. Trees already lie scattered on the ground, crisscrossing my camp area like a handful of uncooked spaghetti and making movement around camp quite difficult. Slowly I start cutting them to length and adding them to my growing shelter structure.

As I work, I'm acutely aware of the noise that I generate and its effect on wildlife. Every stroke of my axe ringing out across my meadow could mean the difference between killing a moose or not ever seeing one. Every crash of a tree could be driving away my winter's food.

The smoke from my campfire is an even worse problem. All of the damp firewood in this swamp seems to generate smoke like a coal chimney. The smoke is heavy and pungent, a constant beacon sweeping the land downwind and begging animals to take a wide detour to avoid me. At this moment, the smoke is blowing straight out to the lake where I spotted a moose this morning. But there's not much I can do about it.

I work all day with that uneasy feeling about my noise and scent. How am I supposed to know when a moose is approaching or lying up in the alders just out of sight from my camp? The brush is so dense that there could be one within a hundred yards on any given morning when I crawl out of my tarp, concealed in the dense veil of willow brush. That one special chance that hunters get would start there for me. The animal is supposed to wander into my realm, remain undisturbed, and feed out into the open. Then, watching from my tree line, I'm supposed to spot it and make a stalk. If I don't see it and start chopping with my axe instead, that moose will head for the hills.

There will only be a few days this fall when moose cross my land, and if I miss those slim chances I will have only fish to rely on. I don't know how long the fish will continue to bite. The pressure weighs on my mind like a ton of rocks.

By the end of today, I have the superstructure of my shelter mostly assembled. My fish lines are still yielding substantial catches, and I have quite a few huge strips of golden fish dried and hung up. I tell myself that I'm doing well.

Day 14

I'm out early with my bow, crunching through a thick layer of frost as I circle around the lake. For a third morning, I'm out here at daybreak to call moose.

A dense fog lies across the surface of the lake and extends back to the spruce forest behind. The fog offers good cover, and the frost is breaking down the stems of the horsetail grass so they don't crunch as loudly. I decide that any moose encounter this morning will happen at close range because neither of us will be able to see far in the fog.

It's an idyllic morning for hunting. Water foul are waking up on the lake, their calls the first sounds to stir the magical calm. Clouds of fog floating from the water's surface are like a dense band of gray cotton. The willows are just beginning to yellow, and the golden tops of the thickets protruding above the fog steam a little as the first morning rays touch them. The silver frost shimmers on the ground. It's like a living painting, and I can just imagine a moose appearing like a wraith out of the mist, slowly picking his way toward me through the frozen meadow and giving me a close shot. If I were hunting whitetails, this is exactly the kind of morning that would have them up and moving. I hope it's the same for moose. I can feel the hunting wind, and it is good.

I call and watch for a couple of hours, then quit for the day feeling deflated that nothing happened. On my way back to camp, I tell myself that I have to forget about moose for now and get my shelter built. It's getting late in the season. I'll still hunt each morning, but otherwise I resign myself to get to work. The noise and smoke I make will just have to happen. I have to make a home.

Reaching camp and hanging up my bow, I unwrap a big chunk of pike from the wet grass I've left it in overnight. I have to scrape a good bit of slime off the skin, but the passing of time has made it easier to enjoy a meal of this boiled fish. I'm not repulsed by it at all, savoring each bite instead.

Yesterday's fire is still smoldering and I stoke it up with sticks. I've decided to bank the fire at night by covering a big chunk of spruce firewood with ashes. To my great amazement, I find that it carries through the night perfectly. All I have to do is turn the log over to expose the coals and then throw some sticks on it.

"Nice!" I breathe as the breakfast fire catches in the kindling and crackles. "If I can keep a fire going like this, it'll save me a lot of energy."

I grab my pot of boiling fish and half stumble over to a log where I can lean my back against a tree and stare at my shelter site while I eat. The tree takes a little pressure off my back, just enough to ease the pain so that I can get through a meal without moving. And from here I can survey my building materials and mentally work through my design while I'm chewing. I get the camera running, thank God for the fish, and dig in.

Halfway through my meal, I suddenly hear a loud crunch in the brush off to my right, followed by several well-defined and very heavy footfalls. It sounds like a big animal very close, not more than ten yards away. I hear footfalls come closer. I can feel that something big is there watching me.

Setting my pot down, I slowly move my head to the right. I keep a sharp eye on the trees while I back slowly to my bow and nock an arrow. I search the trees, but nothing is there. I'm completely baffled. I can see the area well where the sound came from, but nothing is there. Even more confusing, I hear no sounds of an animal fleeing—just nothing.

This might sound insignificant, but I can't begin to explain how defined the sounds of footsteps were, and just how sure I was that a large creature was there. It was as distinct as any sound I've ever heard, and the absence of any animal is actually disturbing me to my core. It's about like hearing a car door close right beside you and turning to find nothing but an empty parking space. But search as I might, I can't find a sign of anything. I even circle out into the meadow, bow half drawn, watching the backside of my grove of trees. Nothing could have moved away without me seeing it. But here I am, feeling like an idiot aiming my bow at nothing. Just empty meadow and the brush around my building site.

Returning to my shelter, I've just hung up my bow when out of nowhere, a grey owl appears in a dive right in front of me, talons out-stretched and aiming for my face. I duck instantly and it whooshes by. I don't know how I'm able to dodge it and keep my eye in its socket. Those talons were so close! The owl was only inches from my face when I ducked. I turn and stare after it, only to find it diving me again, kamikaze style. But on this attack, I have more reaction time to evade his talons.

"What in the world?" I yell at the owl as he lands on top of a dead spruce stub. I grab the big camera and zoom in on it. His eyes are locked on mine, but I return the killer stare. I'm kind of mad, but even more curious about what the creature's actions could mean. My first instinct is that it's warning me about something. But what? The sounds I've just heard spring to mind, and I look around to see if there's a grizzly or something about to pounce on me or steal my breakfast fish. Again, I see no creatures, but I determine to keep my eyes open and stay alert. I don't really know if nature or God is using this owl to warn me off, but I'm going to keep on the lookout for whatever it may mean. I'm feeling really unsettled.

"It's probably just defending its nest," I say aloud. The sound of my own voice settles me a little, but I can't spot a nest anywhere and I don't really believe my own theory.

I decide I'd better finish breakfast, but as I turn back toward my cooking pot, the owl meets me face to face again. This time I only miss getting a talon in my eye by mere inches. The owl's wings actually brush my face as I spin and duck. It immediately dives again, reaching for my eyes with razor-sharp talons.

This has to end! I'm becoming really concerned that he will get me in the eye. The owl is silent as he dives; I can't hear him coming. And I can't build all day on my shelter with this thing attacking me.

Once more he dives, but this time I start waving my arms and he veers away before getting close. He lands in the tree right above my cooking pot. What am I supposed to do?

I grab a handful of sticks and chuck one at it. I miss by a foot and the owl flies to another branch. I'm not trying to kill it, just warn it. I have a feeling that there is some force of nature at work here trying to warn me or something. I want to figure it out but I have to warn the owl away. He's becoming dangerous. I chuck a second stick at it and it flies to a branch farther away. Good.

Stick after stick, I drive the owl away, but with its absence I feel a growing feeling of dread that I've upset whatever force was using the bird to alert me, or whatever. The close sounds of footsteps I heard as the owl arrived weigh heavy in my mind. What did the owl mean?

Some sense of cosmic consequences seeps into my mood, as if I'm playing out The Rime of the Ancient Mariner, bringing a curse on myself by disrupting forces of nature. Is my day totally screwed now? Is nature going to be mad? Am I about to get eaten by a grizzly? Or will Bigfoot pop out to hit me in the head with his big rootwad club stick?

All of these thoughts sound like a joke while reflecting later, but out in the isolation, with an already unsettled feeling that something strange is going on, these thoughts actually occur to me and seem pretty real.

Back at my camp now, my breakfast of boiled fish is cold. No matter how hungry I am, boiled fish is still impossible to enjoy when it's cold. The ever-present pike slime has gelled on what leftovers remain in my pot, and it smells fishy. I could simply throw it back on the fire and reheat it, but now I'm in a hurry to get to work and I refuse to take the time for the sake of a small comfort. I gulp down the six or eight bits that remain, gag on a chunk of skin, and clean my pot with grass. All the while I'm furtively glancing around for Bigfoot and the bears.

The sun is high in the sky by the time I grab my axe and saw. I only have to cut eight or ten more trees to finish my shelter's superstructure. I'm regretting all of the noise I'll make and wondering how far away a moose can hear it as I haul back and prepare to fell the day's first fine tree. But before the blow falls, I hear a sound that freezes me in place. Pausing to listen, I hold my breath and wait.

"Something's out there, I think." I wait for it to come again, and when it does, I immediately recognize the grunting sound that the bull moose made on day five when I called it to me. He sounds pretty far away, but the noise is distinct. I have a moose on my land!

Dropping my tools, I snatch up my bow and dart out into the edge of the meadow where I can see the lake. Almost instantly I spot the moose, and I'm surprised by how far away it is. I can only make out a dark shape way across the meadow. I can't even tell if it has antlers, but I know it's a bull because of its grunting. I guess the lake is helping the sound drift all the way to my camp. Hearing it at such a distance seems extraordinary!

"Okay, okay guys," I whisper excitedly to the camera. "I've got a moose on the other side of the meadow. But how am I gonna stalk and kill this thing?"

At first, I can't see a way to approach the moose for a stalk, then I see that he's slowly heading toward the false creek inlet near the old beaver lodge. That's half a mile away, but if I make it there ahead of him I may be able to ambush him without even calling. It could be ideal. I just don't know if I can get there first; I'll have to run a half mile and he only has about two hundred yards to cover. This hunt will be a race. I creep backwards through the trees toward the river, keeping an eye on the meadow in case the moose turns.

I warn myself not to get too excited. I feel certain that if I make a big deal out of this stalk I could somehow jinx it to turn out like day five. With that caution in mind, I decide to leave the big camera in camp and just grab up the two GoPros. Reaching the river bank, I break into a run, racing downstream toward the inlet.

One GoPro is strapped to my bow and I hold the other in my right hand. It bobs up and down as I run and I feel like the footage is going to be crap. I pray as I go asking God to give me a shot.

"Please let me beat the moose to the inlet! Bring him into range!"

The wind is turning, and it's not good.

"Make the wind go more to the left!"

I pray all the time when I hunt. In the wilderness, so much stuff is outside my control that I just talk to God constantly about it. There's no pretense or empty religion out here in this wilderness, but this place is God's sanctuary, and I know He's watching me run around trying to kill these creatures so I can stay alive. So I'm always looking up and saying stuff like, "Man, I'm hungry today, God," or, "God, I'd sure like to kill that squirrel right there." It's just something I do. So I pray intently about this moose, but I don't record much talk about the hunt on the cameras. I just keep them rolling and run as hard as I can.

I'm getting winded pretty easily, and it dawns on me how much endurance I've lost in just two weeks. But I'm close enough now that I have to slow down and be stealthy. I stop running and just speed-walk through the narrow swampy part and approach the high bank that has sloughed down into the river. As I start to climb over it, I picture myself coming face to face with the moose when I pop over into the inlet. If he's already there, I need to be careful or I'll spook him. I control my breathing and sneak into the inlet channel. The moose isn't there, but when I poke my head over the bank I can see him out in the meadow, still standing almost where he was when I first saw him. He hasn't really moved at all.

I duck below the bank again. Since I have time, I give my breathing a couple of minutes to recover from the run. Now I'm okay. So how am I going to kill this thing?

Checking the wind, I see that it's not blowing directly towards the moose but it will be quartering towards him. Not ideal. If he comes straight at me, he won't smell me; however, if he turns to my left at all, he will be directly downwind and the hunt will be over. I ask God again for success and decide to do a call.

I give a single cow call from below the high bank of the river, hoping that the sound will seem a little distant to the moose. The bank forms a point of high ground that ends with the false creek inlet. The point conceals me from the meadow where the moose is, but the moose could choose one of two routes to take as he approaches; to cover both, I will have to sneak out into the open and down the moose's side of the high bank. Nothing but a small willow shrub is there to provide cover for me. Deciding that a stalk to the willow is too risky, I stay on the inlet side of the bank. Now I'll only be able to cover only one of the possible paths the moose could take, but I'm gambling it will be the right one. My concealment is great as I crouch with my back toward the bank and a clump of bushes on my left hand side hiding me from the moose.

Out in the meadow, the bull is taking his sweet time. He started from about two-hundred yards away, and after ten minutes he has only halved that distance. He reaches the edge of the willows eighty yards in front of me and begins to thrash them with his antlers. Again, just like day five, I'm treated to a majestic display as the bull scrapes and grunts for a good long while. Several times I consider calling again but I'm too close so I just remain silent and patient. I've got an arrow nocked and I'm trying not to hold my breath.

Eventually the bull breaks loose and starts my way again. Instead of coming in a straight line as he approaches, his head swings right for a couple of steps and then left for a few steps. Each time he veers to my left my heart sinks, and I'm filled with a compulsion to leave my position and scramble over the bank to get out ahead of him. But then he swings to my right again and I calm down. It's so hard to guess which route he will take once he reaches the inlet. I slip my boots off just in case. Being in sock feet might help if I have to move.

I have heard that moose make things happen very slowly, and that's proving to be true. This bull is taking so much time to amble toward me that he's wearing on my nerves. He stops every two steps to listen and test the wind. Each time I want to call again and bring him closer but instinct tells me to just let him do his thing. Time is on my side.

I can hear his breathing now. He's just fifty yards away when to my horror he veers to my left and heads toward my downwind side. This path will take him on the opposite side of the high bank from me, in the one direction I can't shoot. I have to move but I'm terrified he will see me, being so close. I move anyway, knowing that this hunt will be over as soon as the moose advances another twenty yards and detects my scent stream.

As stealthily as I can in sock feet, I creep over the top of the bank, outlining myself boldly against the sky.

"How can this work?" I ask myself, praying silently. "He will surely run."

There's nothing between me and the moose now at all. He reaches a little shrub and stops just feet from being directly downwind of me. I freeze in position as his head swings my way. At a distance of thirty-five yards, we begin a little staring contest. He caught me mid-stride so I'm standing on one foot and trying not to lose my balance on the bank. Every fiber of my body is electrified with that surge of hot blood that hunters get right at the crucial moment of a kill. This moment will decide everything. Will he smell me or hear me breathing? Will he allow me to draw my bow while he's staring right at me? Every possibility runs through my head as I try to keep my balance without blinking or shaking.

"You have a three-second window to make a kill." Those are the words my dad said to me after taking down a nice buck, and they've stuck with me forever. More often than not, I find that he was right, especially when I'm using primitive equipment. Primitive hunters get the most fleeting chance to make a successful kill. Whether the hunter is a human with a bow or a bobcat trying to pounce on a hare, there is a window of time when it will work, and it's usually the tiniest window imaginable. It's the killing moment. The most successful hunters can consistently make everything happen in that one moment. If the moment passes, the hunt is over. The chance on that animal is gone. Another killing moment might not present itself for a long time, maybe days or even weeks. And now the kill window is going to either open for me or close within the next few moments.

I just keep hovering there on one foot without blinking, but I want to draw my bow. He's perfectly broadside to me right now and I could shoot if I could only draw on him. But his stare has me pinned down. If I move he will bolt.

Moments pass, and instead of bolting he begins thrashing a little willow shrub.

Awkwardly balanced so long on one foot, I'm relieved that I can gently set my right foot down on the ground. While he's distracted, I draw my bow. The distance is farther than I want to shoot, but there is no way I'll get any closer. I go through my mental targeting routine. I know why I missed the moose on day five: I underestimated his size and shot low. This time I hope it's different.

"Aim like it's a horse," I advise myself silently. "Aim like it's a horse. God, help me kill this moose!"

The arrow flies. It seems like minutes before it reaches the moose. Then comes the hollow "thwack" sound that only a rib cage can make as the arrow hits just behind the shoulder and sinks deep. Time stands still for me as the moose spins and bolts back toward the path he came from. I'm watching breathlessly for a telltale spurt of blood from the puncture wound but I can't make it out as the moose runs.

My first thought is that I hit a little high. The shot was perfect laterally, but just higher than I wanted. Still, I think that the razor-sharp point is in both lungs, and I watch the fletching of the arrow bob up and down with the moose's movement. It's probably slicing vitals inside as he runs.

He reaches his bushes at about eighty yards from me and stops. I can't tear my eyes from him. I believe that he's as good as mine, and I say so to the GoPro which has been recording from the top of the bank, snatching it up to point it toward the moose.

"He's going down!" I half-whisper, half-shout to the camera. The bull's head bobs and he spins around in a circle before falling over. One or two kicks are the last signs of life before the great beast lies still in the deep horsetail grass. It's done, and I can't believe how quickly it happened.

The next few moments feel surreal. I half expect the moose to get back to his feet and take off, but he doesn't. Everything is silent and still. I watch until I'm absolutely sure it's down for good and then I turn the camera towards myself and gush my happiness and thanksgiving.

I never like it when hunters follow up a kill by dancing around, fist bumping and shouting like they're crazy. On the videos they post to YouTube, they like to use intense sound tracks as if they've just vanquished an invading army. I hate it. I could understand it all if their weapon was a javelin missile and their prey a tank, but it seems so tacky when it's just a wild animal that's been killed. However, I'm afraid that I celebrate almost like that when I realize that my nearly impossible dream has just happened. My adrenaline dissipates, and the truth of what a kill this size means for my survival overwhelms me. I'm so thrilled that I can't even talk coherently.

As I approach the moose, I'm careful to keep an arrow nocked, taking nothing for granted. But once I poke him, I can feel that he's good and dead. I come around his front and marvel at the size and beauty of this creature. His antlers are breathtaking; upon examining them, I quickly confirm that this is the same moose I missed on day five. I'm so excited about it all that I can hardly decide what to do next. I take a few moments to thank God for giving me this beautiful creature. The magnificence of this beast and the fact that it won't be roaming the land any more settles in on me. It's a heavy moment and I don't know what to do besides breathe "Thank you" over and over again. I thank God that he trusts me with the lives of his creatures. I wonder if he will miss seeing this animal when he looks down at my land. I would.

I make sure to put some blood on my shoulder tattoo, and then I set up the camera and get a few shots of me posing beside the moose with my bow. I don't take very long with all of this because my work load is going to be enormous beginning now and running for the next few days.

Viewers later may see my moose fall and say to themselves, "Well, it's over now. He has this in the bag." Although it's true that I have a winter's supply of meat lying on the ground in front of me, so many things could happen that would strip that supply of food away from me before I can benefit from it. To begin with, it's a huge task butchering, hauling, processing, and preserving that meat—a gargantuan job for one guy with only a multitool.

Secondly, the things that threaten that meat are myriad, from predators like grizzlies and wolverines to small creatures like mice and even insects. The weather is an even bigger factor with temperature and moisture. I need a way to store and protect the meat from all those foes. As I contemplate all those factors, I feel the sun on my neck and realize the day is warmer than I thought it was going to be. There isn't a moment to lose so I roll up my sleeves, take out my multitool, and dive in.

I know how to go about butchering large animals. I've butchered almost everything that there is to butcher. But I've never tackled something quite this big alone, even cows on the farm growing up. At least one of my brothers was always around to help with those. This time, it's only me and a three-inch multitool blade against one of the biggest land animals in North America.

I work as hard as I can to strip the hide off the bull's exposed side. I'm sweating so I take off my shirt and soon I'm smeared with blood up to my shoulders from reaching up inside the rib cage to take out the heart and lungs. The afternoon passes quickly as bit by bit I break the bull down and stack the fresh meat on a bed of willow saplings.

The sun sets on a scene straight out of the Stone Age. A hunter literally dripping in blood, a fresh kill with red ribs exposed to the sky, a camp fire to keep away the enormous predators, sizzling bits of meat eaten on the tip of a knife blade, the moon rising thin and weak and the arctic wilderness cradling the scene like a secret treasure. It's playing out just like it must have for untold millennia.

Late into the night I work, butchering and hauling loads of bloody meat back to stack it on boughs near my camp. The work is back-breaking in the dark, trying to balance eighty-pound sections of moose shoulder and haunch while I trip and stumble along the river path. The muck sucks me down and roots clutch at my boots. I'm weary and far from finished when I realize how juicy I would smell to a grizzly and how vulnerable I would be in the dark, not being able to see if I'm stumbling right toward a bear. I decide to call off the work until daylight, although that adds to my concern that a bear may find and claim the kill while I'm not there. Then I would be in a fix.

I mark the area with scent to remind any passing bear by that this kill belongs to me. Finally I stumble into camp and get into my sleeping bag, happy but exhausted.

Chapter 7

Work

*   *   *

*"Every man must choose one pain, the pain of discipline,
or the pain of regret." -Jim Rohn*

Killing big game is the beginning of a race. Meat comes with an expiration date. The moment an animal's heart stops pumping blood through its muscles, a timer is set that relentlessly ticks down, marking a lifespan of just hours while its body is usable and healthy. Then it must be frozen or preserved in some way. Otherwise, big game amounts to nothing more than a pile of organic matter fit only for buzzards and crows. Though the amount of meat from a moose is supposed to bring life, food, and energy for a long time, it's all for nothing if it can't be used.

If the weather would cooperate, I'd just allow the meat to freeze. But alone and without any information to help me guess what the weather will do, I'm up against an enormous risk as I butcher the fresh meat, wishing for a refrigerator as one of my ten survival items.

Day 15

I feel the weight of the work I have ahead of me from the moment I open my eyes. It feels good except for the growing suspicion that warm weather may threaten my huge stack of meat. I poke my head out of my tarp shelter and feel a sense of dread. There is no frost. It's significantly warmer than yesterday, and as I begin to stir around I can sense that the day is going to warm up further. Running my fish lines and eating breakfast as fast as I can, I gear up and head down river to finish butchering my moose.

As I approach the kill, I contemplate what I will do if a grizzly has claimed the carcass. Whenever a grizzly claims a kill, it becomes very aggressive and willing to fight to protect its food. The moose carcass is lying on the edge of some pretty thick willows, so a bear could easily be lying up in the shade close by where he can keep an eye on the kill.

I have a little can of bear spray on the safety belt I wear. I'm supposed to use it if a bear attacks *me*. But if a bear is on my kill, I will be compelled to try and drive it away. What will happen if I have to attack *it*. Would this spray do me any good in that situation? My axe is the only weapon I have with me and I say a heartfelt prayer that I won't have to find answers to those questions.

Near the kill, I carefully poke my head over the river bank to survey the scene. I'm relieved that there is no bear in sight, but what if it's lying up in the dense willow nearby with a belly full of moose liver? I start yelling as I approach so that I at least won't surprise it.

The kill is untouched except for a couple of gray jays which keep darting down from the willow tops to snatch a bit of fat and fly off again. I can tell that no bear has visited because the most delicious parts of the guts are totally undisturbed. That's where a bear would have started in.

Beginning where I left off yesterday, I haul the loose hide off of the rib cage and start cutting out huge muscles from the left haunch. Then I strip the rib cage and neck. Finally I can flip the moose over and get to what remains of the lower side. The hide comes off and I drag it a few meters away and spread it out. I'll stack meat on it. I'm sweating and dripping in moose blood by mid morning.

The kill is completely broken down at last. Only the major bones remain intact, the head with its big antlers, the spine, rib cage, and hip bones picked almost clean of meat. I've piled the meat on half of the hide, and I pull the free half over it to block the encroaching sunshine. The day is getting warmer but the thick, black hair on the outside of the hide will absorb all the radiant heat and the meat underneath it should be fine as I haul it away bit by bit.

I don't dare stop working for more than a minute to stretch my back. Chopping a couple small poles, I use them like skewers to spear big sections of meat and lever the load over my shoulders. For hours I'm hauling huge loads from the kill site back to my camp, adding them to the pile and covering the whole stash with spruce limbs to keep the birds off. Each trip kills my lower back where I injured it a few days ago.

I also have to make sure to stop and position a camera to capture shots of me coming and going. Each time I turn a camera on I have to unload my burden of meat, get the camera set up, pick up the meat again, walk past the camera and around the bend, set down the meat and come back for the camera. It all makes for an exhausting day and I even forget to stop and eat until it's almost pitch dark again.

By day's end I'm completely exhausted. My lower back injury is screaming at me. I'm crusted with dried blood and feel ready to drop. I've sweated out a lot of salts too. Losing salt through sweat is a terrible thing to be doing, as I have no way to replace it.

I know I should clean up, but I'm just too tired by the time I boil water and cook some meat to eat. I crawl into bed in such a filthy condition as I hope to never repeat, promising myself that tomorrow I'll clean up well and wash my clothes.

Day 16

When I awake, real worries about my meat settle in, and I realize that it really could spoil. The day dawns warm like yesterday and promises a bright sky with full sunshine.

"Why isn't the weather staying cold?" I keep asking myself. This is the arctic after all, isn't it? On the day I arrived here, the air was chilly and convinced me that the temperature would drop below freezing within a week. Each morning that I've woken up to frost, my confidence has grown that cold weather was here to stay. And yet here I am sweating, the warm sun beaming down, and my meat getting warmer and warmer. I'm baffled, dumbfounded. But I pray fervently that the weather will drop in time.

If things don't freeze quickly, I only have four or five more days of grace before the meat goes rancid. I absolutely cannot let this animal go to waste. I can smoke the meat, but that makes it so much less desirable and nutritious than fresh meat. Building a smoker will also require a ridiculous amount of work. Can I do all of that construction before the meat spoils? More importantly, there aren't any more poles or moss to use for building a smoker. I've cut and used quite literally every usable tree, pole and clump of moss within a quarter-mile radius of my shelter. The rest of the spruce around my camp are more than a foot across. Not ideal. Is it even possible to smoke the whole moose before it starts spoiling?

I come to the realization that I will tap out if it's the only way to keep from wasting this precious resource. The creature and its life that I've taken mean too much to let it rot. But it shouldn't come to that, because within four or five days I can have my shelter finished and it will make the biggest smoker ever seen in these parts. So all I have to do is keep the meat fresh for four or five days. Can I manage that?

My mind grapples with all the possibilities as I rack my brain for solutions. Other than the warm temperatures, the weather is amazing. The sky stays bright and clear. If I were only able to sit down and bask in the sun, I could enjoy this idyllic paradise! But I'm feeling pressured by the massive amount of work yet to be done, so I don't dare stop for more than a moment here and there to savor the amazing adventure I'm living and the incredible setting where it's all unfolding.

Racking my brain for a way to keep the meat cool, I check my fish lines and haul in a small pike about twenty inches long. Since I don't want to eat it right now, I loop the wire leader through its jaw and place it back in the water to stay alive. Instead, I get a pot full of thinly sliced moose meat and decide to add a bunch of fat to get some sort of frying effect.

I have piles of fat, having cut as much from the moose carcass as I could. The kidneys and stomach particularly had huge clumps of bubbly, white fat, and I took it all. I know I'll need the fat even more than the meat later in the season, understanding that fat can keep me alive during the cold months when straight protein won't. However, I've always been on the picky side with food, and I've never liked fat much; when I'm eating a steak, I cut the fat off every time.

Dicing up a bunch of kidney fat, I put it in the bottom of my cooking pot beneath the meat. It starts to sizzle as the fire heats up. The flames are pleasant as they lick around the pot and the smell of the meat is tantalizing. The fat is reducing to hot, golden globs and as I reach over to stir it something suddenly comes over me. I don't know if it's the smell of the fat or the look of it sizzling and oozing oil. But for some reason I become absolutely ravenous for the fat, and I pop a dripping chunk the size of a walnut into my mouth. I bite down just once and the fat bursts open, releasing a stream of warm moose oil flowing down my throat. It's pure heaven!

I'm so into the taste and the feel of the warm oil that I dive in for another and another, burning my mouth when I can't wait for the fat to cool. I'm ferociously consuming those golden globs, and I'm shocked as much as pleased that I like it. This fat is incredibly delicious! It's possibly the best thing I've ever put in my mouth. Something inside me has changed.

When the fat is completely gone, I reach in for the thin strips of meat with my fingers and eat it piece by piece. This one meal changes everything, and now all I can think about is eating fat.

With my belly full of rich moose fat, a warm contentment settles in on me. For just a moment, I allow myself to relax and sink back in comfort, a spruce tree supporting my aching spine. I'm getting a taste of that glorious feeling that only wild men know when they're living on the land: an intangible sense of freedom and wealth. It's the feeling I dreamed about when I heard I was cast on *Alone*. So far I've been working too hard to sense it at all. But right now, sitting by my fire and licking grease from my fingers, I feel it. It's amazing. And then it's gone again, replaced by a feeling of urgency about the work that has to be done to save my moose.

The meal has strengthened me and cleared my brain a little, opening some neural pathway for a helpful childhood memory to emerge. When I was a kid, we had no electricity and therefore no refrigerator or freezer. After milking the cows, we always needed to store that milk for a few days. To keep the milk cool and fresh, my brothers and I dug a pit in a creek bank where the sun couldn't touch it. We lined the pit with stones. Cool water would sit in the bottom of the pit, and we would set the jugs of fresh milk down inside and cover it with a big stone. It wasn't quite a refrigerator, but our cool cache extended the life of the milk by a couple of days.

115

I realize that I can build a similar setup here by digging a pit on the north-facing creek bank, the only place protected from the sun. Cool air settles there, and the sun only touches it for a few minutes at the end of each day. If I dig deep enough into the bank, I can create a cold sump where the ground will maintain a fairly cool temperature.

But even this solution generates another big problem. That riverbank is the one where a grizzly bear and a pack of wolves are constantly prowling. Storing the meat there could draw them in. If they get a taste of fresh meat, they could stick around and cause me real problems...like turning me into fresh meat. So can I keep the meat cool for five days without losing it to grizzlies or wolves?

I decide to dig the pit and barricade it with a system of stakes and logs. It will be the best I can do while I convert my shelter into a smoker. So I grab my axe and start digging into the river bank.

My axe is not a great tool for digging, but I chop down into the bank six or eight times, separating a basketball-sized chunk of dirt. Then I drop my axe and wrestle the large clod free, throwing it downhill toward the water. I repeat the process over and over again, driving myself with sheer determination to protect my meat. I work feverishly, forgetting to even eat. I have fish on two of my lines now, but I haven't taken the time to grab and butcher them. Time is going by, the temperature is staying warm and every moment works against me.

I also have my hands full keeping birds and animals off my stack of meat while I dig. Every time I look at my meat pile, gray jays and mice are squeezing through the boughs I placed on it, snatching bits of fat and running off.

By day's end I have the pit dug out, but I'm filthy and exhausted. There's a layer of mud on top of the crusty blood I was covered in yesterday. Again I close the day too tired to bathe and promising myself that tomorrow I'll finish and clean everything up.

Day 17

I spend most of this day constructing a wooden box in my pit. I've been lucky that no bear has come after my meat during these past three days. I thank God for that as I cut wooden stakes and drive them into the ground like a palisade. Then I cut bigger trees and make a double wall by lining both sides of the stake palisade with sturdy logs. I add a second row of stakes, and I also leave some of the logs really long and stake them down at the ends, far back from my food cache. I'm hoping all this will keep a grizzly bear at bay if he comes through tonight.

As I work, I feel weaker and slower. I'm literally stumbling around now. Apart from my delectable breakfast of fat yesterday, I've barely taken a moment to eat since I shot the moose. All of the work, from handling the huge shelter logs I've been using, butchering the moose, hauling it to camp, and now digging this cool-cache and cutting up logs to barricade it with is really taking me down. I'm legitimately struggling. I note with sad irony that killing a moose could be what eliminates me from the competition. However, I feel like I can't stop even for a meal until the meat is safe.

I also know that I'll have to build another food cache, so my present effort feels wasted to a certain degree. This riverbank cache is the only way I know to keep the meat cool while I make my smoker. But once the meat is smoked, it can't survive the dampness here so close to the river. Later on, I'll have to build another cache up in the dry spruce trees where it's warm right now.

If there's one thing I don't need right now, it's wasted effort. The thought of doing this work twice makes me feel more exhausted, and it reminds me of a year that I worked for a small NGO in Tajikistan.

*   *   *

117

We had a small plane, the only aircraft in the country that could safely do medical evacuation flights to the Pamir mountain villages. We flew out of a small army base, and the soldiers there were always blowing holes in our airstrip with grenades and RPGs. That created a serious risk, not only for aircraft, but also for whoever had to clean up the airstrip that week. When you're digging RPG tail fins out of the dirt, hoping like crazy that it's not a live round, you sometimes wonder if your effort to help is being squandered.

Often the soldiers would use the air strip for training, digging trenches across it everywhere. There was an enormous training field just yards away, so it was clear they were only destroying the runway to be devilish.

But at the end of the day, I remind myself that it may have all been about my friend who sells lumber in the remote town of Khorog, who thanks me every time we meet because his little daughter was able to fly out and get an emergency procedure that saved her life.

Sometimes an enormous task is for just one purpose, and it's worth it, no matter how costly it becomes in energy and time.

*   *   *

Though I can't use this river cache long term, I know this task will be worth it if I can preserve my meat until I smoke it. Still frustrated by the thought that I'm wasting my effort on this cache, I carry on slowly.

Setting up the cameras to capture everything I do takes so much precious time and extra calories as well. Hauling the tripods around, keeping the batteries fresh, making sure the microphone is on me, and explaining my process to the cameras while working - it all feels like a direct threat to my success. And that task of filming remains constant, complicating every survival effort. Only sleep frees me from the burden of filming everything. But I try to film it all anyways, embarrassed by the weakness I'm displaying as my pace of work continuously slows.

I keep at it until there's a fairly solid barricade inside my pit. Then I line it with spruce boughs and start stacking meat inside. I'm so exhausted that successfully protecting my meat inside the cache brings me little sense of relief. I stumble back to camp and collapse at my campfire, as tired and weak as I ever remember being in my life.

Needing to immediately get my shelter ready to use as a smoker, I intend to sit for only a short time. But I'm utterly spent, out of strength. My limbs feel like lead as I just sit here entranced by the flames, trying to eat but mostly staring like a zombie.

I must be a real sight now. I'm filthy with mud, blood, and even gut juice from getting inside the moose. Spruce sap has tangled my hair into wild clumps, and my face is hollow and listless. My brain feels numb but races on endlessly inside me, shouting about the work I still have to accomplish before my food supply is secure and I can face cold weather. On top of it all, my back is getting worse. I can hardly sit through the pain.

I think about my shelter, still far from finished. It will take me a couple of days at least to make it usable as a smoker. I'm finding that obtaining food is the easy part, but having fresh meat out here is like opening Pandora's box. Protecting it and preserving the meat are a real nightmare. Guarding it from predators is easy compared to protecting it from weather conditions. If meat is fresh, it can handle moist air, but not warm air. If I smoke or dry the meat, it can handle warm temperature but not moist air. I know straightforward solutions to any one of these threats alone, but building something in the bush that guards against all of those dangers at once is unspeakably challenging.

The truth sinks in on me that these are my crisis days, the days that will either break me or set me up to go the distance. My whole story out here will be defined by how I manage this challenge, and it's all going to be on film in front of everyone. The weight of that thought almost crushes me in this moment. It's humbling to realize that in just three days from my highest joy of killing the moose, I'm struggling so desperately now and my whole season is at stake.

How did my decisions get me into such a jam? Was killing this moose a bad move? Will I be unable to save the meat, and go down in history as the guy who wasted the biggest animal ever killed on *Alone*?

My decisions have gotten me into jams before—lots of jams. Sometimes the situations were funny, sometimes life-threatening. As I sit beside the fire, zombified by exhaustion, my memory takes me back, cursing me with the memories of bad decision after bad decision.

$$*\qquad*\qquad*$$

One time in a little city in Central Asia, my decisions led me to get involved with a man who nearly got me killed. I was working on learning Russian so that I could take part in humanitarian projects across the former Soviet republics. During a year of language learning, I got bored so I decided to start a restaurant as a side quest to help pay the bills. Going into business with a Tajik friend whom I thought I could trust, I rented a space in a nice area of the capital city and worked for a few months having furniture made, ordering kitchen equipment, and making a beautiful lounge space. Things were going well, and for one season we were the top restaurant for young adults in the capital city.

But there came a day when I needed to import some supplies, and my partner promised that he knew a way to get it done quickly. As I learned later, he was transporting tax-free shipments of hookah tobacco on the side, and perhaps some stronger stuff as well. Happily ignorant of this at the moment, I went with him to meet his transport guy.

"We have to be very careful," he told me as I climbed into the vehicle. "There was a terrorist attack nearby last week and now the police will shoot anybody. They only give one warning, then shoot."

Not five minutes after he said that, we arrived at a police blockade. Instead of stopping, my companion panicked and gunned the accelerator through the barricade.

"What are you doing?" I shouted at him from the passenger seat. "Stop!"

"No! I don't have license!" He shouted back as he barreled forward. The engine screamed and the tires smoked. "If my father finds out about this, he will kill me!"

Away we went, careening at top speed through a crowded bazaar. Behind us police piled into their cars and raced after us. Panicked people fled before us, narrowly missing being run down.

"Stop and talk to the police!" I shouted. "We'll give them some money!"

"No, they will shoot!"

Right and then left, we dodged through narrow streets. Our SUV was on two wheels, ramping over curbs, scattering pedestrians and causing absolute mayhem. I hung on for dear life, not knowing how we avoided rolling over.

"This is how I die," I whispered to myself, "doing something that doesn't matter, making dumb decisions."

As I saw the police closing in on us from behind, I knew that we'd be dead if we stopped now. The time for surrender was past; they would shoot first.

"I'd better start helping," I told myself. "We've got to get away."

My companion was getting stiff shoulders from the stress, and this stiffness would probably cause him to crash. So reaching over to massage his shoulders and keep him loose, I helped him navigate at top speed. Each time we shook off one pursuer, another police car joined the chase.

The race went on and on. At several points I thought we would surely kill a pedestrian. Finally gaining a couple of blocks on our pursuers, we darted down a dimly-lit side street. Abandoning his car, we ran away on foot and escaped.

For days afterward, I shook my head at the close call and how badly it could have turned out. Time revealed more and more that my partner was far from trustworthy, and eventually I had to leave the entire business to him and walk away.

*   *   *

I freely admit that I've made a lot of bad decisions in life. But sometimes things turn out badly, whether our decisions were good or bad. Once I was on a flight with my wife and infant son, going from Singapore to Indonesia. I had decided to save money by using the lowest budget airline. Given our financial situation at the time, that choice seemed to be the most responsible. I had no idea that "budget airlines" could operate internationally with the risks we would soon discover.

After takeoff from Singapore, as we reached cruising altitude, the normal vibration of the plane came to a sudden stop and everything fell silent. The engines had cut off, and slowly we began to lose altitude.

Cara's eyes widened with terror, and a murmur spread throughout the plane.

"What's going on?" I asked.

Suddenly the pilot's voice came over the intercom. "Our engines are off."

There was no need for him to tell us. It's easy to detect when you're at twenty-thousand feet and the engines die.

"Everyone please stay seated. We will try to restart."

After a few tense moments of falling, the engines came back to life. We climbed back to altitude and there was a huge sigh of relief, but in Cara's eyes, I could see that she had lost a year off the end of her life. I felt responsible for putting our family in that situation, even though I couldn't have known the risk. The simple fact that my wife and son were in danger was sobering.

After each bad decision, I spend a lot of time ruminating, thinking over what happened and why. Right now, I'm thinking that it was a bad decision to kill this moose. But was it really? The persistently warm weather is like those plane engines dying: I couldn't have known. I made the best choice I could with the information I had. I've got to find a way to come to peace with the uncertainty of life, accepting the reality that I can't control what happens.

Out here in the arctic, I took my chances and killed the moose. And now the only thing to do is work with the hand I've been dealt.

I could go home right now and just consider this the best two-week moose hunt in the world. I would get to take home hundreds of pounds of fresh moose meat. The meat could be frozen, safe from spoiling. The problems of finding materials to build a smoker would just evaporate. The mental struggles of finding a way to meet these compounding nightmares would instantly vanish.

But if I go home now, I would never get what I've come here for. I think I would be empty and miserable forever. Something tells me with certainty that if I quit now I will never grow beyond the person I am in this moment, and I don't particularly like this man. I'm a stressed-out, often angry guy with hair-trigger emotions. I'm on edge, jumpy, quick to lash out at anything that seems threatening. I'm always dwelling on dark thoughts like the passing of my little brother and the many people who have died near me since I lost him. I have nightmares constantly, and I'm on the verge of tears in seconds when

I remember certain things. My soul is just filled with turmoil and misery. So I'm a bit of a wreck inside; what's worse, I don't really know what to do next in my life. I've come to the point where something has to change. Either I have to change personally, or I have to quit doing what I love to do. Basically, change is unavoidable. But how, and to what?

After a long, silent sit, I come to the conclusion that I'm spiraling downward mentally. I'm getting discouraged the longer I dwell on these things, and I can't allow this to happen to me. But there simply isn't more strength in me to work today. So I change tactics and decide that right now I need to be proactive to care for my body and mind. I have to do anything I can to keep my body and mind positive and able to move forward. But what can I do that will lift my spirits and give me some strength? I look at the reflection of my face in the camera and immediately know where I can start: I should wash up.

Getting to my feet, I grab my cooking pot and fill it with murky river water to boil. Then I rummage around in my gear until I find a piece of clothing I can use as a wash rag. Next, I grab a big handful of spruce tips—the tender, young tips of the branches where the needles are softest and contain the most fragrance. Spruce tips make an excellent antiseptic wash when they're boiled. It's not only cleansing, but healing, and it smells great too.

I sit down by the fire, happy that I've decided to take the rest of the day off to take care of myself. The flames are warm and I begin to feel so languid as I lean back against the spruce tree by my fire. Only the pain in my lower back keeps me from falling asleep.

The water is just starting to boil when the parting words of a good friend ring in my ears. He said, "Remember that this journey isn't all about having food. You are body, soul, and spirit. You are three parts, and don't forget to feed those other parts of you, or you'll weaken."

I think about those words for a moment. They stir something in me, and I know that what I need today is so much deeper than a facial scrub. "Body, soul, and spirit," my friend had said. I agree with him. I think that we are triune creatures. My body is the workhorse that I'm abusing so badly right now, but inside me lies a spirit that should be alive and awakened more than ever before. It's the part of me that's creative, joyful, always happy to be planning some new thing or diving into a radical adventure. Only right now, it's not manifesting any of those things. It's dark, muted, and broken. And that shouldn't be the case, because everything that I love doing and being converges right here—right here in the arctic, being on *Alone*, hunting and fishing. It's the exact way I've always longed to live. And yet I'm not finding the joy I should be finding.

Mentally, I return to the moment I left home, and I again hear my wife's parting words: "Go get drunk on the wilderness. Leave everything else behind. Don't be afraid of anyone's judgment. Scream at the wind, howl at the moon. Be the savage you are. And come home with peace in your heart and the answers that God has waiting for you there."

Wow. What a woman, right?

And I haven't gotten drunk on the wilderness. I haven't taken the time to let go of things and just be. I dwell on that for a moment and ask why. It strikes me that we carry our internal issues with us. I've brought mine here, and my surroundings, even the breath-taking wilderness where I am, can't change that.

Inside me is also a soul. The part of me that hears and responds to the eternal. It longs for meaning and connection to God. Right now it's crying out, reaching for a solid place to start over.

And so I realize that the physical challenges around me are not that big of a problem. It's all just work that needs done. The bigger problem is the battle raging within me. Because of that, I haven't begun to enjoy this remarkable, wild life I'm building. In my wife's poetic words, I haven't gotten drunk on the wilderness.

I know that I need to mentally move back quite some time and think over certain events, to internally process what happened and how it affected me. I've been at war for a long time. I mean that literally and metaphorically. By working in war zones, these past two years have brought nothing but death to me. I've been swimming in a sea of death. So many of my friends have died that it's hard to even count them. And my brother's death lives in my every waking thought.

I don't like to use the word *trauma* because I think the term is becoming a catch-all for everything from bad habits to a lack of self-control. But I recognize that I haven't shaken off the effects of loss, grief, and pain. It wears on me. I think I don't handle it as well as other guys I know. Maybe I'm a little too sensitive. I only know that the peace and answers won't come until I think things through and put them to rest. I can't attempt all of that just now, though. It's too much to face all at once. My spirit wants to survive. However, just like I've realized with the physical side of this survival situation, I can't win it all in one day.

But what I *can* do today is feed and care for not only my body, but also my soul and spirit. My spirit needs something to be excited about, something creative, some problem that does not involve my very survival. So I decide to try shaving while I clean up. I feel a twinge of creative energy about just making that happen, and I quickly decide that the best tool will be the arrowhead that killed the moose.

My soul needs nourishment too, and I instinctively know just where to turn. I bring to mind a psalm I memorized over the summer, a place where I found something that tugged at my soul. I memorized the whole thing, saving it to think through later. And so as my pot of boiled water sits to cool and I sharpen the arrowhead on my leather belt, I begin to quote the psalm aloud:

> "The Lord is my light and my salvation.
> Whom shall I fear?
> The Lord is the strength of my life.
> Of whom shall I be afraid?"

I dip my cloth into the spruce tea and bathe my face. It's incredible, warm and sweet. The blood, grease, sweat, mud, and sap of the past week start to come off.

> "Though a host should encamp against me,
> My heart shall not fear.
> Though war should rise against me,
> In this will I be confident."

I say the words slowly, as if I can taste them. When I get to the phrase about war rising against me, I can barely keep back from tears because of the recent images that leap to the front of my mind. I quickly shove them back. The wash cloth feels so healing and warm.

> "For in the time of trouble He shall hide me in his pavilion.
> In the secret of His tabernacle shall He hide me.
> He shall set me up upon a rock."

By this time, I'm fully convinced that the words I'm speaking are meant for me. The camera is still recording, as it always is. I think for one second about how I may look like a fool on film for quoting all this. But I don't care. I need it. Taking off my shirt, I bathe down to the waist and then grab the arrowhead to start shaving. There's an eight-inch piece of broken arrow shaft still with the head. The moose broke it when he rolled over on my arrow. It makes a great handle and I grab it to begin shaving.

"One thing have I desired of the Lord,
That will seek after.
that I may dwell in the house of the Lord
All the days of my life."

I keep quoting the psalm, and find that it touches all the deep places of my soul, like a healing breath of fresh air.

"When my father and my mother forsake me,
Then the Lord will take me up."

Using an arrowhead to shave while watching my image in the camera viewfinder is a really difficult task to accomplish without cutting my throat. Unlike a mirror, the viewfinder reverses the image I see. It's all backwards and confusing. I see a patch of hair on the right side of my neck and go for it, only to find that I've stabbed the left side of my neck. But after a few minutes of persistence, I have less neck hair than I did before and I'm feeling pretty good.

Washing my hair comes next, soaking it for a while in the warm water before the clumps of spruce sap soften and I can get the tangles out. My hair is getting longer, and I'm happy about that. I've always wanted to see what it would be like if I grew it out, but there's never been a time when I was free to try it. I'm often in some professional setting where I need to look trimmed up. But out here I'll just let it go and be a wild man.

With that thought in my mind, I embrace the adventure and freedom of this experience. This moment is a small breath of life, a promise of savagely awesome days to come. And as I finish quoting the psalm, I know that I'll make it through all of the challenges. I'll

see everything this land has to show me, and I'll be a better man for
it.

> "I had fainted, except that I believed to see
> the goodness of the Lord in the land of the living.
> Wait on the Lord, be of good courage
> And he shall strengthen your heart."

I'm well. I'm here. I'm letting stuff go and becoming a free
man. I can't make it happen in one day, but I believe that it will happen. God sees me running around here in the wilderness. He's happy
that I'm doing it, and knowing that is enough.

Chapter 8

Shift

*   *   *

"Nature never hurries, and yet all is accomplished." -Ancient Proverb.

Day 18

I've dreamed every night—crazy, scattered dreams that are violent and chaotic. But last night's dream was different. I'm standing at a doorway talking to my brother Silas. It's somehow perfectly natural to be speaking from this world with someone in the next. I don't know what we talk about, but time passes until my brother tells me to follow him; I do, right through the doorway. I see an endless atmosphere lit with swirls of blue aurora. It's breathtaking.

"I'm gonna teach you to fly," he smiles. I follow as he dives into the swirly blue lights and glides away. I follow him for hours, soaring on layers of light.

Just before dawn, I wake up wondering if the dream meant anything. I don't know, but I want to think it meant something. The dream stays with me in my thoughts as I set about my routines.

Just like every morning, my first move is to check my fish lines. As I head for the river, I feel wary. My camp smells like a huge pile of bloody meat, so I anticipate bear encounters any time now.

Pretty much every time I go to the river I expect to see a grizzly ripping into my food cache or sniffing around my fish lines.

While I check my lines, I make scent posts as an effort to keep the local bear out of my camp. I walk upriver a couple hundred yards and press dead sticks into the ground like a fence across the bear's trail. Then I soak it all with pee from top to bottom. I do the same thing on the downstream side of camp and out on the edges of the meadow. I'm staying well hydrated by drinking a pot of tea brewed from spruce tips every day. Consequentially, I pee a lot. Every time the urge strikes, I save it until I can go find some stump or tree to soak on the perimeter of camp. I always pee as high as possible so that the bear will think I'm enormous. I have a theory that if he has to tilt his head upward to sniff my pee, he will feel inferior.

I'm opening the lid of my meat cache to grab some fat and meat for breakfast when I hear a noise inside. Listening for a moment, I realize that something is in there with my food, snarling and chewing.

"What in the world?" I whisper. It can't be a wolverine because the cache is intact. Slowly I begin removing lid pieces, expecting to see a weasel or rat, when suddenly a mink shoots out and runs into the trees. He's oddly obese, as if he swallowed a volleyball. I can see that the little stinker has eaten a third of the precious moose heart and half of a fish spine. I curse the bandit under my breath. I'm not supposed to kill a mink, so I'll just have to get the meat smoked and into a tighter cache.

I grab some food, cook it up, and once again eat as much hot, greasy fat as I can swallow. Then I start right in on my shelter construction, hurrying to get it closed in so that I can start smoking the moose. About a dozen more logs extend it to the length I want. Then I cut shorter logs for the front walls and make a door. Finally, I find moss or mud to chink the cracks. It takes a huge work day, but I'm happy, and I feel up for the task now as I set about it.

Hard work is where I come into my own. I may stress out about how all the details are going to come together, but whenever the decisions are done and it just comes down to back-breaking work, I know exactly what to do. My childhood years set me up well, and it's paying off now.

*   *   *

Growing up on an off-grid farm taught me to work hard. We had no electricity, no running water, no neighbors, often no vehicle, and no money. We grew almost everything we ate. Everything needed for life, we either built by hand or just did without. There were no ball games or picnics in our world, and no excuses or breaks. There were cows to milk, wood to cut, ground to plow, weeds to pull, vegetables to pick and can, hay to pitch, and chickens to butcher. When we were sick, weak, cold, or hungry, the work still had to be done. It's like I was born in another century, and I love that fact. I feel like I'm the closest thing there is to time travel.

Poverty motivated us to work hard. We were so poor that I remember a three-year stretch when I didn't get socks. But I'm not ashamed that we were poor, and I'm proud of the work we did. We accomplished some amazing things, pressed by my dad to persevere through adversity.

My dad was a tough guy for sure. Once, I saw him get his thumb caught in some machinery which twisted it until the machine had ripped the thumb half off. The muscle and skin at the base of his thumb were torn right down to the bone. I could see the bone when he moved his thumb, but most of the tendons were still connected. Dad simply walked to the house, got a sewing needle and thread, and stitched the skin back over it all. He was working again the same afternoon.

Another time, we had gotten a trailer load of howitzer ammunition crates to tear apart for the lumber. Dad jumped from the top of the load holding an armful of wood only to land on a nail-filled sheet of plywood. A nail went through each foot, right through and out the top. He didn't even put his load down. He just lifted one foot and then the other off the nails and kept working, blood squelching from his boots and all.

So my dad taught me a lot about working hard and persevering through pain, and he expected no less from us kids. We had to become tough or else.

As a seven-year-old, I remember cutting lots of firewood. At that time, we lived in a barn where one wall was nothing but cardboard. Winters were cold, and there never seemed to be enough firewood to get through. Every day we were out there cutting wood and hauling water. One day while picking up the wood Dad cut and loading it onto a trailer, my little brother fell and bit right through his lower lip. Blood was streaming down his face, and he cried until Dad came over to check him out. I was feeling pretty low myself, with ice building up on my thin, worn-out gloves and my fingers and toes aching intensely from the cold. In my mind, my brother and I were almost dead, staggering through our work like survivors of the Bataan death march.

"Surely Dad will let us quit for the day and go home," I thought.

Dad looked my brother's face over, poked at his lip, and just said, "Yep. Go try it again."

There was no choice but to shake off the snow, wipe off the blood, and keep going.

Oddly, it's a cow that provided me with the mental image which comes to me most often when I need to dig deep and persevere. We had this milk cow that had gotten used to running through fences. She would walk up to a tight, five-strand barbed wire fence, shove her nose between the strands, and just struggle until she got her whole self through. Every time, the barbs would lacerate her milk bag and teats, and then milking her was a real problem. It must have hurt like crazy to have those things squeezed, being full of cuts like they were, and the cow would dance around, knock over the milk bucket, and kick the stuffing out of me and my brother.

So any time we saw her going through a fence, we were invested in stopping her. She would be halfway through and we would both run, one boy grabbing her tail and another grabbing a stick. The one with the tail would haul backwards while the one with the stick whacked her face to get her to turn around and save her teats from becoming hamburger. But the cow would just close her eyes and ignore us. You could see her brain working so plainly. She was thinking, "If I close my eyes and keep my legs going, I'll end up where I want to be." And she did. Every time. No matter the strands of wire stretched taut across her face and chest, no matter the blood running from her teats as the barbs dug deep gouges down them. No matter the stick whacking away and the little boys screaming. She just tuned it all out and plowed forward. Eventually, one strand of wire would pop, then another, and she'd drag us through the fence and take off. She clearly had a broken mind.

Throughout my life, in the darkest and most difficult times, a mental image of that cow has returned to me. I've found that her strategy is the best: just push one leg forward and then the other. Keep them going. Ignore everything else. If I just close my eyes and keep my legs moving no matter what, I'll get through this. I'll end up on the other side where I want to be. Sometimes, it really helps to have a broken mind.

That mentality is how I got through most of my childhood. Many times, I had to just forget the pain and push through like that cow. Because although it was great to grow up with wholesome skills and self-sufficient capabilities, the other side of that coin was that my childhood was not always happy.

*   *   *

But today, I lean into this work with the confidence that I can see it through. Cutting logs, digging, dragging heavy loads—that kind of work has been the mainstay of my life. I may have been bitter as a kid about lacking the things other kids had. But now I'm relying on the things I *was* given, not relying so much on bushcraft tricks or wilderness wisdom. Instead, I'm falling back on the old skill of planning and executing a good work day: probably the must unsung survival skill of all. My dad gave that to me, and I now consider it a great gift.

When I'm up against physical challenges like the difficulties I'm facing here in the arctic, my childhood experience is a reference point that tells me I can push through more, bear more weight, and go on. More importantly, though, my story is a reminder to me that God can meet me anywhere, and he always brings true life. He can turn the bad into good.

Today while I'm cutting trees and hauling logs for my shelter, I contemplate all the mistakes I'm made here already: my bad decisions, weaknesses, and even the baggage I may carry inside. I ask aloud that it will all be redeemed, that it will be turning into something good: a story that says, "God walks with Timber, and the joy of that is better than life."

I work until dark, almost finishing my shelter's woodwork. Grabbing some food for supper, I notice that the mink bandit has returned to my cache of moose meat. He got caught in my snare but broke it and escaped. Offering a silent prayer that he will choke and drown on the loop of wire, I set another snare before I go to bed, this time using stronger steel wire.

Day 19

I'm thrilled to find the meat staying just cool enough when I check it this morning. But another problem has to be solved now. I need some containers in which to store lard. I've been puzzling over what I could pour hot lard oil into as I render down all the moose fat. It has to be rendered as surely as the meat has to be smoked, or it will all spoil together.

Rendering fat involves boiling it down over a fire until the impurities are all floating like a little gooey island and I can dip it out. All that's left is pure liquified oil which will harden once it cools. The resulting lard will be a rich source of fat, packed with good nutrition and also great as cooking oil for frying fish. I have taken quite a few pounds of fat from the moose and it will make great lard if I can boil it all down before it spoils or gets eaten by some animal.

One of the greatest bushcraft challenges is making containers that can hold liquid. I consider using moose hide for a moment, but it would take a few days for me to properly prepare the hide. Another option is to make a burn bowl - a chunk of wood with a dish-shaped cavity made by burning and scraping. I don't have enough time for either option. I have a hunch that birch bark could be a quicker way to make multiple containers if I could only find some birch.

Only one spot remains unexplored on my land, and today I decide to go there with the hunch that birch might be waiting for me there. After a long trudge through swamp and willow, I'm elated to find not only a few small birch trees but also some clumps of moss that are usable. It's a big win, and I gather as much moss as I can carry and chop a few sections of birch bark from the biggest of the trees, which is about four inches through at the base.

Back at camp I put a pot of fat on the fire to render and start shaping a container from the birch bark. I have a good-looking tube of bark, a section that resembles a tall can with a split down the side. So I make two round discs of alder wood slightly bigger in diameter than the tree I peeled the bark from and about an inch and a half thick. Smoothing them carefully, I fit them into the ends of the bark tube. They go in nicely, spreading the split side apart a couple of inches. I tie the end plugs in place tightly with snare wire. Now when

I lay the container on its side I have an open tub about four inches wide and a foot long, both ends corked with the alder disks. It looks almost waterproof.

My pot of fat is boiling down nicely. I dip out the gooey island of gunk and tip my pot to pour the oil into my new bark container. For a second it looks waterproof, but then a leak springs as the oil softens the bark and leaks past one of the plugged ends. I end up having to squeeze the leaky end tightly until the lard cools enough to solidify. It takes a long time, and I resolve to do better on my next batch.

Getting distracted from my lard work, I head to the river and see that I've caught a thirty-inch fish.

For the rest of the day I scrape up bits of moss wherever I can find some and stuff them into the gaps of my shelter. It's a big job. I estimate that there are five-hundred lineal feet of gaps to chink and it's hard to find enough moss. I roam everywhere trying to find patches of it that are substantial enough to mess with. Then I use my axe to scalp the moss up in a nice layer. I end up with more dirt clods than moss. Piling them on my rain jacket, I carry them back to camp and use a wedge of wood to tamp them deep into the log gaps until I have a nearly airtight fit. The shelter is far from finished, but it's already looking cozy.

Day 20

Rain starts just before daylight, and it's still drizzling when I decide to grab some moss and head to a toilet log on the edge of the meadow, leaving the camera behind.

The toilet log is a wet, slippery driftwood log partly hidden in some bushes. It's not comfortable at all to sit on, but it works.

*   *   *

Using a makeshift toilet is nothing new for me. Growing up, we used an outhouse most of the time. It was located down a slippery, muddy path from the house. We did have a toilet inside the log home we built after the barn with the cardboard wall. The bathroom was just a closet where a five-gallon bucket was concealed under a wooden box with a hole in the top, and on cold days that's what everyone used as a toilet. With a family of thirteen, that bucket filled up fast.

It was my job or my older brother's job to empty "the bucket" each day, and I complained loudly and often. It was no picnic, as you can imagine, hauling that thing down to the outhouse and dumping it without getting splashed or rubbing it against my pants. There is just no way to paint a rosy picture of that chore. More than once while I lugged that bucket nearly brim-full of waste to dump, I thought about how weird we were compared to the rest of the world, sitting on their porcelain toilets and pushing a lever to get rid of the contents.

The unthinkable happened to my brother once on a morning trip to dump the bucket. He decided to hang the bucket on the handle bar of his bike while he rode to the outhouse: a life hack that evidently would make the chore easier. He was so pleased to get the job done faster, until he hit a patch of ice one day and went head over heels into the bucket's contents. I still cringe every time I think of that awful sight.

*   *   *

I remember that instance with a grin today as I squat over a log and I thank God that I don't have to face the "bucket" chore any more. Squatting over a log out here in the Arctic is just fine for me.

I'm just getting things moving when I look out into the meadow and spot a young bull moose about sixty yards in front of me. I want so badly to film this but I've left the camera behind this morning and with my pants down, I can't do anything about it. So I just sit there and enjoy watching the moose as he noses around in the horsetail grass at the near end of the lake. It's a spectacular sight, as light fog frames the meadow and the rain-drenched horsetail grass sparkles a little.

"Nice day for a hunt," I think to myself, knowing that the rain would make it easy to stalk this moose. But I've already killed my moose and I'm not allowed a second one. I plan the hunt mentally anyways while I push out a huge log of digested pike. It feels like there are still bones in the fish. I choose which approach I would take for the stalk and determine that I might be able to get close enough for a shot. The moose continues to feed undisturbed in the shallow edge of the lake.

The wind is starting to shift towards the moose and I wonder if he will smell me. I can sure smell me. Fish and moose fat that's been chugging its way through the guts for six days is none too pleasant when it finally decides to make its move and come out.

The wind shifts another degree or two and suddenly the moose's head snaps up and swings my way. I can read what's going through his mind as he stares in my direction.

"Whoa, that's not natural. (Sniff) Somebody over there is in real trouble. (Sniff, sniff) Bear? Bigfoot?" He can't decide what I am, never having met up with a human before. He cranes his neck to get a better sniff. "Phew! Bleh! Not natural I say!" He turns and slowly picks his way off into the willows again, having decided that I'm too busy or too sick to be a threat, but feeling done with the air quality in these parts.

After days of strenuous work, my shelter is finally ready to use as a smoker. It's high time to preserve the meat. But while preparing the meat, I'm battling a whole army of gray jays. My local pair of birds seems to have sent out invitations to the four corners of the earth. Now there's a literal swarm of jays flitting around me in the trees. They fly right up to me and take any piece of meat that I'm not holding onto. The most audacious birds come right up to my face and yell at me. After a little experimentation, I find that they're asking for fat. I set out a little chunk of lean meat and after tasting it, they scold me ferociously.

By late morning, my moose hangs on racks in my shelter. From front to back of my shelter and from side to side, the entire space is filled with big slices of meat hanging about two inches apart. Standing inside, there's the most intense aroma of fresh blood. My mouth waters, and it's all I can do to keep from sticking whole, uncooked chunks in my mouth. I've never before felt such a compulsion to devour raw flesh, but it's real and it's overwhelming.

After I stoke up a fire inside and pile it high with green alder wood, my shelter is belching smoke from every crevice.

While I tend the smoke fire and cut wood, I also render pot after pot of fat as rapidly as I can, pouring the hot oil into birch bark containers to solidify. I find that I have my hands really full keeping up with my fish lines, maintaining the smoker and lard fire, and making containers for the lard all at the same time.

Once, while a pot of lard is cooking, I run off to check my fish lines intending to be gone for just a minute. There's a fish on one of my lines, and it takes me longer than I intended to get the fish off and return. I come back to see with horror that the pot has caught fire and is flaming about twenty feet high. A spark must have popped into the oil. I grab a glove and get a nasty burn as I put the lid on the pot and smother the flames.

Each time I render a pot of fat, it takes a long time for the lard to cool and solidify. But it I'm making such nice, round wheels of white lard. It's easy to store, using birch bark and my nylon gaiters as storage containers. Once all my containers are full of lard chunks, I close the tops and hang them up in a tree.

Night falls, but I have to keep my smoker going until the meat is smoked through. So I sit by my outdoor fire for most of the night while I occasionally look in on my smoker and stoke it with more green wood. Towards morning, I pile the green wood on extra high and go to bed for a little sleep.

Day 21

It's raining again this morning when I finally open my eyes. Droplets splash against the tarp above me and it sounds pleasant. It's one of those days where my natural reaction would be to sleep all day. But I want to check on my meat and see how well it smoked. I lie in bed anyways for another thirty minutes. Then I get antsy, sit up, film my morning update, put on my rain jacket, and head out.

Everything outside is soaked, and a drizzle still falls. Hoping that my smoker hasn't let any moisture get through to the meat inside, I pull the moss away from the door edges and open it up to be greeted with an intense aroma of meat and alder smoke. The fire is still smoldering, filling the shelter with thick smoke.

Once the atmosphere clears a little I go inside, seeing row after row of nearly-black strips of jerky hanging overhead. I find the thickest strips and break them open to find that they've smoked clean through. Not one strip of meat is still moist in the middle. Success!

Coughing and choking, I exit and let out a huge yell of relief and happiness. The weight of struggling to save all the meat, the intense work of the past week—it's all over. I've done it! And it's just in time, too. I believe that the meat would have spoiled after even one more day of this unseasonably warm weather.

I have a winter's supply of meat hanging in my shelter, and lots of lard stashed in birchbark and hung up in my gaiters. It has been one of the most intense weeks of work I can remember, but I can afford to relax a little at last!

I'm beyond amazed that I've succeeded with the meat. It's finally done. I don't have to stress out about the warm weather or work all through the night. The moose kill is now something I can simply enjoy going forward.

To celebrate finishing such a herculean task, I decide to go and fetch the moose head back to camp. I want so badly to see those antlers up on my shelter. I can just imagine what they'll look like over my doorway. Once that huge, bony trophy is adorning the gable end of my lodge, I'll look up at it every morning and feel awesome. So I head downriver with my axe in my hand, happy and doing something kind of non-essential for the first time since I arrived on the land.

Arriving at the kill sight, I'm extremely wary of bears. But after scouting around for a bit I don't see any sign that a bear has been on the kill. The gut pile is still there, the hide is still folded right where I left it, and the head is still sitting exactly how it was when the bull fell.

I admire the head for a few minutes. What a creature! It's magnificence is still very much awe inspiring, even though I've picked its body down to bones.

Taking one last moment to look things over and satisfy myself that no grizzly is going to jump out of the willows, I grab my multi tool and get to work skinning the head. I have to get the skin off and somehow get it down to bone or it will be a rotten mess soon.

The skin on the moose's head is incredibly thick and tough. Not an easy job. Anyone who has skinned a head before knows that you can't just cut down through the hide or you'll hit bone and your knife will be dull in seconds. So I run my knife blade up under the hide and cut while pulling outward. I'm only able to extend the cut about half an inch each time I slice. It's slow work; making the process more distasteful, the brain, tongue and eyeballs have spoiled and they stink.

I'm pretty sad about having lost the brain. I'd like to have eaten it. But I was so hard pressed to save the main stack of meat and fat that I never even had a moment to spare for all the extras. I could have really benefitted not only from the brain, but also from salvaging a lot of the intestine lining, stomach lining and sinews to use for different projects. But I'm too late to salvage anything else from the kill now except for the hide. I'll use the hide even though the fleshy side stinks just like everything else.

The skin is finally off of the moose's head and the brain smells really strongly. I don't want to carry the whole skull full of dripping brains back to camp. So I wade in with my axe, chopping down into the skull in a circle around the antlers. Bits of bone fly like wood chips and when I'm through the bone, brain splashes out at me with each chop. I swing too low once and chop an eyeball, which spurts foul-smelling juice onto my pant leg. With a promise to myself that I'll wash everything later, I keep chopping until I have the skull cap with the antlers freed from the rotting head. Then I balance the antlers on my shoulder and triumphantly bear my gory trophy back to camp.

I feel amazing. I have a huge moose rack on my back, its sweeping tines sticking out on both sides of me like bat wings. It's like I'm an ancient caveman carrying mammoth tusks. I have a bloody axe in my free hand. It's so awesome. In that moment, everything in the world is just right.

I remember feeling this way as a nine-year-old boy bringing home my first squirrel. It sounds like a small kill now, but being exceptionally small myself at the time, it felt like big game to me. I remember watching my shadow as I toted that squirrel home from the woods, imagining myself as a long-ago primitive man bringing supper. I was so proud. I could just imagine the hungry people eager for me to return with meat. Cheers from the waiting villagers erupted in my ears. I was a hunter now, and I would provide for my cave-woman wife and family.

Never once did I think about having kids, experiencing family life as a whole, or even kissing a girl for that matter. Those topics were certainly taboo. I just wanted there to be a girl at camp impressed and happy that I could supply meat for her. I would come home cold, wet, and tired, clad in furs and dragging a bloody something I had butchered. She would be waiting there with a fire going, smiling, happy to see me. And we would sit by the fire for ever and ever, until we wanted to move to some other place. We would only have the belongings that would fit in our packs. It would be mostly weapons, of course. And our life would be one endless dream.

And here I am, living as close to that vision as a man can get. The only thing lacking is the woman. But I know that in my real life, I've married her. She's the woman of my dreams, and she's at home thousands of miles away keeping my fire going. I feel it and know it.

"I'm living a freaking dream!" I shout at the sky. "I'm living my dream!"

Without really knowing it happened, I've started to have fun. I want to just stop and howl at the moon for an hour or two. I would do it if the moon were visible, but instead the sky is a mass of gray clouds. So I keep carrying my prize moose antlers down the long river bank trail to camp.

Reaching camp, I'm about to set the moose antlers up on my shelter when an idea comes to me. Why not plan a big ceremony of some sort, and mount the antlers on the roof in a ritualistic fashion? I could make a production out of it, and it would feel like an auspicious start to my habitation of the shelter.

So I prop the antlers up nearby and try to think of a skit or something to mark the occasion once I move into the shelter in a couple of days. I'm still living under my tarp because my shelter is full of smoked meat. I need to build a good food cache that will keep the meat dry and finish the fireplace, bed and door of my shelter. So I have a few days work before I'll be ready to move in.

After cooking and eating half a fish, I'm back inside my tarp getting comfortable in my sleeping bag. It's been a good day, and I talk about that as I film my evening update with the big camera. I have to do this every evening. Get the camera set up on a tripod in my shelter, clip the microphone on my shirt, and describe everything that happened during the day, including how I felt about it. I talk about getting the moose antlers and how it feels to have all that meat smoked and ready to last the winter. I mention feeling so lucky to have a big food supply and still be catching fish as well.

"I could feed a whole village, but I still need someone to cook it for me!"

I really could feed a village. I'm down to nine fishhooks. Only nine. And I'm catching more fish than I can eat for now. I still have my gill net and fish weir projects which I've put on hold. Now I have this big supply of smoked meat and rendered lard.

"If only I had someone to worry about the cooking, keep the fire going, and help me preserve meat," I lament to the camera. "I could spend one-hundred percent of my time out there getting food, and I'd bring in piles of it! We'd be food rich!"

There's enough here for two, but there's no one to share it with. There's no one with whom to experience the success and struggle. And that's where meaning is truly found in both success and struggle: sharing the whole story with someone who values it.

Feeling suddenly lonely, I decide to take my mind off it by reviewing footage on the big camera. I haven't done it up to this point, but I really want to look back and see how my shots of carrying the moose antlers looked. I'm replaying a clip when I notice how my face looks for the first time. I stare at my image in horror. My face looks gaunt, wasted and hollow.

"Holy smokes!" I mutter under my breath while the clip plays. I knew I was losing weight but I had no idea just how bad it is. It's like looking at someone from day forty or fifty. I look spent, and it's only day twenty-one! I'm horrified. The past week has destroyed me.

Three weeks have passed since I climbed off the chopper and said goodbye to civilization. It's been three weeks of really hard work, but that's basically what my plan was. I've wanted to emulate a bear with my strategy. Right before going into hibernation, a bear will work really hard feeding itself up. He will spend a few weeks gorging for sixteen hours a day. Then one day, when he feels that the time has come, he will go underground and begin his long winter's sleep, resting in the knowledge that he prepared well.

I intended my first few weeks to be all about working like crazy to get everything situated. But with the size of trees I've been cutting, the distances I've had to go for materials and the major task of preserving moose meat, the work has consumed thousands more calories than I expected. I've worked too hard.

The second phase of my plan, my semi-hibernation, has to begin right now. I have to start moving slowly, relaxing a lot, eating as much as possible, and sleeping in. I have to build strength or I'll be a goner. Sitting there in the greenish glow of my tarp camp, I resolve to make the change right now and hope that it's soon enough. From today forward, I'll choose rest first and work second.

I also have to keep feeding my soul and spirit each day. I've been proactive to do that, frequently quoting a psalm or singing something these days while I'm cooking. But I'm going to focus on strengthening my soul even more. As my body weakens, I'll draw more and more on strength from within. I realize that means I'll have to deal with the things that are wrong with my soul. The discouragement, stresses, terrible memories, and bad mental habits I've accumulated will all have to come out.

A verse from the book of Proverbs springs to my mind: "The spirit of a man will sustain him in weakness, but a wounded spirit who can bear?" I hope that the wounds will heal by the time I really need strength to sustain me. With that thought on my mind, I drift to sleep.

Chapter 9

Wild at Last

*   *   *

"I was happy in the midst of dangers and inconveniences." -Daniel Boone

Day 22

Today I wake up tired and sore. I try to sleep in, reminding myself that I need to rest now more than anything. But after a few minutes my back hurts so badly that I can't lie still any longer.

Late morning finds me strolling down to the river to begin my day the way I always do, checking my fish lines. I've caught a nice pike about twenty-four inches long. I'm just finishing and putting my pike on a stringer when I hear a boat motor which sounds like it's coming my way. Scurrying for the bushes as fast as I can, I take my camera, tools and bow along with me. I'm disturbed that I've left sign of my presence on the river shore in the form of my fillet table and boot tracks everywhere.

All my life there's been a compulsion that wells up in me to run for cover whenever I hear a vehicle approaching. I can't help it. It comes from being told as a kid never to let anyone see me, that my life depended on it. That feeling was reinforced by endless drills to perfect the technique of getting out of sight quickly and effectively.

*   *   *

When I was very young, my parents became convinced it would be safer to live off-grid, off-radar, and completely away from society. They had become afraid that forces inside the government were preparing to annihilate splinter groups who didn't fit into the "normal boxes" of American society. They had just learned about various government raids that turned into great blunders and caused tragic loss of life. The siege of Branch Dravidian in Waco, Texas, which ended in the deaths of ninety-two people, was the main case study. The Ruby Ridge shootings and several more incidents were also fresh on everyone's minds. We were already part of a splinter group, and to those heading up our system it seemed like a really dangerous time to be whatever we were.

I was very young at the time, maybe six years old. But my parents and others in our group concluded that we were next. My family responded by "getting out of Dodge," so to speak. So we went off-grid.

When I say we went off-grid, I mean that in the truest sense. We already had no birth certificates or I.D. documents of any type, so no one knew we existed. Beyond that, we went as far out into un-developed land as we could and set up a completely self-sustaining life. There was no electricity, phone, or internet connection. There was barely a road. We ate what we grew and killed, hid out from everyone except a few other families, and we stayed that way for many years. My younger siblings were all born at home, and they had no idea about light switches or flush toilets. We stayed so far from society that when I finally left home at nineteen, I had to learn how to do the most basic things, like order food at McDonalds.

So that's how my siblings and I were raised. I don't blame my parents for anything. They did what they thought they had to do. They wanted to make us not only invisible, but also capable and in-dependent in case we had to live in the woods hand to mouth, kind of like I'm doing now in the arctic. So we did a lot of training, both mental and physical. In addition to survival work, there was training in tactics like evasion, resistance, and escape. There were people who specialized in teaching those things. Some of it was pretty hardcore. Pain tolerance, suffering, and resilience were really important. We were preparing for the apocalypse, for Armageddon. We were preparing for the day the government got rabies and killed or enslaved us all. It's happened in history a lot, after all.

I loved every minute of the hands-on training. Everything from shooting exercises to living in the woods was exactly what I wanted, between the years of five and thirteen. I excelled at that stuff and it was just great. I particularly loved manhunt drills, and thrived at being the one who was given a one-minute head start and then hunted by everyone else.

Sometimes Dad would just take us deep into the woods and have us start fires in the rain or set up a shelter. Those were the second-best memories of my life.

One facet I did not enjoy was being "desensitized" by watching films of various incidents on violence and bloodshed. The film of the bodies from Waco was particularly graphic. That type of media was nearly the only media I was exposed to for years, and it affected me deeply. It ultimately meant that I grew up in fear, having nightmares every night about our family being shot up and burnt and losing my little brothers and sisters to enigmatic black-clad agents.

One film that I saw at that time changed me in a very different way, however. It was a film shown by a man who'd just returned from Africa. It was his first-hand account of a major genocide being committed by communist-backed forces in a couple of African countries. This fellow had been helping wounded civilians as a front-line medic, and the footage that he showed was far beyond gut-wrenching.

The children in his footage stood out to me. What I feared most was to them a physical reality. I saw the looks in their eyes, and I felt connected in some odd way. That notion would come back to me very strongly later in my life, setting the tone for my choices in humanitarian aid work.

*   *   *

I'm my own man now, and I don't live in fear. But when I hear a motor coming around the bend, I still can't help myself. I just have to find cover, so I run for the trees dragging my equipment.

The sight of the production team with a medic coming ashore surprises me. I had forgotten all about the medical checks. However, glad to see them, I emerge from the bushes and offer to help carry their gear.

My hopes for some refreshing human engagement are sorely disappointed. The crew simply reply that they can't engage in conversation. I'm alone, and this brief medical check doesn't change that fact.

I try to engage them in dialogue anyways while they take my blood pressure, weigh me and write down some notes. It's a fun game, at least.

"See if I can trip them up, get some info from them stealthily," I tell myself. It would help if I can get a weather forecast from them. I start asking loads of innocent questions rapid fire, like, "How are things for y'all at camp? Are you guys staying warm? Did you notice that first snow flurry a couple days ago?"

Most people will start talking if the questions seem benign, and then if you keep them going too fast to think, they'll be giving up info before they know it. So I try, but they're pretty experienced at this and don't give much up. They stay tight-lipped while they finish the medical check and get on their way.

They don't even congratulate me when I follow them down to the shore, see a fish pole moving, and pull out a thirty-six inch pike right beside their boat! One of the crew simply shouts as they pull away "Hey, get your camera and film that! Don't go anywhere without that camera!" I do notice a couple of crew members grin though when they see the fish.

One need is becoming very apparent to me: I need to find a source of good quality fire tinder and store up a ton of it before snow covers the ground. Snow could come any day now, and if I don't get enough tinder gathered for the whole winter it's going to get really hard to find. I've stored enough dry tinder for ten fires and kept it in reserve all along, but now I need to store enough for a hundred or two hundred fires.

There are also a few places on my shelter that need to be patched with moss after I used my home as a giant meat smoker. Having the heat of a fire in it has caused everything to dry and shrink a bit. When standing inside, I can see light streaming in through a few cracks that have opened up. All of this means that I have to hike out for another load of birch bark and moss.

After eating I head out across the meadow, taking my axe and bow. While crossing the meadow I get an urge to pee. So I find the latest set of bear tracks and unzip.

"Get a load of this!" I yell as I soak the bear tracks with pee. "Haaaaa! Cross me and die!" I'm infusing my scent with a little aggression. Because it helps.

A grizzly is still always skulking around my territory at night. Even a small bear could kill me easily. But this bear doesn't know that. All he knows is that I can pee higher than his head, so I must be huge. In his little grizzly brain, I'm a monster. Every dry stump or dead stub around my camp as been marked at least once a week. The bear comes strolling around at night. He gets a whiff of dried meat from my camp and he thinks, "Hey I wonder if I could get that delicious stuff?" But every few yards he runs into my silent sentinels of pee which warn him, "I'm way bigger than you and more dangerous. This is my land. I own everything here, and you'd better respect my boundaries!"

It seems to be working so far. Several times I've noticed tracks where this bear has come close and then turned away, making a wide detour around my camp. But I realize that if the grizzly ever meets me in daylight he's gonna say to himself, "What a tiny human! I've been duped!"

If I was still hoping to kill a moose, I wouldn't risk peeing everywhere like this. It could warn the moose away too. But having already killed my moose, I can make as much noise and scent as I want. Just thinking about it makes me want to howl, so I throw a few barks at the sky, listen to them echo and then holler for a minute or two. It feels good just to be alive!

Reaching the tundra zone, I gather all the fire tinder I can, scraping off flakes of loose birch bark and picking any clump of dead grass I can find. Not much is there, and it's all soaking wet, but I'll dry it out in the rafters of my shelter.

The best result of my exploration today is that I find a huge patch of Labrador tea plant. It's a low bush that makes a fine and tasty tea. I've never used it before but I learned about it when I arrived in the arctic. So I pick an armload of it to take to camp, elated that I'll have something besides just warm water to drink now.

Once I get to camp, stomach cramps hit me. I'm not nauseated, but the cramps become painful as the hours pass. I while away the hours beside my fire, cradling my stomach and sometimes moaning a little bit. I'm afraid that it might be caused by the latest batch of moose fat I ate. I had saved a few handfuls of meat and fat to eat fresh as I smoked the majority of it. The fat was on the border of spoiling, but I ate a lot of it.

Hoping that the cramps in my stomach go away, I boil a pot of water for tea, tossing in a big handful of tea bush along with some spruce tips to steep. Maybe the tea will solve whatever's going on inside me.

Someone told me at orientation in basecamp that I should use the tea sparingly, but considering the absence of edible plants on my land, I decide to brew the tea as strongly as it can be brewed. The tea smells delicious, and I'm a believer in the adage, "If a little is good, a lot will be better."

I drink a full pot of strong tea right before bed, hoping it will help my stomach and happy to have found a comfort item at last.

Day 23

The skies have been constantly gray and overcast, and rain falls lightly for hours every day. I haven't seen the sun for over a week now. This weather is driving me nuts because I want so badly to wash my clothes. My t-shirt and pants are still stained with all the blood and gut juice that I got covered in from the day I killed the moose until now. I've been rotating my two pairs of socks, wearing a clean one each day. This worked to keep my feet fresh-smelling when the weather was sunny and I could wash a pair every day. But this morning as I dress everything is so dirty that my socks are stiff and crunchy like corn chips, and my shirt feels like a dog blanket. Every garment I own is begging to be washed, but I'm waiting for a clear day so that they can dry in one afternoon. I don't want to risk my clothes being damp overnight. It would chill me.

I have a second set of pants, a wool sweater, and my winter boots that I haven't touched yet. I'm saving those, along with some socks, to change into once really cold weather strikes. I figure I'll wear my light set out completely in early season when I'm doing all the working and sweating. Then once I'm finished with the hard work and I can feel cold weather setting in, I'll bathe and switch into my clean, fresh winter clothes for my hibernation phase.

Pulling on my muck boots, the stench from inside them is so strong that I turn my head away, relieved when they're corked by my feet. I stand up and feel the blisters on my heel burning. These boots are very damp inside from sweat and its causing problems for my feet. I can't wait to get rid of them.

Not only are my boots wet, everything on the landscape is soaked. Every single bit of kindling, every single stitch of firewood, every patch of grass—it's all drenched. Good thing I've been stashing piles of twigs and wood. I've stockpiled armloads of fire materials not only inside my shelter, but also under every fallen log and beneath every leaning tree where I think it will be dry.

The constant rain is making it impossible to hold my move-in ceremony, for which I need good weather. But the sky remains gray and the rain drizzles down endlessly. I can't complain though. I consider myself absolutely lucky to have gotten two weeks of good weather to start this experience off.

I realize that the gray weather is getting me down, so I focus on feeding my soul as I move slowly along my fish lines. I mostly quote psalms.

> "I will lift up my eyes to the hills.
> From whence cometh my help?"

I haul in each line, check the bait and toss it back out. Some of the lines are tangled in rafts of floating weeds, and it takes me a while to untangle them.

> "My help cometh from the Lord
> Which made heaven and earth."

I've really leaned into the idea that I'm a three part being; body, soul, and spirit. It's helping when I treat myself that way, and I'm developing a system of feeding all three. I feed my body with pike and moose lard. I entertain my spirit with projects like engineering my shelter door and planning my move-in ceremony. My soul I feed with words of life.

Sometimes the words of life come in different forms. I've started what I call "free-style psalming," which is basically just saying whatever comes to mind about God and my soul as poetically as possible. Today it comes out something like this:

> "God I see your glory in the heavens,
> I see your hand at work in the earth,
> I see your life in nature around me.
> Don't ever forget that I'm part of it,
> Keep me and guide me as I wander this land.
> Thank you for trusting me with the lives of your creatures."

Every day I have moments when I suddenly become very aware that God sees me. It's inexplicable, but during particular moments, I know in my bones that he is watching, enjoying what I do here. I can't explain it, but it's as real as stone.

It makes me so incredibly happy to walk along my muddy river shore fishing and free-style psalming. I don't want to stop when I get to the last fish line, so I decide to go on downstream and take a look at the moose kill site. I just keep talking and walking, carrying my bow and smiling. I'm truly smiling these days. Accidentally smiling. That hasn't happened for me in a long while.

Reaching the high bank from which I killed the moose, I see lots of fresh bear tracks. I look out over the meadow, stained with blood and trampled by the bear with splintered moose ribs pointing at the sky. The bear has chewed them up, and he is probably right inside that band of willows at this moment. It makes me feel so alive that I can't even explain it. Drawing the deepest lungful of air, I roar the longest howl I can muster toward the sky. It's intoxicating, just like my wife Cara had hoped it would be.

I'm shouting now, screaming out over Moose Meadow.

"I am the keeper of the wilderness!
I am the speaker for the land!
I am the shepherd of the wild creatures!
I am the wild man!"

I lift my bow and scream at the sky in sheer joy. If anyone saw me, they would think that I have lost my mind. But the camera isn't running, so no one sees.

When it dawns on me that I haven't even brought along a camera, I feel guilty and turn to head home. I'm supposed to film everything. It's why I'm here, and I promised that I would do it. If I have to go home tomorrow, I would like for my boys to have seen me being so free and joyful. It could help them.

Another part of me is glad I didn't have the camera. My walk with God and dialogue about it feels pretty private to me, but there will be nothing private once it gets to TV. It's a weird feeling to be as private as I am, and yet to have some of my most secret moments about to be broadcast to the world.

At last evening falls, and it's time to cook my supper meal. After another mostly unsuccessful attempt to fry fish with my moose lard, I call it a night and wrap up in my sleeping bag. The patter of tiny rain droplets against my tarp puts me to sleep fairly quickly.

Day 24

I wake up this morning to a freezing rain. It's coming down hard as I zip up my rain jacket and check the fish lines. If this turns to snow, which it could do at any minute, there would be several inches on the ground in no time.

The rain makes me determined to move into my new shelter before snow collapses the tarp I'm sleeping under. I can't afford to wait for my big move-in ceremony. I feel in my bones that good weather just isn't coming back.

I spend the first half of the day finding enough straight, slender poles to finish my new bed. It's hard to find even one pole near my camp. I've used every tree that's straight and small-sized. I end up hiking about a quarter of a mile away from camp to find the last couple of small spruces I need.

While carrying my things to the new shelter, I think about the other contestants. I imagine that everyone has moved into their shelters weeks ago. I'm sure I must be the last one to get situated. But that's what happens when you kill a moose and have to convert your shelter into the arctic's biggest smoker.

Rain is still coming down as I rest in my new dwelling later in the day. It hasn't turned to snow yet, but I'm still glad I made the decision to move. It feels amazing to be in a structure so strong and snug. From inside here I can barely hear the rain and wind outside. My shelter feels like a real house and I'm happy. Smiling as I lie down, I bask in the feeling of being safe, warm, and established.

I fall asleep with the lingering aroma of smoked meat making my mouth water. But I sleep fitfully, waking up often after having dreams about the golden fried fish I'm trying to make with my lard. Maybe tomorrow I'll get it right.

"God, thank you," I breathe. "Thank you for all this."

Day 25

My GPS unit beeps its morning alert, and I open my eyes to the see the strong log ceiling of my shelter. I slept better than I have in a long time and I'm feeling settled and snug. It's good to be moved in.

As I send the daily confirmation message saying I'm okay, I run through a mental checklist that I've developed as a way to make sure I actually *am* ok.

"Am I hydrated? Am I warm? Can I feel my fingers and toes? Can I move freely? Can I think clearly?"

Next come the questions that will show me if I'm about to experience an emergency. "Is my gear secure? Are my clothes dry? Is my fire tinder safe and ready to use? Do I have enough wood to burn for three days in case I lose the ability to walk? Is my food secure and reachable?"

I do this every morning and I plan to ingrain it in my muscle memory as a safeguard in case my mental state is compromised later in the season. If I fall through the ice and can't think because I'm hypothermic and almost dead, or even if I just get tired or complacent as I starve in late winter, I'm hoping my brain will be pre-programmed to check on these things and send my body robotically to take care of them. If the answer to any of these questions is "No," that reveals a weak spot in my system and I take care of that item before doing anything else. It's how I plan my day.

After checking all the boxes, I decide to get the moose hide back to camp so I can scrape it before it rots. I hike to the kill site to find hundred of ravens picking at the carcass. They're making such a mess of the remains, but I spot a fresh set of grizzly tracks so I assume he's been here as well. Staying very alert, I roll up the hide and tie it into a bundle.

The hide is huge and weighs a ton, and its hair is full of water from all the rain, making it slippery and even harder to lift. After a brief wrestling match, I get it on balanced on my back. It feels like two-hundred pounds, but I know it's partly because of my weakened state. It's probably closer to a hundred or one-fifty.

I'm completely spent once I get the hide to camp. My lower back is screaming where I injured it earlier. After resting for a minute, I haul the hide up onto a log and spread it out with the flesh side up. My goal is to turn it into rawhide and fold it to use as a bed. However, the wet weather is impossible to fight; the hide will never dry in this moisture. And it's starting to really smell.

For a moment the rancid hide with it's spoiled fat smells bad, like something rotten. But as the moments pass it changes for me from a bad smell to something else. It smells like something…kind of *good*!

Never in my life have I wanted to eat a rotten hide. But I can't help myself. I'm eyeing the dripping, rancid fat and actually considering licking it. Now I'm thinking about taking a big bite. My stomach rumbles, and I have to walk away or I'll really start eating this foul thing.

I spend a couple of hours scraping membrane and fat from the hide. It's easier than I expected, and I fall into a rhythm. I'm using my axe head, and holding it in both hands, I can half-scrape, half-cut the membrane away without too much trouble.

As I work, I'm pleasantly reminded of my trapline days back when I was a teenager. I feel like that kid again, wearing worn out, smelly clothes, aging rubber boots and scraping away at some animal skin. I was happy doing that, and I smile to myself just thinking of it.

After two hours I decide to take a break; when I attempt to stop the camera, I realize that I hadn't ever pushed record in the first place. I'm aggravated with myself. It's about the millionth time this has happened. On so many occasions, I've gotten the camera all set up, filmed a lead-in to whatever I was doing and then did a task that was difficult or interesting only to find that the camera was never rolling. Sometimes I push record and go through it all again, but more often I just forget about the scene and let it go.

I'm cleaning the fat from my axe and thinking about frying a big fish for supper when I hear something that pulls me upright and alert. A mournful howl drifts to me from across the lakes and meadow. It rises, growing louder, lilting and falling in a long, doleful moan. There's not a moment's doubt that it's a wolf.

Racing out to the edge of Moose Meadow, I listen intently, trying to locate the wolf. The sound is electrifying, being the first time I've ever heard it. I've been around wolves before in the mountains of Central Asia, and I've seen them darting into villages to scavenge scraps or eat pet dogs in the winter time. But I've never heard them howling until now. It's so much more baleful and sad than I had imagined. I'm entranced.

Two more wolves join the howling, more high-pitched than the first. None of them are very far away. In fact, it sounds like they're right where my moose kill took place.

I strain my eyes as I listen to wave after wave of mournful howls. But try as I might, I can't see anything moving over where the moose bones lay. I guess the wolves are in the timber just beyond the kill.

As I lie in bed tonight, the wolves strike up their howling again. They're definitely on my moose carcass now. I wish I could see them, but without a powerful light I have no chance. The music of the wolves goes on and on. One wolf's voice rises while the other falls, their melodies crisscrossing into patterns of beautiful and savage invitation. It's a sound my hunter's soul has always understood, even though I've never heard it before.

At first I'm eager to listen, but after a while it lulls me to sleep.

Day 26

This morning I see a lot of fresh wolf tracks in the mud where I fish. They've sniffed around but haven't disturbed anything.

Even my buried cache of pike guts that I save for bait is untouched. As I follow their footprints along the river, I keep a wary eye, hoping to spot them. But they're long gone from my territory; eventually, I give up.

I spend most of my energy today hauling armloads of horse-tail grass and thatching my shelter roof more deeply. With the straw-like horsetail looking golden-brown and draping all around my eves, the shelter is starting to look like a red-riding hood style cottage. There's no doubt it will be warm and would shed rain perfectly even without the tarp that's buried under the thatch.

As I survey the shelter, I realize that I could call it finished. I should be resting instead of working hard throughout the day. But each time I think that, I get a mental picture of my shelter looking even more snug. Back to the meadow I trudge, gathering more heaping armloads of thatch. I cut more poles, haul more moss and drag more boughs inside as thresh to line my floor. I know I'm over-building it, but I just can't stop.

There are other projects that need to be done, too. I have to make a food cache that will keep my jerky dry. I'm at a loss to figure out a way to do that, with the rain falling every day and the entire landscape soaked through. So for now I leave my jerky in my shelter and hope a bear doesn't decide to raid me.

I'm clearly failing at resting. No matter how resolute I am about taking things easy, I just can't make myself lie down for any length of time. Any moment I sit still turns into anxiety for me as my brain churns me into a frenzy and sends me back to work. Even when I'm feeling light-headed, which is happening more and more every day, I can't make myself stop and sit down for more than a minute.

Why am I feeling light-headed so often? I have never dealt with light-headedness like this before. I tell myself it's because I've sweated out all the trace minerals from my body, making it difficult to hydrate. What else could it be?

I'm not having any trouble concentrating or keeping my balance. What does bother me is that I'm feeling weak and slow, like an old horse that's been used up and is about to die. When I work or hunt, I don't scamper around the land anymore. There is nothing light and fast about my movements. I trudge slowly, halting often and generally acting frail. I hate that. Is this the new normal for me out here?

I know that I'm weaker than usual and it will probably get worse the longer I endure. My land has provided no greens to eat, no sugars, and no carbs. Passing time will diminish the available food and nutrition further. But I have a hard time mentally adapting to being less capable and energetic. Something about being weak just hurts.

Most men probably feel the way I do. We want to be unbreakable, indefatigable. Even eternal. We are men: our backs are made of iron and our faces of flint. And yet we're all stuck in a reality where weakness is part of our being at all times. We deny it, hide it, and try to prove it's never going to get us. But inwardly, we all know that it's in our DNA.

It's how we deal with weakness that's important. I've seen men exhaust and destroy themselves trying to prove that they're bigger than their weakness. Others melt and surrender passively. Some men become angry and mean, secretly unable to cope with their own weakness.

"What is weakness?" I wonder to myself. "What will I do if I go down?"

Weakness is mortality. It's a confrontation with the fact that we're not God. We break and fail. But the beauty is found in the fact that our physical bodies don't define us. Our spirits tell us that we're more. And the spirit is where true strength can be found. Our bodies may fail and even die, but the spirit can bear it all and remain unde-feated. Its strength comes not from calories, but from the eternal Creator. The body's frailty and the spirit's resilience are themes in the story of my oldest son, Levi.

*   *   *

When Levi was two years old, he was diagnosed with muscu-lar dystrophy: a genetic disorder that causes muscles to degrade until a person becomes a vegetable and eventually dies from lacking the strength to breathe. That's the definition of weakness, the pinnacle of betrayal by our mortal bodies. It's cold and unfair.

I was in Kyrgyzstan the day I found out about his condition, but I hurried straight back to China, where my wife and son were staying. I got home late at night; as I hugged my wife, I found no words of strength or comfort to give her. We were so heartbroken that we cried by the hour, envisioning a future where our son de-clined and died from muscle deterioration.

He was two years old and had just been learning to walk. Watching his hard-earned walking abilities fade and then disappear was more heart-rending than I can ever explain. My son was going to die early and never get to experience the things that make living in this world so brilliant and fun. And I couldn't fix him.

I went into his room and stared at him, sleeping soundly in his bed. I promised him that I'd be his strength, I'd carry him up mountains so that he too could see out over the world. I would carry him through the woods to hunt. I'd carry him across this earth. I promised and promised. But all along I knew that my strength would never satisfy my son inwardly. There would come a time he would want his own strength. And it would never be there.

Then one day as I was feeling sorriest for him and for myself, he came crawling into the spare room where I was working. I had a bunch of expedition gear spread out and as Levi crawled around playing, I kept an eye on him to make sure he didn't hurt himself with an ice axe or camp stove. The juxtaposition of his weak body amid the rugged gear made me turn away and cry silently, seeing the tools of adventure he may never enjoy, unable to escape my mental vision of his poor future.

Then his little voice broke in on my thoughts, and I saw that he had climbed into a tent and was arranging some gear for camping. For a while I watched him. He was so thoroughly happy, although at times the pain in his legs would make him stop and cry for a minute.

Then he poked his head out through the tent flap and asked if I'd camp with him. So I did. We "camped" for a long time and while he played I learned some lessons. My son didn't care in that moment if he ever camped in the high mountain peaks. All he wanted was to be happy with someone he loved. He was inviting me to join him in happiness, lifting me up. Me, with the healthy body and no pain in my legs, being lifted up by my little guy. In his own way, he was extending love. And I saw a strength in my son that I didn't even feel in myself: the strength to be more than whatever his body was. The strength to be happy and kind, the strength to think of someone other than himself. That's the real strength. It's the strength of love. And it's the strongest thing there is.

It took a special strength for Levi to go through what he was feeling, although he didn't even understand it. I realized then that although my son may never have my strength, he had the strength to be *him*, and to love someone else while he was doing it.

*   *   *

Feeling my weakness in this moment, I reflect on the gift of strength. It's good to glory in physical strength while you have it. We find so much joy in going up against an impossible task, bearing the heaviest load, going the longest distance, enduring the most pain and torture. It's satisfying to take on something insurmountable, to try, struggle, groan, dig deep, to fail or win…then to stand on a cliff and roar at the world, rejoicing in the simple feeling of being strong.

Physical strength is a gift from God. He likes to see us put it to use in spectacular ways. Ancient Israel's King David, a true warrior and a savage, said something like, "By my God I have charged through a shield wall and leaped over defenses. He teaches my hands to war and my fingers to fight, so that a bow of steel is broken in my arms."

But all of that strength and pride fails when our body starves, sickens, or breaks. Then, the inner man is revealed. Physical strength can make someone a legend, a hero. But it's inner strength that makes a *man*. It's the only thing that can make someone do what's best for others when we have to ignore what's best for us, even ignoring our very survival. In a word, true strength is love.

"What is my inner man made of?" I ask myself as I contemplate all this beside my fire. Once upon a time, I thought I knew my inner man. I guess I'm going to find out once again. It might not be pretty.

I'm boiling a fish, creating sustenance that will give my body more strength for tomorrow. But when my body fails, who will I be then? I decide to prepare my soul for the coming weakness, and the ugliness I may see as I come unmade. I start rummaging in my memory for more psalms, more words of life. I find some.

"My flesh and my heart fails, but God is the strength of my heart and my portion forever."

Chapter 10

The Loose Ends

*   *   *

"When you arise in the morning, give thanks for food, and for the joy of living. If you see no reason to give thanks, the blame lies only on yourself" -Tecumseh

Day 27

    The rain clears off early today and I find that I'm in a great mood. For the past couple of days, I've been in a dreary mood that matched the drizzly, gray clouds. Now with a little sunshine, my spirits rise and I immediately take advantage of the sun by washing and laying out my nasty socks, shirt, and pants. Cleansing away the awful grime and seeing them spread out, clean and drying, brings me immense relief.

    As I try frying half a fish this morning, I can't quite get the crispy, fried effect I'm hoping for. My fish turns out like boiled fish, just dripping oil instead of water as I swallow it in rubbery chunks. At least the taste is somewhat different, being moose flavored instead of river flavored.

    Later, I'm walking along the river with my bow. It's a splendid day. The water flowing sluggishly beside me steams a little as the light touches it. A group of ducks startles as I round a bend, squawking as they skim away and take flight. Only a few leaves remain on the willow tops, and those still clinging on are crispy brown.

An early morning sun is shredding away wispy strands of cloud. The rocky cliffs visible to my north are glowing. The broken boulders up there must be coated with a skim of ice. They sparkle, reflecting the light as if they're piles of silver coins. I wish I could stand up on those cliffs just once and survey the delta I'm living in. But all I can do is appreciate the beauty from this distance.

As I pass my fish lines one by one, I realize that I'm feeling the thrill of the wild at last, deep and real. All along I've been surprised by the lack of the electrifying happiness I had expected to feel. I've been doggedly doing work. But now it's here and the only thing to mar the ecstasy of this thrill is the lack of energy I have left to revel in it. I'm living the dream. These may be the best days of my life. If I only had my wife to talk to, I would never leave.

My last fish pole is just ahead, and I can tell there's something on it. The line is not moving, just stretched tight, the way pike sometimes act when they've been hooked for a while.

Hauling the line in, I see that I've caught I nice pike about twenty-eight inches long.

"Thank you, God, for this beautiful fish!" I shout, holding the fish up to the sky.

I don't know why I've started holding the fish up like this when I thank God. I'm sure he can see the fish when it's lying on the bank. But somehow it just feels right to do it. So I hold it up to the sky and take a minute for God to admire its beauty one last time before I eat it. Its streaked and speckled skin is so unique. Then I bury it under a log where nothing will get it until I return and take it to camp.

After I stash the fish I get an idea in my head that I could find one of the arrows I lost on day five when I missed the moose. Up to this point I haven't even looked for them. The place where I shot the arrows is a sea of hip-deep horsetail grass. The arrows would've disappeared without a trace, and they're probably buried up under the roots. The chance of finding them is practically non-existent. But after thinking about how God has been giving me things I need, I just can't dislodge the thought that if I ask I will find one of the arrows I shot away. It's a weird belief that borders on absolute certainty the more I think about it. If I walk over there, explain how I need the arrow and start digging around, I'll be walking back with it this afternoon.

I often talk as if there's no question that God is listening. It's not like I avoid asking myself the question "Is God there?" I do ask. All the time. But it just keeps bouncing back with a "yes" answer. It may annoy some people who think I'm acting sanctimonious or pious. But that couldn't be farther from my mind. I'm a guy who has no time for "organized religion." I approach life practically and I don't care what people do as far as drinking, dancing, and all the things religion forbids. I wish everyone were happy enough to dance. Let people enjoy life. It's good to be human.

Inwardly I simply know that there's an eternal aspect to my existence, and that it's created by something very real. I'm convinced that it's God. I've reached out and felt his presence over and over. Although I don't have evidence I can hold in my hand, I'm beyond certain that God is real and has interacted with me. I've seen some things happen, signs and experiences that can't be explained.

*   *   *

When my son was diagnosed with muscular dystrophy, we watched his little body get weaker and his muscles decline for months. At that time, I did not pray asking God to heal Levi. Truth be told, I may not have even believed that God would do a tangible thing like that. But lots of other people prayed for him.

169

Because it's a genetic disorder, muscular dystrophy is irreversible. But after people started asking God to heal him, Levi began to mend and become stronger. His doctor was baffled. He hadn't yet been given any medicine besides pain killers. Without treatments, his condition continued to improve. Eventually the tests started showing results totally opposite from before.

"There's nothing wrong with this kid except for the residual muscle damage," the doctor finally said after running every test imaginable. It was the most beautiful sentence I had ever heard. Even though I hadn't believed in miracles a month before, I knew beyond a doubt that God had done something in my little boy. If I didn't own up to it, if I interpreted God's part as simple chance, that would be an injustice. What happened in Levi's body was beyond this world, and I felt it existentially.

To this day, when I look at Levi running and playing, I breathe a prayer of "Thank you" to God. I'm never embarrassed that I talk to God, or when I say "Thank you" for this or that. Because you can't even imagine how grateful I am that my son has his life back, that I have his life back. I just love the fact that God did it, and I want him to know that.

*   *   *

That's why I'm always saying "thank you" out here in the arctic too. I want to be grateful for everything.

Knowing that all of this has happened in the past, I'm curious today whether God will show me my lost arrow. So, considering the certainty I feel, and weighing that against the odds of actually finding it, I head out to search.

I have to cross the area where my moose carcass lies, and as I pass through the ragged and trampled willows, I see that the ground has been picked clean of any remnant of the great beast. Every scrap of guts, every bone, even the huge spine with it's heavy hip bones is gone. Only raven droppings remain on the flattened grass.

This is unmistakable sign that a bear has taken over the area. From the tracks, I read that the bear has dragged the kill back into the brush where it can be eaten in peace. Bears like to get their kills hidden away in the trees where ravens can't annoy them so much.

I'm extremely alert. It's likely that the bear is nearby, guarding the carcass. So I shout and sing loudly as I pass through.

Eventually, I'm standing at the place from which I took the ill-fated shot on day five, the shot that ricocheted off a willow and disappeared. My feeling of certainty that I'll find the arrow diminishes a little as I survey the area. The horsetail grass has fallen down due to the frost. It's an impenetrable layer of vegetation, and searching for an arrow beneath it is exactly like looking for a needle in a haystack. I don't even know how far the arrow went or what angle it took after it ricocheted. There's less than a one percent chance of finding it, and I admit that to the camera. But somehow I still feel like I'll be walking home with it.

"God, I'd really like to find this arrow. I know I'll find it if you point me the right way."

I feel stupid for a moment. What if I can't find it and the producers put this prayer on the show anyway? Will my faith seem dumb? But I keep on kicking up clumps of grass hoping to see something.

The horsetail grass has fallen over, and lays about a foot deep like a dense layer of thatch. Nudging clumps of grass aside with the toe of my boot and feeling less and less certain, I kick through a thick clump and suddenly there it is, the blue and pink fletching of my arrow. Even though I knew I'd find it, I truly can't believe my eyes.

It takes a minute to pull the arrow out of the mud and grass roots without breaking it. But soon I'm holding it up for the camera to see.

"Look at this! There's no way! Absolutely no way!"

It seems like a small thing, just finding an arrow. But aside from the awesome benefit of having another arrow to shoot at things, there's an elation deep inside me from just knowing that when I say stuff, God hears me. I'm certain that I wouldn't have found it without asking Him.

As I return toward camp, the air around my moose kill buzzes with an electricity. Something is present here for sure, and I actually see a daytime vision as I walk. The vision hits me suddenly, and shows me a bear charging me from the willows and knocking me down. I feel a pain in my foot as the bear crunches down onto it and drags me.

Clearing my head with a quick shake, I start talking loudly and hurry out of the moose kill zone. I realize there's a strange pit in my stomach, and muse that after asking God for help and actually finding the arrow, I'm worried about a bear jumping on me. But I really am.

I shake the vision from my head and continue forward, carrying an absolute certainty that the bear is just inside the willows watching me. Nothing happens though, and soon I'm back at camp, happy with my new arrow and buzzing on adrenaline.

As I approach camp, I see a squirrel dart across my path and stop at the base of a big spruce tree. Noticing a pine cone in the squirrel's mouth, I estimate that it will sit still and eat as I approach. And that's exactly what happens. I drop my stuff and quietly sneak right up to the squirrel, zapping it with a quick shot from my bow.

"Nice! Thanks, God!" I say under my breath. "Could this day get any better?"

Once I grab the squirrel, the tunnel vision I get when I'm killing stuff wears off and I realize that I dropped the camera, failing to film the kill. I'm disappointed in myself. It's the same thing that always happens to me when I'm hunting with another person. Like forgetting the camera, I forget that they're there and I steal the shot opportunity from them. It especially happens when I'm trying to teach someone else how to hunt.

*   *   *

Back about fifteen years ago when I was dating my wife Cara, we went squirrel hunting. Squirrel hunting with a .22 is a great way to date a girl, take my word for it. This time wasn't truly a date though, because we brought along another girl who wanted to learn to hunt. Cara and I had each killed a squirrel when we came across a pecan tree that was full of ripe nuts. Nine or ten squirrels were up in the tree cutting ripe pecans. Since it was our friend's turn, I put the rifle in her hands and pointed at a squirrel that had just descended with a nut in its mouth. It sat in the crotch of a tree and ate while it looked us over.

The girl took aim for about thirty seconds, and as each second ticked by I saw the killing window slipping away. It was painful to stand there and wait for the shot. Second by second I was drawn in to that animal, losing sight of everything else around me. Cara and the other girl ceased to exist; I could only see the squirrel, and I knew that any second it would finish its pecan and dart away.

An unexpected rifle crack sounded, and the squirrel fell down.

"Good job!" I whispered to the girl, who looked back at me in confusion. That's when I noticed that the rifle was in my hands. I had snatched it and fired.

"Oh, I'm so sorry! Here!" I handed the rifle back and pointed to another squirrel up in the tree. The animals were alert now but not fleeing, and I knew she would get a second chance. She aimed for a whole minute that time and still didn't fire.

"Crack!" The rifle went off and another squirrel fell down. Again I noticed that I had snatched the gun, and again I apologized and gave it back.

Three times the same thing happened. She took the gun and aimed, time went by, the squirrel was about to get away, and I unwittingly took the gun from her hands and fired.

Eventually all the squirrels were gone from the tree. Three were dead and the rest had fled. Cara was laughing, but I was feeling so embarrassed and sad for the other girl. I tried to put the rifle back in her hands and promised that we'd find another tree full of squirrels. But she wouldn't take it. The hunt was over and we went home.

*　　*　　*

That's when I realized that I go into this zone when I'm killing something, just like today. I forget that the camera exists and I go kill something. Then I feel stupid because I really want to film this stuff! I want to get amazing shots of hunting so my boys can see it when they watch the show.

Setting the camera up, I present the squirrel and do my best to describe the shot. Then I put some of its blood on my tattoo like I always do and head to camp.

The whole day has been so perfect, and I top it off by filming my moving-in ceremony. I make several torches, finding a gnarly-looking driftwood stick for the torch I'll hold in my hand. Splitting the tops of the torches and stuffing them with spruce resin, I light them up and place some in front of my shelter while I hold up the gnarly torch and start chanting.

I've removed my shirt and donned a headband to make the ceremony as primal as possible. Three of my cameras are set up to catch the action.

174

"Brothers!" I shout after taking a dramatic moment to stare at the camera. "The time has come to usher the spirit of our tribe into this new village, which shall be called Fort Moose Head!"

I chant rhythmically and in my mind's ear, a whole village joins in with me. They're just thrilled to have a chief. They love their chief.

Turning to my right, I shout to a warrior standing by.

"Place the moose head!"

The warrior puts the moose antlers above the door, and we all chant again, raising a chilling, thrilling echo that rings across the arctic.

"Now when this torch of fire and a weapon crosses the threshold, our spirit has entered!"

I grab up my axe and hold it above my head with the torch while the whole village screams and chants. It's a magical moment as the torch passes through the doorway and lights the first hearth fire. Everyone screams and happiness streams throughout the camp. And with the last of the chanting and howling, I've finally and officially moved into my shelter, Fort Moose Head. It's a proper camp now. I feel at home and I imagine that all my fellow warriors and villagers do too.

I fall asleep tonight wishing that there actually were other villagers here. But I smile, just glad that I'm living in the wildest land on earth, glad that I'm free and savage, and finally having all the fun a man can have.

Day 28

I'm snug inside my shelter these days, but it would hold heat better with a thicker roof. So even though it's unnecessary, I spend most of the day hauling huge armloads of horsetail grass from the meadow and thatching my shelter with another foot-thick layer. I just can't stop building. The roof is now at least two feet thick, built in five layers with moss, horsetail thatch, tarp, more thatch and the spruce boughs that top it all off.

A better door would also be nice. I've come up with an idea for a door hinge from something I saw in a remote village in Afghanistan. I take the last straight piece of dead spruce which I've been saving, and with it I make a vertical post. This hinge post is a little higher than the door and as big as my arm. I sharpen the lower end of it to allow it to spin in a socket. Then I make the socket, which is just a chunk of spruce wood with a deep dimple carved into it. I bury the socket in the ground where I want the door hinge to rest and drive stakes to hold it in place. The post will stand with its sharpened end in the dimple and spin easily when I open and close the door.

I affix horizontal cross members into the hinge post with dovetail notches. It's surprisingly strong and rigid. Now all I need is to split some wood into rough boards for door paneling.

*   *   *

The house in Afghanistan where I learned this trick for door construction had a sheep skull placed on top—a huge, Marco Polo sheep with double-curled horns. The Marco Polo is the world's largest sheep species, a majestic symbol of Asia's mountains. The people place the heads over their doorways as a sign of power and good luck.

My son Elliot saw a Marco Polo head placed above the doorway of a house we stayed in once when he was really small. The skull was half-rotten, but as Elliot looked up at the empty eye sockets, he struggled to understand.

"Don't worry, sheep!" Elliot said, his little two-year-old voice filled with compassion and kindness. "It's okay, sheep! Don't worry! It will be okay!"

The skull just stared back, of course, with its ragged bits of flesh dangling from white bones. It would not be okay.

It was a cute moment, tender and innocent. Today, I take a moment to wish that Elliot would never have to lose that sweet innocence.

While I work on my doorway, I look up at my moose skull and wonder if I've done right by bringing my family through so much trial, exposing them to so much suffering and death.

When we arrived back in the States just months ago, our plane was descending into Indianapolis airport when Levi asked in a trembling voice, "Daddy, is there a war here too?"

"No, buddy," I assured him. "There's no war here."

"Oh, good!" he sighed with immense relief.

As I drove to the house we would stay in, Elliot saw a combine picking soy beans. Dust billowed from it, and the long grain chute protruded from the dust cloud.

"A tank!" Elliot shouted, ducking down to the floor.

I cried when that happened. It breaks my heart that they have learned the truth about life: it won't be okay.

I've done the only thing I know to do for them in the face of such stark realities: I've tried to give them hope. When Silas died, it affected Levi deeply. Silas, "Uncle Ice," had been Levi's best buddy. How do you explain to a little boy that Uncle Ice can't come back? Where are the words that make sense?

Building up to the funeral, I spent lots of time trying to explain. Eventually I found myself telling him these words, which Jesus spoke to a family grieving the loss of a beloved brother: "I am the resurrection and life. He that believes in me, though he were dead, yet shall he live."

The verse goes on, but Levi interrupted me with a shout.

"Daddy, those words are good!"

"Yes, son. They are good. They are so, so good."

*   *   *

I'm just finishing the hinge post of my door, using my saw to cut a notch when I carelessly slip and cut my left thumb. It happens fast, and for a couple of moments I can't feel any pain. I know it went deep though, ripping straight through my glove like tissue paper. A dull aching sensation runs from my thumb up to my elbow, and that could mean my bone was hit. I take off my glove and get a look at the damage.

The thumbnail is cut right in two and there's a mangled mass beneath it. I can't tell if it hit the bone or not. But there are bits of skin and muscle hanging out and it's starting to bleed a lot.

I'm not worried about the bleeding or the pain. The big worry that sinks into my mind is the thumb getting infected. I'm constantly in and out of the nasty river water, gutting fish and generally struggling with cleanliness. I already have multiple infections where pike teeth have gone through my gloves. Those infections aren't serious, and I'm dealing with them by just milking the puss and letting them heal. They show, however, how quickly things get infected in this setting, and an infection in a cut this deep could really mess with me. I yell in rage at myself, angry that I've gotten careless.

A little emergency medical kit was given to us as part of the safety gear. It's a small kit, containing only a small quantity of basic supplies. There are three iodine wipes, a few patches of gauze, half a dozen bandaids, a half-roll of medical tape and a tourniquet. The bandaids aren't big enough to keep the wound protected and clean. It would be nice to find some liquid iodine to cleanse the cut with, and wraps that would be watertight, but there are none of those commodities.

After a couple more minutes of pacing around my yard, I decide to do the only thing I can come up with. Scraping bits of spruce sap off of logs and stumps, I daub the wound until I have a pretty good cap of gummy resin sealing the entire end of my thumb. Then

I wrap it with a little medical tape, taking care to use the bare minimum, because the crew will not replenish any item from the medical kit if I run out.

The tape is either too old or too cold to be sticky and it just keeps unraveling from my thumb. But it's the best I can do.

Back down at the river shore this evening, I've caught another pike and I'm trying to keep my thumb out of the slime and water as I flay the fish. I find that it's impossible to keep the thumb dry. By the time I get the fish done and my multi tool cleaned, the medical tape wrapping my injury is soaked and slimy. I hope that the spruce sap is doing its job and I ask God again to look out for it.

Day 29

Working on the moose hide is dull and monotonous. I work inefficiently, tired and trying to protect my thumb from getting bumped or infected by the rotten hide fat. Only the gray jays break up the boredom by flying in and out to grab pieces of flesh that fall from my axe head as I scrape. My efforts to tame the birds has failed because I threw sticks at them again when they tried to steal another string of fish eggs from me. They don't trust me now, but they'll still come pretty close as they snatch fat and scream at me for more.

I'm working on the moose hide when a moment of inspiration strikes me. Why not use the hide as a way to seal my food cache? I could make a structure out of big logs to keep out bears and then line it with the moose hide like a pool liner. It could protect the meat, keeping it safe from rain and snow while keeping out small animals like mink and mice.

The idea immediately cheers me up. It could be the answer to my nagging problem of storing the jerky. So I immediately switch gears and start chopping trees for a permanent food cache.

It takes a lot of effort, but as I slowly cut logs and notch them log cabin style, the cache takes shape. I lay the logs up in the shape of a box, positioning it between two big trees. The trees will come in handy when I make the locking system I have in mind for the lid.

Later, once I'm tired of notching logs, I check the fish lines again and haul in a pike. I'm still catching more fish than I can eat, so put this one on a stringer near my fillet table.

I've developed fish stringers that protect my fish from the eagles. When I used a normal stringer, eagles would swoop down and grab at my fish. Now I use a long alder pole and tie a short stringer to the end of it. Then I push it out into the water and stake it down where it will hold the fish down near the bottom.

By day's end I'm worn out again and disappointed in myself because I can't seem to make myself rest. I've already decided that rest should be my main strategy, but since making that decision I haven't really changed anything. I just keep working. Only once have I laid down to rest in the middle of the day.

Each evening I'm supposed to film a rundown on the days activities and describe how I felt. But today I haven't felt like talking at all. I've just passed the day, not melancholy or down, just silent. It's like I have nothing to add by using my voice. I just feel like listening to the silence. It feels good in a way I don't fully understand.

For a long time I just stare at the camera until I can muscle up the energy to say a few brief things about the work I did.

Finishing my update, I turn the camera off, thinking about how it's just me out here. Just one guy to look after everything. All the needs of a successful camp are a lot of work, but I don't mind it. I'm managing. The success means I can make it another day, and I'm grateful for that. I decide to say so to God as I get my calendar string out and tie another knot.

"Thank you God for keeping me alive, safe and well for another day. I've made it through my crisis days. Thank you."

I've been using a piece of orange paracord as a day marker. Each day right before I go to sleep I tie another knot. It's a routine that gives me a sense of closure to each day. Now there are twenty-nine knots. But what are all these days supposed to mean? My wife is glad I came out here and she encouraged me to enjoy the wilderness, but am I enjoying it enough to make it worth the extra work she must be handling at home? Am I making each day meaningful to anyone but myself?

Human beings are meant to live as part of a community. A village. You can see it just from a practical standpoint. All the needs of a successful camp—stuff like building shelters, preserving food, cutting firewood, managing food harvest—all of those things are most effective when they're shared. The benefits of that work can always be shared by more than just one person, and having a second person to share them with is where you find meaning in it all. We're designed to care for something more than just ourselves.

I'm the same as everyone else in that I need a village. Except in my case the village can be very small, like just two people. Just my wife and me. Occasionally three or four close friends are nice. So I'm almost a loner, but even *I* need another human to struggle and succeed *for*. Someone to make it all meaningful.

I decide to get out my family photo, my one luxury item from home, and I stare at my wife and kids for a bit. They're beautiful. I don't always look at the photo at the end of the day. Dwelling on their picture too much puts me into a really lonely frame of mind that weakens me. But I do always, always pray for them, my wife and my two unspeakably perfect boys.

"Please keep them safe and well. Let them sleep tonight with the peace of God."

I quickly put the photo back inside my pack before it makes me tear up. For now I'm a bachelor, a hermit living back in the woods. I decide to embrace that notion and try to enjoy it.

Day 30

Two long lines of geese pass overhead, winging their way south in huge, V-shaped skeins. There must be thousands. Each day several groups have passed, but today I witness the last of them.

Once the wedges of geese are out of earshot, the land is left feeling empty. It's quieter, lonelier now. The absence of waterfowl noise makes me antsy. If I were really living by instinct I would be heading off somewhere right now too, following the birds' example and seeking a better winter habitat.

Thinking of a better winter home makes me glance toward the cliffs on the north-west horizon. That's where I'd like to be, over there on the sheltered side of those hills. But today I notice an ominous edge of clouds hanging over the hills and they're inching my way. A smell on the air makes me think this weather front will bring something cold and wet.

The weather has been merciful so far, and I've made good preparations for snow. I have an armload of fire tinder drying out in the rafters of my shelter, loads of kindling, and a bunch of moss for wiping and cleaning. There's also my huge supply of moose jerky and lard.

One thing remains to be done before the cold weather front hits, and it seems really important. I want to take a final bath in the river. I'm planning on switching to the fresh underwear and socks that I've saved for winter and I want to clean up really well before I do. If I miss my chance at decent weather and it spits freezing rain for the next week, there's no way I'm getting in that river. So in the late afternoon as I'm about to start cooking supper, I force myself to strip down and bathe.

Getting into the river is no fun. I'm standing here at the water's edge, naked but hesitant to get in. I have my handful of spruce tips for scrubbing and I've got clean clothes laid out on some bushes above the muddy bank. But I realize I'm procrastinating when I find myself checking fish lines and tracking a mink down the shoreline instead of washing.

"Aaaaaah! I scream as I rush deep into the near-freezing river. I start scrubbing like a mad man. My bristle brush of scratchy spruce tips feels like razors slicing me all over and certain body parts don't like it at all.

I've hated swimming in cold water all my life. I'll dive into it if there's a good enough reason, like if a child is drowning or if there's an animal in it to kill and eat. I did it once for a dead deer. My brother had shot a buck and ended up losing it. We tracked it for several hours and came to a lake, where we spotted the deer. It was just visible in the icy water, dead and floating way out there. So I stripped off and went after it. Towing it to shore was way harder that I had expected, with the deer being full of water and stiff. But after a struggle I made it to shore, shivering, blue, and barely male. Turns out, it wasn't even the same deer we were after. It had another hunter's crossbow bolt sticking out of its ribs.

I've also fallen through the ice a time or two on my trapline. So I can do cold water if there's a good cause, but for just a bath?

"Graaaaaah!" I yell at the water again and try a kick of protest. Rage helps warm me up. But I've sunk into the mud and I'm stuck. The water is up to my chest but most of the depth is mud. The sucking morass has swallowed both of my legs up to the knee or higher. As I try to pull one leg out, my weight makes the other go deeper.

Yanking and thrashing to get my legs free, I race up the bank shaking mud from my legs and feet and soon I'm in the thick alder trees where I left my clothes.

I'm struggling to catch my breath when I glance to my right and nearly jump out of my skin. A huge, green eyeball is staring at my naked self from just four feet away. After the initial shock I see that it's nothing more than the big pike I caught right before bathing. I had stuck the fish into the crotch of a willow tree so that a mink couldn't drag it away while I washed. It's sitting there in the tree at head-level, huge eyeballs just staring me up and down.

I have to laugh at myself for a second, but it feels simply amazing to get into clean, dry clothes. They're not crunchy with sweat and blood. They don't stink. A deeply luxurious sensation washes over me as I slide the fresh socks onto my feet. My clean shirt is like a gift from heaven. I feel like a brand new person.

Chapter 11

Tremors

*   *   *

"There is more to life than the avoidance of death." - Jonathan Sumption

The word "arctic" holds a certain mystique to all of us who live in southerly climes. It's like an escalation word, similar to the word nuclear. Just like nuclear war makes all other war seem paltry and insignificant to our minds, so arctic winter is on another level too, hardly imaginable to normal folk.

I'm sitting here in the woods knowing that it's not just winter coming around the bend, it's *arctic* winter. How will this arctic winter be different from regular winter? I don't know what to expect, or just how bad it will be. But I'm seeing all the birds flee, the plants and trees shut down, and nature basically battening down the hatches. Everything has shut down completely for winter. Everything except for me.

I'm a country boy from Indiana, and although I've experienced cold temps and savage winds on mountain peaks and high deserts in Asia, I've never spent an arctic winter in a handmade shelter with only my wits to keep me alive.

But I can't leave. As winter rumbles and sends out its first blast of icy breath, I have to face whatever comes. I feel like I'm tied to a railroad track and around the bend I can feel the ground start to shake. All my instincts rise up against staying put in the path of what's coming. But all I can do to alleviate that instinctual surge is to cut more firewood and kill more animals. So that's what I do.

Day 31

Each day that I wake up, I open my eyes to be greeted by absolute darkness inside my shelter. It's like being inside a cave because it's sealed so tightly. So I'm surprised this morning when I push my door open to find snow falling thick and fast. It has already carpeted the ground a couple of inches deep.

I love snow. It makes me feel happy and savage. I'm about to start howling when I spot a dark shape out in the meadow. I can barely make it out through the thick snowfall, but I creep closer and see that it's a moose. And it's not just one. As I get the camera set up to start filming I count *three, four…five* moose out in my meadow!

The falling snow is masking my movement, allowing me to get my camera in position and film without spooking them. Two bulls are chasing a cow moose, being that it's the middle of breeding season for these creatures. A big bull about the size of the one I killed stays right on the cow's tail and a smaller bull circles constantly around them looking for an opening to get his shot at mating. Every time the younger bull gets too close the big guy charges to drive him off.

The cow also has a set of twin calves which hover nearby in confusion, not understanding why these dudes are chasing their mommy all around the place.

I get lots of footage, elated that I'm fulfilling one of my kids' requests. They asked me to film moose, bears, and the northern lights before I come home. This footage should make them happy.

As I film, I start narrating the bull's attempts to mate with the cow.

"Oh, Baby, you look great! Love those hips!"

"I said not now, Bob! I'm hungry and Junior is over there eating all my salad!"

"Come on, baby! Slow down!

"Stop it!"

"Whoa, love the way those hips move when you run!"

"Get off me, Bob!"

"Hold still for just a second. I just wanna…"

"There are children present!"

"Uh, huh?"

"Shush! I just heard something!"

My narrating has grown louder and evidently attracted her attention. The cow spins and looks my way nervously, but the big bull is preoccupied with charging the small bull. They seem oblivious.

Eventually the wary cow leads the whole group away into the willows and I'm left alone in camp. Snow is falling faster as a winter storm sets in. The wind gets stronger.

With the snow, I move my fire inside the shelter. The mud firewall that I built has dried without crumbling, and it looks nice, but it is untested. Eager to shift to indoor cooking, I stoke up the fire and prepare myself to feel cozy and comfortable.

Suddenly I find that the vent hole I made in the high gable end won't ventilate. I rush outside and leave the door open. Thick billows of gray smoke swirl just inside the doorway but won't come out.

I try leaving the door open and stoking up the fire for a cleaner burn. I also switch out the wood I'm using, hoping dryer wood will generate less smoke. Still the atmosphere inside is too smoky to breathe or see anything. Soon I'm coughing and choking, with tears streaming from my eyes.

Pressing my eyes closed, I feel around the vent hole, making sure it's not blocked. Then I tear out a couple of logs to make the vent hole bigger. Nothing seems to help.

One problem is that the savage north-west wind is gusting right through my smoke vent. So I block that vent with moss and open a similar hole in the south gable of my shelter. No difference. I try opening an air hole below the fire so that it can draft oxygen more readily, hoping that it will start a flow that purges the smoke. Still no change.

Solution after solution comes to mind, and I try them all. Each time I stoke my fire back up to see if it will burn cleanly, but the smoke is absolutely smothering. It can't be endured.

I've been working with indoor fires all my life. Going back to the time I was a little kid, I was responsible for keeping the house warm and the water heated. I had to use barrel stoves, cook stoves, handmade stoves, open fires, and even a jerry-rigged contraption made from an old tool cabinet and a stainless steel trough. Designed to heat our water outdoors in the summer, this contraption was difficult to use, but I had to continually fire it for making hot water available to the kitchen. My life was largely consumed by operating fires and cutting the wood that fed them. But I've never encountered anything as difficult to figure out as this. Why won't this smoke vent? It defies logic. I think the shelter got used to being a smoker and just doesn't know what else to be.

By the time I'm done poking new smoke holes, digging draft holes and rearranging everything, my shelter isn't nearly as tight and windproof as it had been. One last option remains. It could be that a taller chimney structure right in the peak of my shack would be enough to defeat the wind and start a draft that would suck the smoke out. But I don't have any rocks or non-flammable materials to make a chimney from, or I would have already built it.

After some deliberation I decide to cut short logs and lay them log-cabin style as high as I can over a new smoke hole in the peak of the building. I spend the rest of the day racing back and forth to the river hauling armloads of mud and climbing up my shelter roof to plaster the mud inside the log chimney.

The snow keeps falling fast and wet, drenching everything it touches. The ground is just starting to freeze and handling the cold mud bare-handed is no fun. Every time I put a handful of sandy mud between some logs, it crumbles and falls out. But I keep going.

As I work, I imagine that I'm paying for one of the mistakes I made as a kid, when my brother and I started shooting bricks from the chimney one day with our .22 rifles. It was stupid, I know, and since then I've developed much better powers of target selection. But it was during my angry days, when I was a mad and sullen mid-teen. As we shot the bricks out of the chimney they toppled and slid down the metal roof making the best racket ever. It was fun. But Dad didn't feel amused at all. It was one of the few times that I totally understood his anger. And now here I am, cold, soaked, and struggling to patch this chimney. I put up one handful of mud and the last handful tumbles out, sliding down the roof and crumbling to an irretrievable powder. It's frustrating and miserable. I'm definitely paying for my sins.

By day's end I have a fairly substantial chimney structure, but it's the one part of my shelter I'm ashamed of. It's been done in a rush, haphazardly and it looks terrible. And still I can't make the smoke clear from inside my dwelling.

Feeling defeated, I stop work and clean up at the river, tired, sweaty and soaked. Most of all I'm alarmed that cold weather could come and find me unable to keep a blazing fire indoors. It's not good.

Day 32

When I push my door open this morning I'm pleased to see a blanket of snow covering everything two or three inches thick. The ground has frozen during the night and yesterday's wind has vanished, leaving the landscape silent and still.

"Winter is here!" I say under my breath.

Ducking through my doorway I turn and look at my shelter. Snow draping the roof boughs makes it look cozy. The moose antlers are covered and tiny icicles hang from the lower tines. The overhanging spruce trees look all Christmasy with their frosting of sparkling white. It's so beautiful. I only wish there was a thin wisp of smoke curling form the chimney. It's the only way the picture could be better.

Thinking of the smoke problem and the fact that I haven't kept a fire indoors through the night starts to get me down again. If I can't figure this out, what will I do when it's forty below? I sense a lot of leftover discouragement from yesterday rising up inside me. But I decide that I'll find a way no matter what. During mountaineering expeditions I've camped in negative thirty with no heat. I can do it again if I have to.

I'm not leaving here until it's *really* cold—until there's something impressive to endure. People should be watching the show and saying, "Oh my gosh, how is he doing that? How is he keeping alive?" So I'm staying. I won't let a little problem like this get me down. I'm glad for the snow, glad that the situation is looking wintery at last. This is the weather I expected on day fifteen, when instead it warmed up and I had to smoke the moose meat.

The snow is wet so it has stuck to everything and the firewood is soaked. But before long I have a fire blazing and I go to the river for a pot full of water. The mud along the shore is frozen, and the hard ground is nice because I don't sink as I reach out and dip up my water. Soon I'm back in camp cooking half a pike.

I'm carrying my bow everywhere again, and today it pays off. I see a squirrel and kill it. Then once I'm back in camp I notice a field mouse dart across the path, and I take a quick shot. To my surprise I nail it. Now I have two rodents to cook for lunch.

A couple sets of mink tracks wind their way along the river shore, but nothing else. I've been eagerly waiting for a chance to track hares and start a snare line, but even after taking a long scouting trip upstream I don't come across a single set of hare tracks. This lack of tracks doesn't bode well.

By mid afternoon the snow is thinning. Most of the ground is bare, and I take advantage of the situation by finishing my food cache. It only takes a little while to cut and notch a few more logs, and now the main part of the structure is complete. I only have to line it with my moose hide and make the lid.

The moose hide has not dried. With the daily rain and moisture, it hasn't dehydrated like rawhide should, and it smells. Normally I would say it smells bad, but out here the smell of the rancid fat is kind of pleasant; I still have to hold myself back from licking it as I roll the hide and heave it onto my shoulder.

It takes a lot of grunting and heaving to get the hide to the cache and spread it out. I'm not worried at all that the rancid fat will hurt my food. The fat will be on the outside with the hair side inward toward my food supply. The hide will freeze and then it won't even stink anymore. It's going to make a perfect liner to keep out the smaller animals like mink and mice. They'll chew on the outside, but the skin is so thick and tough that I doubt they'll get through. There's only one hole, the place where my arrow pierced it. So I sew that hole shut with snare wire and then climb into the food cache, stomping the hide down into place.

I finish the lid and make a locking mechanism to keep it safe from bigger animals like bears and wolverines. I create the lock by fixing a strong log over the cache lid, just inches above the lid pieces.

The log is notched and wedged in place between two trees. I've built my cache between two huge trees for just this reason. With the locking log notched into the trees, I can remove the lid pieces from under it to access the cache. But once I put the lid pieces in place and drive wedges in between them and the log above, the cache is incredibly sturdy. The wedges keep the lid pushed down so tightly that I doubt a grizzly could pry it up.

"Ha!" I shout at the camera once the lid is wedged in place. "That's what I call a food cache! Bring on the bears! Bring on the mice! Just you try to get at my meat!"

I smack the lid with my axe for extra emphasis. The solid feel of the structure reminds me of the word "steadfast": a word I like. It brings me mental images of an unconquerable fortress or a sturdy shield wall of warriors. A verse comes to my mind, so I launch into it.

"My brothers, be ye steadfast, unmovable, always abounding in the work of the Lord!" With every phrase I smack the food cache with my axe.

"This thing is steadfast, unmovable! Always abounding with food!"

It never crosses my mind that I may look like an idiot to the camera which is silently watching me from its perch on the tripod a few feet away.

"Steadfast! Unmovable!"

I feel a surge of happiness. Maybe it's because I have finally created a solution to the overwhelming problem of food storage. Maybe it's because with the completion of this project, my heavy work is finally and truly done. I don't know. I'm just caught up in a moment.

Each time I say the phrase and smash my axe against the lid of the cache, I feel more and more happily violent. It's intoxicating.

"Be ye steadfast! Unmovable!"

I'm growling and yelling now.

"Steadfast! Unmovable! STEADFAST! UNNNNNNMOV-ABLE!"

I'm dancing around the food cache, beating it like a drum. It's been too long since I talked with an actual human. Maybe I'm beginning to lose my mind.

"Haaaaa! Come on ye grizzlies! Do your worst! Come and dash yourselves against my unfathomable fortress of food!"

After a while the frenzy wears away and I switch the camera off, feeling a hint of embarrassment but not much.

My thumb has been wrapped ever since I cut it with the saw a few days ago. This evening as I sit in my shelter I unwrap it, knowing that it needs some fresh air.

Other than looking suffocated, it's healthy. The spruce sap under the tape has sealed the cut closed really well, keeping it from getting infected. No dirty water or fish guts have reached the injury. I'm amazed by how well the sap is working.

After doing my bedtime routine of frying half a fish and drinking a quart or two of Labrador tea, I pull out my family's photo. Looking at the beautiful faces of my wife and kids is getting harder and harder.

"God, keep them safe and well. Help them sleep tonight in the peace of God."

I thank God for the spruce sap and the fact that my thumb is healing. Then I tie another knot in my calendar string and slip into my sleeping bag.

Day 33

Fishing is still the biggest part of my life, and this morning I catch another hefty pike. I haven't deployed my gill net or weir yet. I'm also down to just seven hooks, since occasionally a really big fish gets on and snaps my lines. Yet somehow, the fish just keep coming. There's never a day that I don't have a fresh one to eat.

Pulling this monster out of the water, I see that he's at least three feet long. This is the tenth fish I've caught that's over three feet in length. Hoping to save this fish alive, I take out the hook and get him on a stringer.

Pike are delicate creatures in a way. They seem so big and savage when they're gobbling up other fish, tugging at my line or biting holes in my leather gloves. However, if you grab them by the head, they go dormant.

Just behind a pike's eyeballs, there are soft pressure points. Squeezing these points puts the fish to sleep. It's nice to have them lying still as you take the hook out, but the problem is that they fail to wake up sometimes. If the fish die, I have to eat them right away. So I've learned to take my time reviving them.

Setting this fish in the water and keeping him upright, I move him slowly back and forth, making water rush past his gills. This time it takes almost ten minutes before he wakes up and swims angrily off into the river depths. The stringer tightens, the pole bends around as he pulls and I can tell that he's going to be just fine.

I'm insanely pleased. I have two big fish waiting on stringers now, and still half a fish in camp ready for supper. I'm smiling as I grab my bow and head downstream, thanking God and just having a good time.

"God, you promised I'd have food for each day. But you've given me food for more than just a day. I'm super happy about that!"

I actually have food for a lot of days. It staggers me when I think about just how long I could last without catching one more thing.

"God, I'm having the time of my life! This is such a dream!" I shout at the sky.

Another pike wriggles on a line half-way down my stretch of river, and I manage to get it to camp and put it on a stringer before it dies.

Tomorrow, I'll eat the one that's been caught the longest and work my way through them from the oldest catch to the most recent. I worry for a moment that a family of otters will find these fish and rob me some night. But it's the best I have.

Day 34

Another enormous pike is waiting for me when I get to the river this morning. It's on the line nearest my flay table. Almost half of my total number of fish have been caught on that one lucky line. I guess its because I'm constantly chumming the water there with fish scraps and guts. Occasionally I look inside the stomachs of fish I'm catching and find that they've swallowed the scraps and heads I tossed yesterday. So my flay table is really helping to attract these fish and keep them here.

Using the measuring scale on my multitool, I find that today's fish is forty-four inches long. It's really fat too, and I thank God aloud as I put the fish on a stringer.

I have so many stringers in the river now that I'm afraid some of the fish will die off before I can eat them.

"How am I catching all these fish?" I wonder. I'm not known as a fisherman in life, but I'm killing it here. I think God is bringing these fish in.

I find myself really wishing my son Levi could be here to experience all these pike. He loves fishing more than just about anything. Levi is my outdoor sidekick. He has come to really love nature just like I did as a kid, and it's probably because his life has been difficult too. He's experienced hardship very different than the stuff I faced growing up. We all tend to mess up our kids in our own special way, I guess.

*   *   *

I'll never forget the time I stopped being just the person who caused Levi, and became his dad. I think it happened one moment when I ran outside to shoot a raccoon. We were living in a cabin I built; since we were surrounded by woods, coons were perpetually tearing open trash bags and chewing on stuff outside. I had taken to shooting them, and early one morning I heard a noise and ran outside with my rifle. I was focused on the chase, so it took me a minute to realize that Levi had seized a Nerf gun and come along beside me.

I looked at him and cracked up. He was wearing nothing but a diaper but trying in every way to imitate my movements. His Nerf gun was poised and he searched for a target, occasionally checking my stance and adjusting his.

In a squeaky two-year-old voice he asked, "Daddy, are we dangewous?"

There we both were, me in my underwear and Levi in his diaper, looking serious and aiming guns at the woods. I laughed, and something happened that made me swell with pride and feel a new depth of responsibility in fatherhood.

"Yes, son," I replied gravely. "We are very dangerous."

Not long after that, Levi told me, "Daddy, I want to explore the whole entire world." Each time I went out with him that summer to a park or even the grocery store, he would ask earnestly, "Is this the day we explore the whole entire world?" We already traveled a lot, but ever since then he has believed that we traveled just because he came up with the idea.

Levi has been through some insane difficulties while our family did aid work overseas. When he was just two months old, we took him with us on a trip to an Inuit village above the arctic circle. By the time he turned four, he had been in twenty countries and endured over a hundred flights.

After he started having his muscular issues, the stress of travel and moving really took a toll on him. Even after his muscular problems healed, he stayed somewhat sickly. We kept working in remote countries where medical access wasn't good, and many nights brought sudden sickness to him. He was often so sick that my wife or I just stayed up, sitting beside him all night to make sure he kept breathing.

Then when he turned four, he fell from a swing in another remote country and broke his femur in a long, splintered fracture. I took him to the local hospital, and they allowed us to wait in a little concrete cubicle that was littered with pop bottles and trash. I watch them treat another girl with a broken arm. Her arm was black and half-rotten from being untreated for so long. She was entertaining herself by swinging it back and forth like a rope.

Two nurses came in and one pulled her arm tight and held her head back while the other tightly wound plaster wraps around the arm and let them dry. Then they scolded her away from the room and beckoned Levi to come. I just picked him up and walked out.

I ended up carrying him in a make-shift splint for several days to reach a good hospital. He was put into a body cast, but the bone came loose again and I ended up carrying him from one hospital to another looking for more specialized treatment until we ended up back in the States.

That episode spiraled downhill and became a month-long ordeal, one of the most heartbreaking things I've ever seen. Passing so much time hearing my son scream in pain, carrying him on and on hoping to find a better solution and dwelling on how my life choices were causing so much suffering for him is one of the most terrible things I've ever faced. For Levi, it was many days of abysmal pain. For me, it meant I fulfilled my promise that I'd carry him around the world, the promise I made back when he was diagnosed with muscular dystrophy. But I'd have given anything to spare Levi the experience. To this day, I just wish I could erase the whole thing.

Injury after illness, the difficulties went on and on. But with each interval we spent in America getting seen by doctors or taking time to heal, we went out to the creek and we camped and fished. It calmed him, and our outings turned into Levi's best core memories. And so the wilderness has become a sanctuary for him, like it is for me—a place of wellness and peace.

*   *   *

When I left home to go on this show, Levi told me he plans to spend every night sleeping in the shelter I set up for my Alone audition. He also made me promise I wouldn't tap out from loneliness. My kids are the ones I want to impress here. I want to make them proud. They're also one reason I'm choosing to follow every rule, to stay inside the lines, so to speak. I have ample opportunities to cheat in some way. I could go outside my territory to the beaver colony I've seen and trap them. I could try to get a second moose. And I could work it all so that no one would know. But I want to sit on my couch one day watching this show with my kids and be proud of every single moment. I want to cut an image with every action that will inspire them to be good men.

Thinking about the image that I make on camera, I decide to spend some time washing up again this afternoon. Anything that touches my cooking pot gets blackened, and the blackness inevitably gets on my face as well. I can tell by looking at the camera's viewfinder that I look pretty much like a chimney sweep. So I grab a handful of spruce tips and set up to boil a pot of bathwater.

I'm pretty good at sponge baths. When I was a little kid, my family sponge-bathed out of a two-quart pot like this one for a couple of years. It was the only thing we had. No matter what work we did or how dirty we got, we each had a turn twice per week to bathe with two quarts of warm water and a rag.

Washing with spruce tea is a true delight. It simply feels luxurious, like a spa treatment. I've never experienced a spa treatment, but I think it must be close to what I feel as I wash up in my warm shelter using a piece from my overalls as a rag.

The scent of the spruce steaming from my pot is amazing. In addition to being wonderfully aromatic, it's cleansing and healing as well. The spruce bristles make fantastic exfoliating brushes for scrubbing between toes. I think everyone will be doing it in the future.

While I wash, I see how skinny my arms have become and I moan about that for a while. But all in all, I'm feeling good. I've accomplished all the major work that must be done before winter. I'm living large, eating enough food and feeling successful. There's nothing to really stress me. The pressure is off.

Day 35

These days I can afford to do the little projects that make life more convenient. This morning I carve a spoon and a spatula from a nice chunk of alder wood.

It might seem crazy that I've eaten fish soup for over a month without making a nice spoon. But it reflects my survival philosophy, which is all about priorities. I don't believe in making spoons when my energy should be spent getting food. It's possible to eat the barbaric way, grabbing at food with my fingers. But I could have a thousand spoons and starve.

I'm using spoons as an example but the idea extends to all other convenience items like chairs, baskets, tables, and boxes. Crafts don't win the game of survival. Having a basket won't help me if I haven't collected food to put in it.

But now with my food seen to, I sit back and enjoy some carving. It will be nice to finally have some good utensils.

As I carve long curls of alder wood from my spoon, I mentally run through the words of a song that's been slowly shaping itself in my mind. I start singing it aloud.

> We've got a lot of time to kill
> Lie here with me and just be still
> The moon that's in the sky so bright
> Shines down on us tonight

It's a song to my wife. The first phrase and the tune came to me unexpectedly on day thirty, and it's been flitting through my head ever since.

> Outside there is a frosty chill
> The arctic snow lies deep and still
> The northern lights are overhead
> Lie close to me in bed

I feel like an imposter singing it because I haven't seen any northern lights yet and the snow is not very deep. But I figure to have experienced all those things by the time the song is ready. The chorus isn't finished yet but it's going to go something like,

> Then I reach out from where I lay
> We're miles apart, you're worlds away
> Na na na na
> Na na na na na...

I can't figure out where the chorus should go after the first two lines.

Finishing a couple of nice spoons and a spatula, I chop some wood and prepare for bed. My new song, which started as a mental diversion, has started depressing me. But it's stuck in my head now and I can't dislodge it.

Music is always running through my head. Songs get stuck in my brain for a week or two at a time, playing endlessly day and night until I'm sick of them. But they don't sound beautiful. I can somehow hear my heart beat as the blood courses through arteries of my inner ear. It's like a high-pitched, searing whistle rhythmically pulsing with the beat of my heart. The music in my head gets mixed with the timing and sound of the blood pumping through my ears, and it turns the songs all circusy and jangly. I'm powerless to play a song cleanly in my mind. It's a mess.

By day's end, the lyrics of my song have gotten through to me and are affecting me emotionally. It seems ridiculous that something I invented, a simple song, could get me so depressed. But that's exactly what's happening. I can't stop the lyrics from replaying over and over, and they highlight just how alone I am, how far I am from my wife and kids.

I'm sensing the isolation more keenly than ever before. The absence of other human life is like a void I could fall into, and the barrier of time and space separating me from my loved ones feels almost as infinite as death.

There have been many missions and aid projects that have kept me away from my wife and kids for months at a time, but never was I unable to communicate with them at all for this long. The only thing I can send and receive is prayer.

"God, please get some love to my family tonight. Send them love that they can feel."

The prayer feels like too small a thing, like a drop thrown into the ocean. The love I have for my kids and wife and the level that I'm feeling their absence borders on unbearable. It seems like it's been months already. I'm so depressed that I can hardly face the camera as I film my evening update and slip into bed.

Day 36

The wolves regularly visit the moose kill site now, and they set up big howling concerts each time. I think it's cool. But last night, the noise of their howling was too much to sleep through.

Once during the night, I heard them come close to my shelter, so I went out with my axe and scouted around in the darkness hoping to spot them against the backdrop of snow, but I didn't see anything.

This morning I see that the wolves have skirted around my camp, exploring very close and sometimes walking in my tracks. They undoubtedly smell the meat I'm protecting.

I haven't been able to shake off the lonely and depressed feelings that followed me to bed yesterday. An unstoppable current of memories want to be processed, and they besiege my thoughts all day, taking me straight to the depths of the things I've done over the past few years, both good and bad. I didn't ask for this barrage of memory, but I knew it was coming. The producer who warned me was right, and I ponder his words before launch:

"You've got a lot to think over out there," he had said as we concluded a pre-launch interview in base camp. I had just explained to him some of the events in my life leading up to being on this show. "I hope you've got what it takes to mentally face all that. Good luck."

As I robotically perform today's survival tasks, I decide that I'll just get on board for the ride and let it all happen.

Chapter 12

Turmoil

*   *   *

"You just keep living until you are alive again." - CTM

The fabric we humans are made of is complex and in-scrutable. It's like a tapestry woven with horizontal threads of thought and knowledge criss-crossed by vertical threads of emotion and experience. Under normal circumstances we don't notice any of the individual strands that comprise us. Our inner processes are inter-twined with our community, normalized and sustained by the effect of other humans as we experience interaction and conversation. This interaction camouflages what's truly going on within us, and we expe-rience only the tip of each iceberg that floats through our ocean of being. But under certain circumstances, we're brought face to face with the reality of our life's fabric.

I've seen extreme stress, pressure and heartbreak expose my raw edges before. But I've never experienced anything like I am going through right now. Out here in complete isolation, I find that I'm fac-ing all of the individual fibers that are strained or broken. I feel everything, piece by piece, and there's nothing to mask the effect. No conversation, no media, no input of any type exists to help me skip over the tough parts.

The effect I feel is a roller coaster of ups and downs. When I'm up, it's the highest I've ever been. When I'm low, there's no bottom to it. It boggles my mind how I go from one extreme to the other in just hours. Every feeling is amplified.

This morning I wake up as low as I can remember. One of the painful threads has been plucked. The broken thread I can't move past is the death of my little brother not many months ago. I don't know what causes me to dwell on it, but it comes up a lot here in the wilderness. Some days it's a definite feeling that he's watching what I do, enthralled by my journey as I hunt and fish. But other times, like today, it's just a sense of absolute loss.

*   *   *

His name was Silas. He was lost in a drowning accident when a freak current took him under and never let him go. For me and for my other siblings, it was a core thread of ours being severed early and without warning.

When I got the call, we didn't yet know if he was alive or dead. The search and rescue crew was still searching for him, and I just got in my truck and drove the four hours to his place as fast as I could. When I arrived, they had recovered his body, and I went to the hospital where he had been brought.

No one else was in the room as I went inside and hugged him, absolutely unable to process what was happening. His body was stiff, but I held onto him tightly. I could smell his hair and lake-water soaked clothes. His stillness and the reality of his departure was unspeakably stark and so unfair.

He was about to turn twenty, a kind and incredible kid. In just one week, he would have been in my truck headed with me to one of those ten mile obstacle races. His first time. He'd been so excited when we signed up together.

I hung onto him for a long time, stunned, unable to move or think. I stayed until I felt a presence touch me on the shoulder from behind. Somewhere inside me I thought I heard him saying, "What are you doing? Don't grieve like this. Eternal life is real, and I'm okay."

At that point, I stood up and dried my eyes. Some very respectful paramedics had been waiting to move him to an ambulance for transport. I motioned that they could go ahead, and I stood by until they drove off into the blackness of the early morning hours. The parting salute I offered him seemed like too little, a paltry way to say goodbye. But I gave it with all the respect I could muster.

Death is without question one of the hardest things for us to fathom. The shock we feel from it is a sign that we're designed to be eternal, but we're betrayed by our bodies' adherence to the natural course of life and death.

I've asked myself countless times since that day, "Why couldn't I have died? Why am I the one still alive after the countless ways I've prodded death?" There's no real answer. I really shouldn't have survived a lot of things. And I always come back to the question, "Is it a good thing that I'm still alive? Am I living a life worthy of…well, worthy of *life*?"

Silas's passing was not the first time I had experienced death, but it turned out to be the first of many, many to come in the following months. Only a week after his funeral I was sitting on the Afghanistan border and death seemed to be on a rampage.

I was working on a long-term literacy and research project and happened to be living right on the border of Afghanistan at the time. The Taliban had just launched their effort to retake Afghanistan, and their offensive was gaining momentum daily. Waves of refugees fled as the Taliban advanced, driving people out by the thousands and killing scores.

The American embassy in Kabul was evacuated. Thousands of Afghans and hundreds of American citizens, including a few of my friends and coworkers, became trapped in a stampede of humanity that descended on the Kabul airport desperate to get away.

The section of border that I lived on at the time, usually peaceful, suddenly became a hotspot as people tried to get away. They poured across the few bridges until those bridges were closed. Then they tried to swim across to safety. Some made it and many didn't. In many cases they were shot at from the 'safe' side of the river while they tried to swim across. Then, being driven back to the Afghan side, they were sometimes killed right on the shore of the river.

My best friend and his family were living in a border town and we went to check on them first. He had just been through a harrowing incident helping an American girl cross the border with a Taliban contingency right on their heels.

Not everyone in that party was rescued at the time. It turned into a case where hard choices forced some people to stay behind and face the consequences of helping an American. My friend, Grayson, not knowing if his people were alive or dead after helping with the rescue, looked haunted as we helped him get his own family packed up and ready to leave. His wife was about to give birth, and they had to leave for maternity care.

As we left the border, we saw hostile forces arriving from deeper inside Afghanistan, driving new American Humvees and flying Taliban flags. They secured every post and bridge crossing, fortifying their positions.

Grayson and I took the time to photograph the Taliban forces as well as we could using our hunting scopes. We saw that many of them carried new M4 rifles, probably drawn from US supplies in Kabul just days before. The info we gained helped to inform rescues for the next few weeks.

I took my own family to a safe city far from the chaos and got an apartment for them to stay in. Then I turned my attention to the border and lived there almost full time for the next few months.

I worked with official aid groups and with underground channels, and with an awesome group of Marine buddies from a group known as Free Burma Rangers. It was then that I met Sky Barkley, the friend who later encouraged me to get on *Alone* and tell my story. He is the quintessential Marine and a fantastic combat medic. We became fast friends as we rolled up and down the border river for weeks together.

We tried anything we could that might help someone. Two separate efforts to broker a deal to fly Afghan helicopters loaded with food and medical supplies and return them with American citizens and other high-risk people fell through. Finding money and official connections who would allow the rescues was almost impossible.

My friendships among the officers manning the free side of the border came in handy sometimes. I also worked privately with one of the late Shah Massoud's close allies in an effort to create an underground corridor out of the Panjshir Valley, the last remaining free position in Afghanistan. I put a lot of money into that channel. But the problem of finding friendly governments to receive the people we would carry persisted, and government reluctance shut down effort after effort.

Our efforts did result in a few people escaping, one bus-load here, a couple of people there. But more than anything it was a frustrating, maddening pursuit. Sometimes we would hear of a group of refugees trying to cross the river and head toward the spot, only to find that they had already been either rounded up or killed on the Afghan side. Some were beheaded and tossed into the river. Once we heard that two young girls who had been caught in the river just before we arrived. As they tried to cross, the Taliban cut their throats and let their bodies drop.

In the end, it's fair to say that nothing we did really changed the situation. We worked constantly from July to November, but by the time activity died down, my friends and I were exhausted and without the satisfaction of having accomplished anything significant.

Once the leniency of surrounding governments wore out, the rescues shut down. At that time lots of people started arriving from America to "rescue somebody." I've seen that there are books written about it now—books being sold about rescuing people there on the border where my home was. I met the people who came and shared with them my photos of Taliban positions. I know the real stories and it's not always the same as the printed version.

For me, I had thought that rescuing some people, that "punching death in the face for somebody," would help me process the death of my own brother. That didn't happen. Instead, the grief all descended on me at once after the adrenaline was gone, and it was only compounded by all the failure I had experienced during the Afghan effort.

We had little time to rest. A few weeks after I stopped working on the Afghan border, Russian invaded Ukraine and I found myself headed there.

Sky and my Marine buddies do front-line medical mission work, and they had called me weeks in advance. Guessing that the invasion was imminent, they wanted me to go along and help. Since I speak Russian, I would interpret and do logistics.

My wife and I prayed together, asking whether we should help the aid efforts if the invasion happened. I'll never forget the evening my wife looked at me and said, "Of course we help. It's what our life is meant for."

So Russia invaded. I woke up early on February 24th to so many messages—videos of KA-52 helicopters pouring across the border, tanks rolling in, and a message from Sky that simply read, "It's on. Come."

The feeling that landed in the pit of my stomach can't be described: a heavy, sinking weight that I chalked up to simple fear. It stayed with me until I walked across the border of Ukraine to link up with my team.

The Ukraine war was real, and still is as I write. It's the kind of war you've seen in videos of Poland when Hitler destroyed it during WWII. Entire towns and cities were being leveled, and more than ten million people were driven from their homes in just two weeks.

I left for Ukraine on the morning that Russia invaded and joined my friends, all former combat medics. We linked up and worked together for a long time.

We were there to help set up casualty collection points and care for injured people who were fleeing from the front lines but were still too close to danger for regular medical services. We ended up helping mostly refugees, and training additional medical personnel.

Many of the displaced people had just seen their homes destroyed and even family members killed right before their eyes. At one point, a woman arrived to tell us that her ten-year-old daughter had just been decapitated by an artillery shell as they were getting in the car to flee. She had felt no choice but to race off, leaving her daughter's body in the street. Another came into the church we were operating out of, having just helped pick up a grocery bag of fragments left from his friend's bodies when an artillery shell landed right on their vehicle in an evacuation corridor. A father, mother, and two kids, the pieces all collected in a small bag.

Day after day, I was on the phone translating for people who needed evacuation. Sometimes we were able to talk people through a series of moves that got them away from their buildings and into the waiting hands of good Ukrainian church people who had left everything to take their vehicles to the front and help.

Sometimes people on the other end of the phone were still stuck in buildings surrounded by enemy. They wanted desperately to get out, but I had to advise them to stay put. They would cry on the phone and beg for answers. And what could I offer? Usually I could offer only words of encouragement, which seemed unscrupulously little. I prayed with people; I cried along with them and tried to assure them that things would be okay.

That really made me check whether I believed in prayer or not. How could I pray with someone who was facing fear of death from artillery strikes and assure them that God would hear and do something? In my own life, I haven't been given answers to every prayer I've made. Many times I've cried and begged God for an answer, never to hear a thing. But what of all the times when he *did* give me the answer? What about the times he came with healing, peace, and deliverance? So I reached into those times and prayed with people, praying with all the dedication that I could.

I thought that God would save everyone we prayed for, but he didn't. People died. I remember driving our lead vehicle through a huge puddle of blood where ambulances were being loaded. It seemed wholly unacceptable to have people's blood being squished around by our tires.

Describing my experience during the Ukraine invasion is difficult. I wasn't everywhere witnessing the battles and observing the destruction and killing. Most of the people who came to us were fine, uninjured, just scared and trying to get out of the country. By the time I left, I wasn't sure if I had even done anything constructive. But I was there long enough to soak up a little of what war is. War is human suffering. And as wave after wave of people fled from the Russian advance, it wasn't just the injured who were suffering. It was an entire people. The deep gashes of grief and trauma were everywhere, on everyone and everything.

I saw kindness during that time too. People reaching out to one another, doing what they could even as they themselves suffered. The kindness touched me most. If there's one trait I value in humans, it's kindness. Seeing one suffering person reach out selflessly to another really gets me. If I were God, that's the basis I would judge people on. It's a good thing I'm not God. Being that I'm not, I do my best never to judge. But kindness still remains the thing I admire most.

From Ukraine, I heard that the usually peaceful country where my wife and children were waiting for me had erupted into some kind of political conflict. I hurried to leave Ukraine, sad to leave my friends still facing the work there. It felt like cheating to leave. How could I run off, when Sky and the rest would still be working and facing the threat of the Russian advance? But I had to reach my family, so I left Ukraine and headed to where my wife and kids were waiting.

It was then that, riding though Poland in a train crammed with refugees, I stared out the window and dreamed of disappearing into the wilderness.

I arrived in the country where my family had stayed and found that the main events of violence were dying down, but killings were still taking place in the street. This time it was many of our friends and neighbors who were being killed. It was folks who felt like family, after the years we'd spent among them.

Ethnic unrest is such an ugly thing. Whenever one group of people believes that the world would be better without the other and starts killing to prove it, it leads to such darkness that even the devil probably throws up a little.

The house we were living in had been in the epicenter of violence; when I got there, scores of families were mourning the loss of husbands and brothers. In one massacre, even preteen children had been stabbed by bayonets. One crowd of men and teenage boys were mowed down by the guns of an MI24 helicopter, and a few men who later lay wounded in the hospital were finished off with a simple pistol shot to the head.

I won't go into details about this incident. It was bloody hell. It sent me into a bit of a spiral, being the first time I'd been around a conflict where my own friends were being destroyed. It was my house, my yard. My friends. I've heard the phrase, "One you know is worth ten you don't." That shouldn't be true, but it kind of is.

I know guys who seem to handle this stuff so well. They rush from one horror to the next, helping people without ever breaking stride. They're tough, indefatigable. I usually feel like one of them. When we're running a mission, getting no food and less sleep, making hard decisions, I can pull my weight and more. But today in the arctic, as I allow all of the scenes of conflict and human suffering to roll unchecked through my brain, I feel like I don't deserve to stand among those guys. I'd be embarrassed for any of them to hear me or see me weeping a little today. I evidently don't handle this stuff as well as I thought.

I heard a retired US colonel talking once to a group of men. Brain trauma was his topic, and he approached the discussion like a true warrior; no squeamishness or blubbering.

"Brain trauma is something you'll face," he began gravely. It's a hilarious side note to mention that when he first said the words "brain trauma," one of the tribals preparing a meal nearby killed a pig, smacking it in the head with a large bolt. Our conversation was completely drowned out by the pig's squealing and the crunching blows of the bolt.

Finally the squealing stopped and we could hear the Colonel again. Actual brain trauma had interrupted, and he had to start over.

"Brain trauma is something that happens. But you can heal and get over it. Where the real damage happens is internally. Not from explosions or bullets. Being men, we like those things. But damage happens from the constant weight of heavy responsibility. Long term responsibility. The kind where you're responsible for people's lives. You're making life and death decisions. That will harm you over time, and you have to find ways to deal with it."

His words rang true. I hadn't been blown up or even touched by a bullet or piece of shrapnel. My kids hadn't been the ones who died. But after a few months in the conflict zone that had been home, I was ready to get away.

I may have gone further down a mental spiral, but one Scripture about eternal life in God grabbed my attention and kept me level. I was in a Southeast-Asian country after I auditioned for *Alone*. I was sitting among a mixed group of refugees and medic buddies, listening to someone talk about the needs of one particular village area or another. The afternoon was warm and I felt tired from having run a lot the previous day. My mind drifted off sleepily and somewhere in a subconscious ocean of thought, a verse popped into my mind: "Death is swallowed up in victory."

I sat bolt upright, completely roused from my daydreaming. The words instantly connected with each occurrence of death that had brushed me. I looked up the page in my phone and read:

"So is also the resurrection of the dead.
It is sown in corruption; it is raised in incorruption:
It is sown in dishonor; it is raised in glory:
it is sown in weakness; it is raised in power...
Oh death, where is thy sting? Oh grave, where is thy victory?"

God spoke to me then, the words forming inside my head like puzzle pieces falling together. It felt like coming to a conclusion that you instantly know is right, and has been right forever.

"I make all things new. I redeem what's broken and I raise what's dead. I am life."

I drank up that reminder from him. It really impressed me, deep enough that I went to a tattoo place the following day and had them put those phrases on my arms. "Sown in weakness, raised in power." The words will be there eternally to remind me why I'm okay, and if they dig up my mummified body someday they'll read the words and say, "This guy believed in life."

*   *   *

Cold and hunger makes my mind snap back to the present, back to the pristine patch of wilderness I call home now.

"Wow, get a grip," I tell myself, getting to my feet and shaking off the reverie. I didn't ask for all of these things to bombard my mind today. I would have been happy to just shove it all into a mental box called "stuff that's happened" and move on with my day. If I had the tiniest morsel of outside input like music or conversation, I would have been able to do that. But in this isolation I can't silence the voice of my memories. They've all been marching toward the forefront of my psyche like an army of shadows. No way to dodge them.

"I need to get some fresh air."

It's the fishing time of day now, so I head down to the river. Each afternoon when the sun hits the water just right, the fish are going to bite. The sun's rays create a magic moment, and I always make sure I'm there both to see the fish strike my lines and to catch a few rays of sun for myself. Today I could really use some sun.

The sunshine hides from me today, but when I reach the shore where I flay fish I immediately see the nearest fish pole bending over almost to the waterline. Something is on it and pulling hard.

Setting up a camera, I reach the line and haul it in hand over hand. Getting the fish near the shore, I can see that it's massive.

Setting up cameras has cost me quite a few catches. It's maddening, knowing I'd get a lot more fish if I just ignored the camera and pulled them in quickly.

I'm expecting this fish to get away, being that the past three have. Instead it stays hooked as I drag the line toward me. It's so heavy that the line breaks the instant I get the fish to shore. This is too nice a fish to take chances with so I dive on it and wrestle it in.

Holding the fish up, I guess that it's four feet long. An absolute beast! I can fit both fists into its mouth side by side. It's ridiculously fat too, and I figure it will make about ten big meals worth of food. I can barely hold it up as I go through my ritual of thanking God for it.

Putting the pike on a stringer, I survey my shoreline. The place is all jammed up with pole stringers sticking out into the water, each one holding a live fish. They're all waiting for me to butcher them. It's a lot of food.

"Wow!" I marvel. "You don't see that every day! Thank you God!"

Before I go into my shelter for the evening I stand outside and watch as the light fades. The sun has begun to set much earlier. It feels like mid afternoon, but the shadows are getting long. An endless blanket of clouds has been suffocating my spirits, but now a hole breaks open in the cloud cover far to the southwest. The sun is streaming through and casting orange-red flames of light onto the horizon. Even though the light is only a tiny portion of the otherwise gray sky, it's breathtaking.

I stare for a long time, eventually walking out into Moose Meadow to be as close to the sunbeams as possible. The sun is quite low, just a red glow illuminating the dark trees that form a ragged horizon beyond where I killed the moose. The golden light poking through the clouds feels like a promise to me—a private sign that good is going to break through. Although the effects of death have weighed me down so heavily, life is going to spring up again. I can't make it happen, but it just will.

I decide to quote a psalm while I'm staring at the fading sunbeams. I start with the psalm that speaks of living through war without fear. But tonight it holds nothing for me. Instead a new psalm has taken its place, implanting itself in my mind. I let instinct take over and begin to quote.

> Bless the Lord, oh my soul:
> And all that is within me. bless his holy name.
> Bless the Lord, oh my soul,
> And forget not all his benefits:
> Who forgiveth all thine iniquity;
> Who healeth all thy diseases;
> Who redeemeth thy life from destruction;
> Who crowneth thee with loving kindness and tender mercies;
> Who satisfieth thy mouth with good things;
> So that thy youth is renewed like the eagles.

Just like my eye is dazzled with the beam of light I'm watching, so my mind becomes dazzled by the psalm. "He redeems my life from destruction." I think I'm experiencing that.

"He satisfies my mouth with good things." I know that part is coming true for me. I'm incredibly grateful, and I say so, lifting my hands up to the sky. No one is here to see me or interrupt as I talk to God for a long time.

I fry my fish tonight thinking about the good things I'm getting to eat, and I wonder how the other contestants are doing. Are they getting anything? Are they well fed? I consider praying for them to get something to eat. But then I change my mind and just pray for their safety. I don't *really* want them to be well fed, because I need to win, and I don't want to stay here all winter.

Chapter 13

Life

*　　　*　　　*

"So live your life, that the fear of death may never enter your heart."
-Tecumseh

Day 37

A fresh layer of snow blankets the ground when I wake up this morning. It's deep enough to slow me down as I walk along the river shore checking my fish lines. Every vestige of foliage has fallen from the alders; the land has fully shed its autumn cloak, laid bare for the cold. Ice is forming a long band of silver along the edges of the water.

The majority of waterfowl have long vanished to the south. Their raucous calls no longer keep me company. But surprisingly, a little clutch of ducks remains on the open water. They don't quack or squabble like before. They just sit silently in the unfrozen middle of the river, wary and apprehensive, as if they've missed their ride south and don't know what do to. But they won't let me close enough for a shot. As I approach this morning they flush and circle around to an open stretch of water further upstream.

Getting to my fish stringers, I immediately feel a stab of panic as I see that one stringer pole, the one with yesterday's huge fish, is missing.

I can't believe my eyes. I thought I had checked every stringer knot twice over, but there's not a trace of the stringer anywhere. I check the surface of the river upstream and downstream. Maybe otters pulled the stringer loose, but I don't think so. If it were otters, they'd have stayed until every single fish was gone. There are no marks or tracks on the muddy shore. I think the stringer simply came loose and was pulled away by the fish.

Ordinarily when I lose a fish I think to myself, "Aw man, that sucks." But this loss feels closer to devastation. The amount of food that has just escaped is significant, and the impact tremendous. What was I thinking? Why did I leave these fish and so unprotected in the first place?

Of course I know why. I'm leaving them here to keep them alive. But with today's loss, I decide not to leave my fish in the river for a moment more. I set up the main camera and hold a little strategy conference.

"I can't afford to lose any more fish like this. I'm just sick at losing that huge one." I pause for a minute and stare at the water.

"I think I'm just gonna whack em and stack em."

My strategy is sound, as long as the weather stays cool. But I'm afraid it will warm up just like when I killed the moose. Then I'll have forty pounds of fresh fish all set to spoil.

I gamble on the weather staying cold. Hauling the fish out of the water one by one, I start whacking them on the head and tossing them onto the shore. I'm not going anywhere until every one of these fish are safe inside my impenetrable food fortress.

Soon the fish are all dead and I set about flaying them. It's miserably cold work, being barehanded and constantly having my hands in and out of the water. My skin is already cracked and full of sores. But I work at it until all the fish are processed and locked in my cache.

As I walk along the shore checking more lines, I'm still smarting from the loss of the big pike. Suddenly I remember the arrow I found after having prayed about it. I decide to pray about this fish. But considering the width and depth of the river, the current, and the live fish pulling at the stringer, I have no chance at all of finding it again.

"God," I begin, recording my prayer with a GoPro. I'm reluctant to film because I'm not sure my prayer will be answered. "If that pike got away with my stringer, it'll just die and be wasted at the bottom of the river. I'd really like to have it back. I need it bad."

The camera keeps rolling and I walk along the shoreline dwelling on my gloomy thoughts. Then something catches my eye in the water to my left. In an instant I recognize the missing stringer pole. It just floated to the surface right beside me. I can't see the fish of course, but there's a chance that it's still tied to the pole.

This stretch of water is one I've been searching all morning as I've gone up and down the river shore, with no sign all day. The fact that my stringer pole appears right beside me feels more like magic than reality. But I respond quickly to try and drag the pole in.

The pole is beyond my reach, out in deep water. But using a long alder tree, I caress it towards me very gently, knowing that if the fish feels a sudden tug he will take off into deeper water and I'll lose him.

Once the stringer is within six feet of me I dive on it, getting water in my boots as a consequence of going in too deep. I yank it toward shore and my elation is complete when I feel the huge fish come to life, tugging and thrashing to get away.

Holding the fish up to the camera, I'm dumbfounded at what just took place.

"I just caught this fish twice!" I yell. "I caught this freakin' fish twice!"

I can't help crediting God with the catch. It's inexplicable, and I'm ecstatic with happiness. I whack it and stack it with the others.

Now, I want to make it clear that I don't believe that prayer is like Karma. I don't just generate prayers and then watch good happen. In fact, it's often been quite the opposite in my life.

*   *   *

I remember the exact moment I realized that Karma either isn't real or doesn't work for me. I was walking through a crowded bazaar somewhere in the Middle East, when I noticed a man with no legs begging beside the busy entrance gate. People were pushing past him, and his little perch on a box looked so sad that I decided I'd give him a little money.

The walkway was crowded with every type of product and good being taken in and out of the market. Carts passed by loaded with fruit, young boys lugged along boxes of sandals, and men pushed a broken-down vehicle by hand. A man with a cart loaded over head high with scrap metal was rumbling by.

I fished a few bills from my pocket for the legless man. Leaning over to hand them to him, I tried to keep my left foot within the lane of traffic to hold my place. At the exact moment I leaned over to hand the money, a big piece of iron tumbled from the top of the load of scrap metal and landed with its sharp end on the tip of my shoe. It cut right through the shoe and bit deep into my big toe. I yelped and danced around a bit, dropping the money in the beggar's lap. Blood was soaking my sock and seeping out of my shoe, and as I hopped around the man pulling the cart looked back and laughed.

"Well, so much for generating good will by handing out money," I thought to myself, and right away I wrote off any ideas that Karma was a thing. So I approach prayer very differently than the concept of Karma. I'm not generating good through the effort. I'm just asking my Father for stuff, and sometimes he gives what I ask for.

*   *   *

I'm back at the river to finish checking my fish lines when I get the idea that I should ask God for ten more fish before the river ices up. After the prayer, I pull a fish line in to find that it has been broken. The end is frayed where it chafed against the ice, and the hook is gone.

Each time I lose a hook I feel a pang of anxiety. Now that I'm down to just six hooks, I have to do something to ensure I can still catch fish.

I consider my gill net and my weir for a moment. They're both almost done and I could deploy them, but now the level of the river water is fluctuating wildly. Both the net and weir would be either swamped or dry every other day. My bank lines are the only fishing method that works no matter what the water level does, and I need to find a way to keep my lines working as I run out of hooks. A solution comes to my mind, and I decide to make gorge hooks to supplement my diminishing supply of steel hooks.

Gorge hooks are basically long splinters made of bone or very hard wood. They're affixed by their middle to the line and baited. Whenever a fish swallows the bait and pulls, the tip of the splinter catches in the fish's throat and turns the splinter sideways, stabbing into both sides of the throat.

The trick with making gorge hooks is to find a material that stays hard while it's soaking underwater. I immediately make plans to use the bones of my moose and grabbing my bow, axe and a camera, I head out into the snow to get them.

Taking great care as I approach the kill site, I'm wary of the grizzly, remembering the tingling sensation I felt last time I was here. For a long while I stand on the high river bank surveying the area.

The land seems empty. There are no signs of animals present. Usually when a predator is on a kill, birds will come and go, keeping an eye on the predator and hoping to snatch scraps. No birds are overhead today, and no sense of threat emerges from the dense willows.

Reaching the kill site, I find that the moose carcass has vanished completely. Kicking around in the snow, I can't turn up a single scrap. The bones have all been eaten or dragged off.

"Must have been a good sized bear," I tell myself, searching around for any clue.

Wolf tracks are apparent everywhere, and mentally I kick myself for not stashing the bones up in a tree.

"So now what do I do?"

Spotting a feint drag mark, I follow it into the willow thicket. A layer of snow has fallen since the kill was dragged away, making tracking difficult. I follow until the trail peters out and the marks vanish.

I'm about to give up hope when I come across another set of wolf tracks, and I follow them deeper into the thick brush. Three wolves came through here, a huge one with paws the size of my handprint, and two smaller ones with tracks you'd expect a Great Pyrenees dog to make.

At last the tracks empty into a little meadow, and I immediately spot a couple of splintered rib bones sticking up through the snow. Hundreds of wolf tracks have rendered the snow a churned, packed surface underfoot.

Only the merest scrap remains of what had been an enormous carcass—about five of the largest vertebrae with the shattered stumps of rib bones attached. Bones the size of my wrist have been chewed straight through or eaten down to nubs.

"It takes a lot of jaw strength to do that," I say, lifting the remaining chunk of spine up to show the camera.

"What could crush and eat bones this size? Must have been the bear. Could wolves do that?" Judging from the tracks, I estimate that the larger of these wolves could fit my whole head in his mouth with no problems. Maybe a wolf that size could chew up such large bones as these. Either way, the predators here are enormous.

Without wasting time, I beat the rib stumps off of the spine with my axe. It takes some really hard swings to break them free, but in minutes I'm heading back to camp with a pocket full of splintered rib chunks: exactly what I wanted.

On the way to camp, I come across an unexpected treasure— a moose antler stuck in some brush. It's a shed antler from last year, and I had never spotted it before, though I've walked this way a hundred times. I'm thrilled to haul it back to camp and prop it up in front of my shelter, planning to make something cool with it later.

In my shelter, I have a stump of wood standing on its end, stationed in front of my fireplace as a surface for chopping food, cooking, and doing projects. Laying my moose bones down on that table, I use the back of my axe head to smash one of the rib sections to splinters. Choosing a few likely pieces, I shape them down with the file from my multitool. Eventually I have several three-inch needles of bone. They look splendid to me, with long, slender tapers and razor-sharp points. But whether they'll catch fish remains a mystery.

It's late afternoon now. The light is fading as I bait the gorge hooks carefully with three-inch sections of pike stomach. The sharp tips of the hooks are barely exposed from the bait, pointing backwards and waiting to catch in a pike's throat once he tugs against the line.

224

I make sure all my lines are in order then I head to camp and cook supper. Sitting in the light of my crackling fire, I start to realize what a life I've made out here. My shelter is sturdy and can withstand any weather. My food cache is convenient and secure. I've created routines, established systems that keep me warm and fed. I'm refilling my food supply faster than I can eat it. I'm enjoying jobs and doing projects. I'm not suffering through an endurance contest. I've created an actual life that's as valid and successful as any other. If only there were someone to share it with, I might be perfectly content here forever.

Day 38

Freezing temperatures greet me as I open my shelter door this morning. The snow that's fallen is wet and clingy. It has stuck all over my firewood and kindling, soaking even the hidden stashes of wood I've placed under cover. I'm annoyed.

While cutting dry wood, I notice a fresh pair of hare tracks running between my camp and the river, indicating that today is a good time to start my snare line. I've waited so eagerly for this, hoping that deeper snow will reveal good hare runs. But after much scouting I discover no other tracks. So I set up a handful of snares over the one trackway.

Heading to the river, I find massive flows of ice chunks floating along the shore. These ice flows make it nearly impossible to fish with my throw lines. The lines are constantly getting snagged and deposited against the shore by the drifting ice.

One of my lines has been broken by a fish and my closest line is now snagged on what must be a log. I try everything to free it but the line eventually breaks, robbing me of another hook. Now I'm down to only four steel hooks. I hope desperately that my bone gorge hooks will work.

I spend the entire afternoon hours running back and forth to check my lines and free them from ice. Several times I get fish close to shore only to lose them, but in the end I get three nice pike for my efforts.

"Thank you God," I breath as I stack the fish in my cache." My food supply is growing every day. These fish make four more since I asked for ten.

Now that I'm keeping my meat secure in my food cache, the local pair of gray jays are beside themselves. They clearly feel that I've let them down by failing to provide scraps.

I've never seen birds more expressive than these guys. Today one of the jays seems intent on teaching me about the virtues of dropping food. He starts from a tree branch near my fire and gets a little piece of bark in his mouth. Once he knows I'm watching, he drops his morsel of bark on the ground where my pot used to sit. Then he rushes down and picks it up in his beak as he happily chirps and hops around. He drops it and picks it up over and over again, each time expressing happy chirps when he gets it and pretends to eat it.

It's almost as if he can speak. "Do it like this, stupid human! Drop the food!"

If I turn my head away he gets really angry, and when I get up and walk off he goes into hysterics, flying in front of me and doing his best to let me know that I'm a selfish butt.

"Go get your own food!" I yell. "If God loves you, he'll feed you."

It sounds harsh even to me, bringing his relationship with God into question. Poor little bird. I might be a little more understanding if these jays hadn't robbed me so ruthlessly in the early season. I sometimes hate them, but other times they're really entertaining.

Day 39

I fight rafts of drifting ice all day as I try to keep my fish lines working. I want them to stay operational right up until the river freezes solid. Each morning I come out to find that the ten-foot wide rim of ice along the shore has seized my lines, so I break them all loose, rebait them, and toss them out. Then throughout the rest of the day the fluctuating water level breaks the ice up and it drifts downstream, causing havoc for my lines.

The fish are slowing down, biting less energetically. They constantly steal my bait by nibbling it. Finally I reach a line that has come loose from its bite indicator and is stretched out into the current. Something has pulled it.

I hate taking my lines in when they haven't been touched. It can make the bait come off. So I've taken little pieces of my softest wire and made hooks that I fasten to the pole about two feet down from the top. Once I bait a line and toss it in, I hook the string in the wire. If anything pulls on the line at all, the hook straightens and the line comes free, indicating that I should pull the line and check it. This system has been saving me from a lot of useless lines checks.

I can't reach the line because the river has risen; the water is deep where my fish pole is pressed into the mud. So I quickly cut a forked stick and reach out, hooking the line and towing it towards me.

As I pull the line in smoothly, a nice pike breaches the water and swirls to get away.

"Don't come loose, don't come loose!" I beg. "Come to papa!"

I've started praying each time I pull a fish in. They're coming loose so frequently now that it's maddening; I just want God to hold this one still while I get him to shore.

This fish doesn't come loose, and soon I'm holding up a pike about twenty-six inches long. My thrill is even deeper when I open it's mouth and see that I've caught it on a moose-bone gorge hook!

The bone splinter I carved has worked perfectly. When the pike swallowed the bait, it went just inside the entrance of its throat. Then, the line came taught and the fish pulled backwards. The tip of bone protruding from the bait stabbed into the side of the pike's throat; as he pulled, the gorge hook came perpendicular to the line. The dimensions of the gorge hook worked perfectly, being longer than the width that the pike's throat could stretch to accommodate. Now both ends of the bone are piercing the pike's throat, holding it completely securely.

"No freakin' way!" I yell, absolutely ecstatic with this catch. My excitement rivals the moment I killed the moose.

"Check this out! It went in this way and stabbed right through there…" I turn on a GoPro and shove it into the fish's mouth, trying to film exactly how the gorge hook made the catch, and getting the camera all slimy in the process.

The significance of this catch is huge. It means that running out of steel hooks won't shut me down. I can keep fishing with these throw lines endlessly, making gorge hooks and keeping the fish rolling in. I bet they'll even work under the ice after freeze-up.

I'm excited beyond all reason by this catch. My happiness carries me through the rest of the day: I find myself whistling, humming, and feeling awesome as the day closes and I tie another knot in my calendar string, closing the book on yet another fantastic day of arctic adventure.

Day 40

I wake up today feeling true hunger for the first time, as my body adjusts to doing without carbs and sugars. The sheer amount I've eaten has offset the lack of vegetables and grains in my diet. But now, for the first time since I arrived in the arctic, actual hunger strikes me.

*   *   *

I'm not exactly a stranger to hunger, or living hand-to-mouth. Growing up extremely poor, everything was rationed. Everything that is, except oatmeal. Oatmeal is the cheapest stomach fodder there is, and an efficient way to fill the bellies of eleven growing kids.

There was only so much food to go around, and I was constantly worried that I'd eat some morsel that I should have saved for my younger brothers and sisters. But I credit my parents with always putting *something* on the table. Three times each day there was something there for each of us. It wasn't always pretty or delicious. In fact, once when things were particularly scarce, my family ate up all the raccoon bait I had been saving for my trapline. But there was always something to eat. From a survival standpoint, that's success.

*   *   *

Being poor is not a sin. It's even good for us, I think. The confidence that springs from knowing you won't die without three meals is a golden thing. I'm benefiting from the confidence and abilities I gained during my childhood days. I know how to get food from the land and do without. But I also know not to eat up everything at once. So I've started to ration my portion sizes. I no longer eat all I can hold at each meal.

I have a lot of fish in my food cache and a ton of moose jerky, but it gives me mental peace to know that I'm saving for the really hard days. The price I pay is the nagging hunger that enters my world today. It will probably be my constant companion for a long time to come.

I find a thrilling surprise waiting for me at the river when I check my fish lines this morning. The lucky line beside my flay table is stretched taught and I pull it in to find the first burbot I've ever seen. I can tell it's not a pike even while I play the line in, because this fish is swirling in tight circles instead of tugging directly away in a powerful rush.

This is the first time I've caught something other than pike, and as I get it to shore I'm dazzled by experiencing a brand new type of creature. Burbot are built unlike any fish I've seen. They're more like giant tadpoles. Their skin feels exactly like frog skin and overall I'd classify them as amphibians rather than fish.

This fish makes ten since I asked for ten, and I take an extra moment today thanking God.

Later in the day, I find that the burbot tastes truly fantastic. The meat is buttery and the variety it offers me after eating so many pike overwhelms me with gratitude. So I sit in my shelter for a long while, basking in the glow of my fire and enjoying the last remnants of burbot flavor still hovering on my tastebuds.

In this moment, I simply enjoy the sensation of being well. My body feels good everywhere except my hands, which are all cracked and bleeding. I put them in and out of freezing water so much that the skin is swelled and split. Under each knuckle there's a big crack that bleeds sometimes and all across the back of my hands I'm raw and red. Blisters are opening and oozing. I wish I had brought a pair of rubber gloves for cleaning fish. That would really help. I also have a thousand infected pinholes in my skin from pike teeth. No matter how careful I am, they get me.

Seeing my lard container hanging from my ceiling, I'm inspired to start treating my hands with it and I wonder that I didn't think of it before. Taking a small piece of lard, I warm it with my breath and smear it all over my skin. It feels wonderful.

I'm full of other cuts and gouges from working through the fall season. The thumb I sawed a few weeks ago is totally blackened by dirt that's stuck to the spruce sap I cover it with. But at least it's not infected.

Though my hands are in worse shape than they've ever been, I know that fishing time is ending and soon I won't have to put my hands in the water so much. I'll start wearing my soft, winter gloves and I'll heal.

Thinking of my winter gloves, I grab them and put my hands in experimentally. The soft, clean sensation is so amazing that I recline again inside my shelter, just enjoying it.

The languid relaxation washing over me is superb. I'm feeling the effects of not only a warm meal and soft gloves, but of a successful existence as well. I'm thriving in the wild. I'm living well, meeting all my basic needs. I'm facing and overcoming each challenge.

The smoke in my shelter is the only challenge I have no answer for. It plagues me every day. But now a sudden spark of creativity flashes in my brain. I could use my moose hide to make a big curtain in the roof of my shelter, partitioning off a space above my fire for the smoke to become trapped in, and then forced out through the chimney. It could work. But do I have enough moose hide?

Immediately I get up, breaking the nice siesta I've been enjoying. When I arrive at the cache, I see that there are several big folds of hide hanging over the lip of the cache box. Overjoyed, I quickly get to work cutting them off with my knife.

Aside from being thick and tough, the hide is almost as hard as a rock. I'm afraid of breaking my knife blade. But eventually I've cut away every excess scrap of hide, and I come away with a pile of strangely shaped bits to work with.

In order to affix the hide to the ceiling of my shelter, I use the one man-made item I've found since I arrived on the land. We were told by some locals that we might find barrels, cans, buckets, boards, and shovels lying around in the delta. But since I've been here the only signs of man I've detected have been one axe mark on a tree, and a short board with some nails. That's it. My land is otherwise pristine and perfect.

The board, which I found a week ago in a pile of drift wood, is about two feet long and rotten, but there are ten or twelve nails sticking out of it. I couldn't have asked for anything better.

So using the nails, I tack the biggest pieces of moose hide to the inside of my ceiling, creating flaps that section off the space above my fire. Then I sew the flaps together with snare wire, punching holes with a special awl I made from the screwdriver of my Leatherman.

The hide warms up and droplets of rancid oil drip from its lower edges. I'm getting soaked in the oil as I work. It stinks a little, but I'm tempted to lick it. The oil seems to soothe the splits and cuts all over my hands.

Once the moose hide curtain is finished it looks ghastly, but in a pleasant kind of way. I could light a fire and test it, but I realize that testing the contraption is such an excitement point that it's kept me happy all day. So I choose to save the test for tomorrow so that I can ride this wave of excitement for as long as possible.

To kill the rest of the afternoon, I decide to unload my food cache and count my fish. It's been a while since I made a full inventory of my meals.

Hauling a panel of my unused fish weir to the cache, I use it as a mat to set fish on and I unload the food cache completely. I'm amazed at the amount of food I have. Mentally dissecting each fish into meal-sized portions, I count out fifty meals of fresh fish. It's an incredible feeling and I just stare at my lineup of gutted pike, feeling amazed.

"Wow, God! This is awesome. Thank you for giving me so much food to store."

Feeling uplifted by my food situation, I decide to eat a bigger chunk than usual this evening. It's a celebration of sorts. Lighting up a cooking fire outside, I fry my supper fish and boil my daily pot of Labrador tea. It's been a fantastic day.

Chapter 14

Peace

*   *   *

Then-in my childhood-in the dawn
Of a most stormy life—was drawn
From every depth of good and ill,
The mystery which binds me still...
                    -Edgar Allan Poe, "Alone"

Day 41

    I'm thinking about my new range hood from the moment I open my eyes. In the darkness of my shelter I can smell the aroma of slightly tainted fat still dripping from my moose hide. It smells a little like breakfast, making me instantly hungry.

    Today I've caught a twenty-four inch pike, and I have to break through a layer of ice to haul it to shore. Half of it goes into the food cache, and I bring the rest back to camp for lunch.

    Striking my ferro rod into a bundle of dry grass, I blow it into flame and set the ball of burning grass in my fireplace. Then I add handfuls of delicate, dry twigs. I top it with larger sticks until I have a nice blaze going.

All the while I'm doing this, the smoke from the fire goes straight up and seems to draw through my chimney. I keep a wary eye on the smoke as I get my pot of water going, afraid to get my hopes up too much. I keep fretting about it while I cook. The peak of my shelter is full of smoke again, but all in all, it seems bearable.

After eating and becoming convinced that my fireplace is going to work out after all, I put a pot of water on to boil and enjoy a nice afternoon indoors. It's bright and warm inside, so cheery and welcoming. My firelight dances against the logs of my roof and a glow of happiness grows in me until it sweeps me away in a paroxysm of joy. I feel so good that I can't stop smiling. I'm happier than I remember being since I started this adventure.

I keep expecting something to darken my thoughts. Usually some memory of a mistake or a messed up image from the past chops its way into my mind and tempers the joy I experience. Surely something will steal this moment from me. But nothing does, and suddenly I realize that nothing is coming for my mind anymore. There are no shadows marching in, there's no buildup of emotion, no unnatural logjam of memory. Nothing emotionally charged is lurking in the past.

Nothing inhabits the past now but experience—a long track of experiences, all mottled with twists and turns, ups and downs. Some parts are marred by shadow and others bathed with light, but it's just my story and that's all. Nothing more, nothing less. The peace of this moment boggles my mind.

Throwing some extra wood on the fire, I set up the camera and wonder what to talk about. I'm supposed to film hours of footage per day, and I'm nowhere near my quota. So I just smile at the camera and throw sticks into my fire for an hour or so.

It's ridiculous how comfortable I've gotten with the camera. No longer do I feel weird in front it. Whether it's baring my soul in deep conversation, taking a leak, or just sitting here staring at my fire,

I've lost all sense of embarrassment, and I even find myself missing the camera's companionship when it's turned off. It feels worse not to have the camera experiencing things with me.

Eventually I find myself thinking about all of the other contestants. Having gotten to know them for only a few days in base camp, it's hard to guess who they truly are or how they'll handle things out here. I feel sure that there are at least seven of them still left in the competition.

"And what do they think of me?" I wonder to myself. I have no idea what they think of me, but being a small guy like I am, I could understand if they thought I'd starve out early. One thing I learned in base camp was that several people thought I worked for the CIA or some government agency. It cracks me up, and I laugh a bit just thinking about it. But then the realization strikes me that I never really explained what it is that I do.

I'm a humanitarian aid worker, and that could mean a lot of different things. I guess it could sound flaky from the start. In base camp with the others, I did reference some war-related anecdotes and talked about some battles and rescue attempts. They heard me speak in a couple other languages as I sent out my last phone messages. So in a way, I can kind of understand why they were suspicious.

Opening up is something I find difficult. I don't like explaining myself—having to do so really annoys me. But somehow, I want to give a clear record of who I am. Since I'll be portrayed on TV, the world will see some version of me. But right now I have a chance to say what really matters to me and what my life is all about.

More than anything, I just want to hear myself tell my story. I want to see if it makes sense, if it means anything cohesive or special. I also have Sky's words ringing in my ears: "Don't hold back. Tell what God has done for you."

"Hey," I break the silence, turning toward the camera. It's been rolling for a long time already. "I'm gonna tell you exactly who Timber is."

The camera stares at me, a dark Cyclops offering no feedback at all. I'm wishing it would say, "Alright, just say what's on your mind." But that one dark eye only stares.

In the back of my mind I know that this camera represents people, viewers who could watch anything I say and judge me or be offended. But I push those worries aside. This camera is getting pretty easy to talk to.

"I do humanitarian aid work," I begin lamely, still a little unsure. "But what does that mean? And why do I do it?"

I take a minute to allow my memory to reach back to where it all began.

"It's pretty much about fear. I've seen fear in the eyes of kids fleeing from war, fear in the faces of families going through hell. I do aid work because I know what it's like to live in fear. I know what it's like to feel no hope."

The words that come out of my mouth have not been spoken more than once or twice before. I've rarely admitted these things even to myself, or faced the past that built and broke me. But these words are the truth, so I forge ahead talking to the camera.

"I grew up in fear. Every day of my life was controlled by it."

I realize that this might not make sense to most of my friends, who know that I grew up on an off-grid farm learning wholesome, self-sufficient skills. We were way out in the country where life is supposed to be nature-based and life giving. It's great to grow up that way, living off the land and all. But the flip side of that coin is that life was not always peaceful or happy.

*   *   *

The reason we lived off-grid was out of fear. We feared that society would destroy us and the government would torture and kill us, so we ended up hiding from everyone. And going off the rails in fear, our family went down a long spiral of destruction and heartache.

I spent the formative years of my life in a militia training camp preparing for Armageddon. Because of certain beliefs, almost everyone in our group rescinded their citizenship, disappeared, and had their kids trained as tough and sometimes as violently as possible. I was one of those kids, a five-year-old boy who believed everything he was told. I'm lucky I made it through those days. Of the other kids I knew, several didn't make it through. Some died, and almost all have broken lives now.

We stayed entirely isolated, fearing that people would turn us in and give the government the opening they wanted to take away the little kids and kill everyone else. As a small boy, the few times I did get out were terrifying. Every time I saw a police officer or soldier, I hoped and prayed they would die so they couldn't kill us.

Now, while I'm not convinced that the government has our best interests in mind, I can't forget the lesson I learned of what a life based on fear can lead to. Fear has a way of blinding its victims and causing them to become something they never imagined. They end up hurting and even destroying themselves and those around them. When I ask myself what made my growing-up years so miserable, I point to fear.

Maybe I was a kid prone to fear, but the environment I grew up in feasted on it. There was fear of being punished more severely than I could take, fear that I'd never do anything but fail and fall short. I feared that I'd eat too much and one of my siblings would starve. I remember fearing that I'd not be needed enough to be kept, that my productivity would drop and I'd be kicked out.

Fear was there when I woke up: would I be able work hard enough? Fear was there when I ate: would the food run out? Fear was there when I slept: constant nightmares that my younger siblings were being killed or punished. And fear kept me from running away, because I thought that the authorities would get involved and they'd take all my siblings away. We might never see each other again.

As I grew older, I learned that I could get by through conformity. That may have been the point of all the punishment anyway.

I know this sounds like I'm broad-brushing an entire childhood, and in a way I am. My story, just like anyone else's, is a mixed-up ball of both good and bad, and throughout it there was the scarlet thread of love. There is no single word that can describe the entirety of a kid's life. But the word 'fear' is as close as I can get.

I also pictured God hovering over me with a frown, angry and barely able to keep from squishing me. It seemed true at home—seemed true of my dad—and mentally putting God in the same position was not much of a stretch. Everyone and everything in my universe seemed spiteful and angry. I could never amount to anything or get away.

Despair grew so overwhelming that for several years I dreamed of killing myself. Imagining the act of suicide became a sort of past-time for me and I thought I'd do it with my rifle, inside a culvert where I often hid for a bit of peace and relaxation. But I was afraid of what might happen to my siblings afterward, so I didn't do it.

Then one day my fear turned into anger. And anger felt a lot better. I feasted on anger, letting it give me power until I lost myself in it. For most of my life I had really wanted to please Dad and everyone, to do the right thing and be a good kid. But I suddenly shed that attitude like an old coat. My plan became to endure whatever I had to until I could leave, then join the Marine Corps and never look back or write home. My main intention was to get into a place where I could hurt other people. And I became so bitter that I began to hate even myself.

Just before I left home, something happened that changed things. A group of volunteers was going on a mission trip to Ukraine. The trip was promoted in church along with the question of who wanted to join in. I had been listening with contempt, dwelling on how dumb the whole thing sounded, but when they asked who wanted to join the trip my hand went up.

"What? Why is my hand up?" I asked myself. I didn't want to go at all. I thought the whole thing was stupid. But there was my hand sticking straight up in the air and something inside me said, "Just go along with this."

I tried to pull my hand down but couldn't, and soon I was too embarrassed to say I had made a mistake. So I went along with it. They wrote my name down, and weeks later I found myself in Ukraine, traveling around to orphanages with a group of Christians.

We were supposed to be ministering to orphans but I remained aloof, sure that associating with these Christians demeaned myself. And then as I met the kids in those orphanages, I was immediately struck by the fear and hopelessness in their eyes. Some were abused, some were near starving. Some had birth defects from radiation poisoning during the Chernobyl explosion. Most were simply abandoned by parents, unwanted and seemingly unvalued by anyone. All of them lived without much hope of a more meaningful life.

Being full of fear and emptiness myself, I couldn't miss what I saw in the eyes of those kids. I knew instantly what it was, and I felt connected. It shocked me that these orphans and I could have anything in common. I saw myself reflected in their eyes, and it was darkness. It made me very uncomfortable.

The volunteers I had joined sat with the kids, talked with them, and brought them food. They listened to the kids' stories and sang, did puppet shows, and made the kids laugh. Day after day they worked.

It surprised me to see them serving so freely. I had thought that all of Christianity was just a show, a way to prove that some people are better than others. But for these people, it was real. There was nothing for them to gain by doing what they were doing. No prizes or notoriety awaited. They just expressed unpretended love for those kids.

What happened next shocked me even more. It was something almost unnoticeable taking place in the eyes of the orphans right in front of me. One of the older boys in a particular orphanage had asked a team member why we were there, why we were helping them, singing and giving out candy.

"Well, because Jesus loves you, and so do I," the worker replied. "I just want to love you and bring you some happiness."

"Jesus?" The boy asked, having probably never heard the name before.

"Yes, Jesus." The worker replied, "For God so loved the world that He gave His only begotten Son, that whosoever believes in Him should not perish, but have everlasting life. That's Jesus."

I knew the verse well, but it seemed to carry new meaning as the boy listened and tears rolled from his eyes. It may have been the first time anyone had told him he was valuable.

As that boy listened, little lights turned on in his eyes: the light of hope, the light of peace, and the light of being valued. It looked to me like the light of life.

That little change happened over and over again, and I watched it as we traveled and ministered to the kids. In face after face, I noticed fear subside and life spring up. It was the realest thing I had ever witnessed. I wanted what was taking place for those kids; I wanted it for myself. There was life there. I wanted to run in that direction, and so I did. Not all at once though, I held on to bits of anger for years. But inside me, life had begun.

My worldview changed, and instead of a perpetually angry God waiting to strike down the fearful and broken like me, I saw a compassionate God longing to raise us up.

"If all this is from God," I silently promised myself, "I'll ask for it too. I'll reach for it." And so I did. I asked God for some meaning in life, for some light.

The light came to me in the words of Jesus: "For God sent not His Son into the world to condemn the world, but that the world through Him might be saved...I am the resurrection and life: he that believes in me, though he were dead, yet shall he live." Those words saved my life, and I trusted my soul to them as well.

Seeing the value that God places on humans changed everything for me. "That must be the difference that God makes," I told myself. As clear as crystal I saw that without God, the only value to a person's life is whatever value that person and their circle place on it. In my case, that was extremely low. But from God's perspective, a person's value is unquestionable. It can't be reduced by slavery or failure. Even when no one else values you, it is God who whispers, "I see something in you so beautiful that I would die for it." Like a father. And with that thought I understood a basic truth: God is love.

Slowly I began to enjoy being with the Christians, talking with the orphans and singing. It amazed me that I was feeling happy.

And then came a day when our team took a little side trip to a WWII memorial. It wasn't really a memorial, but more like a spot in the woods with a maze of half-filled slit trenches and shell craters. No fences or markers where there to explain the site, but as we walked around, it was plain that fighting had taken place and defensive positions had been built and destroyed. Series after series of little ditches, now only knee deep, showed where soldiers had dug in zigzag patterns to keep artillery and grenade shrapnel from blasting down a long stretch of trench. Large, round craters pock-marked the forest here and there and I guessed that they were from bombs dropped by one side or the other. Mesmerized, I walked a long way through the woods.

All at once I found myself standing on a little rise of dirt that was grass-covered and partly caved in at the top. A stone at the center of the mound was the only official marker on that battlefield, unceremoniously stating that beneath the mound lay two-thousand civilians, rounded up from the nearest town and murdered by the Nazis on their drive toward the heart of the Soviet Union.

A chill traveled up my spine. I was standing on the top of a mass grave. The sinking ground at the top showed where the mound had collapsed as the bodies decayed.

Looking around, I saw several more similar mounds topped with stone markers.

I quickly retreated and stood at the foot of the mound, but I could not turn to leave. As if glued to the spot, I waited there for a long time, lost in thought. The tragedy that had happened to these people was the exact situation I had been taught to fear all my growing-up years. It was the event I had prepared and trained against all my life. And here was the evidence that it could happen for real. There seemed to be no point. This was just senseless death, a meaningless loss of life.

It seemed for a moment that we humans may be as valueless as this waste, just as valueless as all the orphans I had met—poor people with no future, who would not have a chance to dream and chase their dreams. In my mind, I was separate from them now because I had my dream of joining the Marines and escaping from home. I could do all that in a very short time. And I could go on toward my goal of doing everything in my power to hurt people. But suddenly I didn't want to hurt people anymore, and I realized that my anger and desire to hurt

Childhood home. Our family of thirteen lived completely off-grid, with no electricity or running water.

By age fifteen I could pop a squirrel at 100 yards, but had no idea how to place an order at McDonald's.

Timber cutting timber at 16.

Dating Cara in Texas. I took her everywhere except
on a normal date.

Silas and I with his archery buck. His first deer, not long before his passing.

Reaching the summit of a peak in the Fann
Mountains, Tajikistan

Me and Cara resting in a village during a long drive
to the remote Wakhan Corridor.

Cara preparing supper with her Pamiri sister, and
loving village life.

Levi and Elliot with their friends overlooking
the Wakhan Corridor.

Piecing together a water system for Cara's kitchen in
the village home.

Having tea with my awesome warlord landlord.

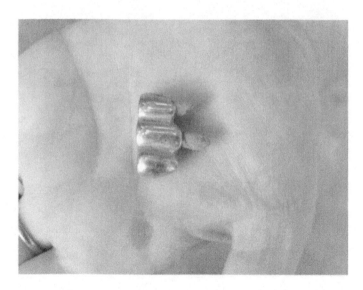

Human gold teeth that fell out of a butchered
goat's head. #NormalDayInTajikistan

Loading up medical patients for evacuation from a remote mountain village.

Rocket propelled grenade fragments and 12.7mm shells dug out of our dirt runway.

Observing Taliban positions during rescues on the border in 2021.

Taliban fighters taking over a defensive position.

Ukrainian apartments damaged in an airstrike.

The "train to nowhere." Leaving Ukraine with thousands
of refugees.

Smiling but weary after a long stretch of relief work.

My prize from *Alone*, and a thrilled smile of satisfaction
at having lived a dream.

people had already left me days ago, at the moment I saw kids coming to life because they learned that God values them.

Though I had never felt valued, the thought that God values people was changing me. If God valued humans as much as these Christians were saying, and I was starting to think He did, then He saw and valued each one of the people lying beneath this mound of dirt. And brutal people had driven them here and killed them all. The thought made oppression and murder seem so much more wrong than I had ever imagined before.

Something came over me then, a feeling as strong as the changing of summer to winter. I recognized it as an intense need to stand against anyone who would commit the atrocity of wasting or even suppressing human life. It was a need to show people that they really *do* have value—eternal value. I wanted everyone to know the truth I had learned just days earlier: that God sets the value on human life. If only people knew this, it could change everything. I was becoming free, and the value of each human life created by God was very real to me.

I prayed a prayer and made a promise to God that day in Ukraine. I said that if He could free me from darkness and use my life to free others such as the people in the mass grave right before my eyes, I would give Him every scrap of my life and my person. I meant the words for sure, but I had no idea what I actually wanted as I prayed. I just felt moved and so I prayed. Years later that prayer would come true in unimaginable fashion, and with uncanny accuracy.

After that trip to Ukraine, I completely stopped contemplating suicide, and step by step, my life turned toward the love I had found in God. The best way I can describe the whole episode is in the words of Jesus: "I am come that they might have life, and that they might have it more abundantly." If God is love, then Jesus is the divine messenger of that love, for without the words of Jesus I would not know God.

*   *   *

Sitting here in the arctic, recounting my story to the camera, I'm struck with the realization that although I understood all those years ago the value God places on humans, His creation, it's taken me until now to fully admit that it extends to me. God loves me.

The experiences of my childhood had shaped my view of the world, but God changed the theme of my story when his love reached me. I had found life and purpose, and I would never be the same.

*   *   *

After returning to the United States from Ukraine, I left home. My dad and I reached an understanding and made peace, so to speak. Against all odds, I was lucky to leave home on good terms. While I had been transformed in Ukraine, Dad had been changing as well. We shook hands and were friends. Then I hit the road with a bag of clothes and four-hundred and fifty dollars in my pocket from selling my horse and some coyote furs.

I had nothing to my name, but I was happy and determined to be as unlike the folks I grew up with as I could be. Wide-eyed at everything I experienced, I headed across the country to Texas. I had decided to pursue an education, so choosing something that I believed could lead me into international aid work, I enrolled in a specialized linguistic program.

I immediately found that the coursework was a breeze, but interacting with humans was a serious challenge. Nothing they said made sense to me, and it seemed that none of my words made any sense to them. I was in America, speaking English, but I might as well have been from another culture entirely. I think that's why I connect with immigrants and multi-cultural people so easily. I understand the challenge of being immersed in a world that's foreign and in-scrutable. I understand being unable to communicate.

Sick of being laughed at, I pressed myself to the task of studying the humans. I watched and learned, accepting the jokes and the confused expressions. In time, I started to understand more, and to be understood. But even to this day, I have to focus with all my might to communicate with anyone but my siblings.

Always fascinated by language and culture, I enjoyed my education immensely and graduated eager to put my skills to work. Having excelled at all of the courses, I was asked to return as an instructor. I spent a few years teaching linguistic courses in the States and then traveling to college programs overseas to teach. I credit the responsibility of teaching with why I'm able to interface with humans better now. I studied my students more than they studied the material, and it helped me to become a communicator.

It was on my first teaching job in the US that I met the girl who would become my wife. While teaching a special workshop on research linguistics, I was enjoying a conversation with someone between class periods when suddenly I heard the 'tink' of something metallic hitting the tile floor and I looked down to see a 5.56mm rifle cartridge rolling toward me. It stopped at my feet and I looked up to see that Cara, a beautiful blonde girl from Texas, was the person who had dropped it.

"Wow!" My mind spluttered while I picked up the round and handed it back to her. "Why would she have this in her pocket? I like it. I'm going to marry this girl!"

It was a lot more than just a stray rifle round which attracted me to Cara. Our values and life goals were similar, and soon we were madly in love. I took her horseback riding, hunting, and pretty much everywhere except on a normal date. She wanted the same things I did from life, to be where we could make a difference, and we knew right away that we were soul mates.

After marrying, we pursued international opportunities to do projects in tribal areas where literacy development was badly needed. We found that all throughout Asia, tribal languages were disappearing, and most of those tribes were either grieving the loss of their language, or struggling to keep their language and culture alive. In most cases, poverty and addictions were part of the situation as well. We found that reducing a language to writing and producing literacy materials could help both to preserve it and fight poverty and hopelessness.

Since alphabetizing languages had been part of our major, we felt suited to help out, and worked with various hill tribe languages from Central to Southeast Asia. Most of the time I spent teaching tribal folks the processes necessary to alphabetize their own language. But occasionally we got to do the work personally. This allowed us to utilize our linguistic training, and it also led us into all sorts of crazy adventures in backwater places all throughout Asia. As often as I could find free time, I would disappear into the backcountry, exploring the mountains or jungle of whatever country we happened to be in. Some of my most memorable adventures happened during those days, because I was young and always eager to run off into the wilderness.

While working near the border of Northern Pakistan, I headed into the mountains often for periods of alpine mountain climbing. I solo climbed one peak that had never been climbed before. At that time, I was no good at pacing myself, so I ended up summiting the mountain way too early and came down with a bad case of altitude sickness. That night, camping alone in the upper atmosphere, my sleeping bag's zipper failed and left me exposed to frigid temperatures and intense wind. Sick and weak, I sewed myself into the sleeping bag using a small knife to poke holes and push paracord through. Somehow I survived the night and then began climbing down. To my knowledge, the peak hadn't been climbed before, or even named.

On a subsequent climb in the same area with a German friend, we got caught by a winter storm and nearly died while trying to summit a major peak. My friend became sick and feverish during the descent and disappeared behind me while I was breaking trail in some deep snow drifts. I found him an hour or two later, almost incoherent, undressing himself and cursing in the -20°F temperature.

"You've got to get up and move!" I shouted while 50mph wind tore at us. I knew he was suffering from altitude sickness and some kind of delirium. He would die if he didn't start moving, but he just kept on cursing and taking off his things.

"Put your boots on and let's go!" I screamed over the wind.

After a lot of cajoling, he dressed again and started walking behind me. Eventually we made it to a lower altitude and his faculties slowly returned during the long, long walk back down the remote valley through which we had come. Later, he didn't seem to remember the struggle on the mountain at all.

I've described some of the perils already, but death and danger hasn't been the whole story. Our work has also given me a host of happy memories I wouldn't trade for anything. Honestly, some of the funniest things I could imagine have happened to me in Central Asia. Truth really can be stranger than fiction.

I was crossing the border from Tajikistan to Kyrgyzstan when we stopped our land Cruiser right at the border gate. An enormous guard armed with an AK-47 approached and started to look through our things. We didn't have anything to hide, but I was sure he would find some issue and ask for a big bribe.

"We'd better settle in for a while," I told my friend. When the guard heard me speaking English he turned and asked in Russian if I knew Mike Tyson.

"Mike Tyson!" I shouted in response, raising my arms in the air. I have no idea why I did that. I don't know Mike Tyson, and I wasn't trying to make him think I did. But some odd urge just made me shout the name.

What happened next took me completely by surprise. The guard threw his arms around me and picked me up, grinning from ear to ear and shouting "Mike Tyson!"

I was flopping around like a rag doll in the guard's arms as he danced, but I joined him in the shouting. Eventually he put me down and shook my hand.

"You are my birth brother," the guard said sincerely. "I'm not even going to search your bags. Have a good trip!"

I didn't know what to do next, I was so stunned, but the man motioned toward the gate and said we should go through. So I personally opened the gate to Kyrgyzstan, hoping that the guards on the other side wouldn't shoot me. They didn't, and on we drove, my buddy and I laughing for hours about the incident.

Another time in Tajikistan I was staying at a good friend's house in a really remote village. They wanted to honor my family by killing a goat to make a feast. But as it turned out, the person who normally killed goats was missing, so they asked if I would do it.

"Sure," I said, taking out my pocket knife. "I don't mind." I cut the goat's throat; after it bled out, I cut its head the rest of the way off. As the head hit the ground, a set of three gold teeth, human teeth, came out of somewhere and bounced away from the goat's head. I just stood there in shock, wondering where the teeth could have come from. But the lady of the house had noticed them too and she made a dive to snatch them up.

"I'm rich!" She shouted as she raced off toward her house, clutching the gold teeth tightly in her hand.

To this day I haven't figured out where the teeth could have come from, or how they materialized from the goat's head.

I've also learned that some of the most frustrating and aggravating experiences can become the ones we remember fondly later on. Once a group of police stopped me at a checkpoint in the Pamir Mountains. I was in a hurry, but they told me I would be detained for a while.

"Why?" I asked with some aggravation.

"So that you don't miss the wrestling match!" They replied. "It's going to be so fun!"

I was forced to go along with them, but the day turned out to be one of my most fun and memorable experiences, watching the best local wrestlers duke it out to win a vehicle, and then catching a quick wedding afterwards where we all danced and ate boiled sheep head. Once I got back on the road, I was only too happy to have been detained by the police.

During a mandatory health screening I had to take in Central Asia, I was offered a ride home by some Uzbek guys who asked where I was from.

"Texas," I replied.

"Oh, Texas! Do you ride camels and milk them in Texas?"

"No, we don't milk our camels. I've never had camel milk."

The guys were shocked, and insisted on taking me far out into the mountains. The ride dragged on and on, and as we crossed through a huge cemetery, I feared they were taking me to a cliff to kill me. We eventually arrived at a Kazakh camp where a herd of camels was corralled nearby. They shoved a jar of steaming camel milk into my hands and I drank it, complete with all the green specks that fall into hand-drawn milk. It didn't bother me. I grew up milking cows and drinking unstrained milk.

Each time I finished a jar, they sent a camp girl to milk another camel and we had refills. It was a relaxing afternoon, resting in a tent and drinking copious amounts of fresh camel milk.

For my family and I, our best times have happened in those out-of-the-way places—drinking tea in some village on the edge of nowhere, chatting with army officers on some of the remotest borders in the world, or sitting with actual warlords and discussing whether the moon landing was faked by America. I have a picture of my eight-month-old son squirming in the arms of a village elder. I found out directly afterward that he was known locally as "Bin Laden's Brother." I thought they were joking, but they swore he was a wanted terrorist.

During those years, my wife and I worked together to develop an alphabet for a tribal language which had been unwritten up to that point. It was rewarding to see people reading stories in their language for the first time and talking excitedly about chronicling their history in this new writing system.

Our life often brought us face to face with people who were living in conflict zones, suffering from war and poverty. Seeing so many people who were living in fear and desperation we began to ask ourselves what we could do to alleviate this a little. Without massive resources to spend, it was hard to help much, but we began doing water projects and small things for communities, mostly in the border areas of Afghanistan and Tajikistan.

Since then, our family has gone from project to project, doing things where we feel most useful. We try to meet needs directly and honestly, showing Jesus' love as well as we know how. At times we have partnered with big aid organizations, but the benefit of being independent is that we can choose which crisis we feel best suited to respond to, or particularly motivated by. Our limited budget is always a pain, but the freedom of choosing exactly what we want to do seems worth the trouble.

The only part that has been unbearable is the constant goodbyes that take place in such a life. My wife and I have moved thirty-eight times and counting since we married in 2011, and each move is accompanied by its own galaxy of goodbyes. There are goodbyes to the folks at home, and goodbye again in each place where we make a home and then move on. Goodbye to a place that was special, goodbye to the object memories my kids create. Goodbye to this or that project we put our whole souls into and might never see completed. Goodbye to this dream or that one, and more recently, goodbye to those who die. Goodbyes freaking suck. I'm tired of them.

The Taliban re-took Afghanistan in 2021, and we happened to be present on the border for most of the crisis. Afterwards, Russia invaded Ukraine, and I got the call to go help my medic friends. I hadn't set foot in the country since I was a teenager. Back then I had arrived angry and bitter, but left having found hope. This time as I entered the country with hope and joy in my heart, but terrified of getting blown up.

As the invasion progressed, the very orphanage where I had been when I found God all those years ago contacted me. They had heard I was doing evacuation work with a group of combat medics, and they called for help. Their town had come under heavy missile attacks. Along with my friend Sky, I got to help them in a small way as they fled to safety. It was one of the most surreal moments of my life, remembering what had started me on this path, and now brought me full circle: I had stood at a mass grave filled with victims of Hitler's war and earnestly hurled a prayer toward heaven.

The words were still fresh in mind: "God, if you can conquer the darkness in me, and use me to help others in this type of situation, I'll give you everything I am."

It was right then, realizing that my prayer had been answered so specifically, that I knew for sure that God hears me, and I felt I had found my niche. That day was one of the greatest gifts I've ever received. I might have cried a little later as I thought on it.

I love working in conflict zones. The effect of aid is so direct and the need so apparent. I'm also fine working under heavy stress and chaotic environments. I'm built for it. But somehow I've also ended up torn and weary. Looking back, I can clearly see where I erred. I've dwelt on it all too deeply. I've thought too much of myself.

Thinking of oneself is the most unhealthy state. Somehow, while helping others, I began dwelling on my own thoughts about it all. And that's where I went wrong. I dwelt on my own feelings about my brother's death too much. I let my mind stay locked on the images of war too long. In the end, dwelling on one's own thoughts is self-centered, and it destroys our natural ability to heal, because it minimizes the healing light from God and makes things all about our own experience. And so I'm healing now, finally healing, by feasting on the words of life that lie buried in my memory.

These strange events that have shaped me are just a few of the adventures and misadventures I've experienced. It has never been an easy path. And all the while, I've worked like a dog to fund our life's work. There seems never to be enough money to buy the necessary plane tickets, fix the vehicle, rent a place, finance the playgrounds, water wells, construction projects, or human needs we find and want to meet. Whenever I'm back in the States for a while, I've built houses and barns, just to scrape some more funds together.

But it's all worth it to me if our story means something, especially if it points any other struggling person to life and light. Though I've erred and made foolish blunders, everything I've struggled through has been in the pursuit of something meaningful or eternal, hoping to have some effect that will last beyond my short and insignificant life. Hoping to bring reality to the words I pray, "Let your kingdom come, let your will be done on earth, as it is in heaven." I want to see the world become a better place, with less fear and needless suffering. With more hope and joy.

*   *   *

"So there it is," I tell the camera, wrapping up my life's story. "That's Timber, for whatever it's worth." I'm alone in the quiet of the arctic wastes, alone in my shelter, but I still feel weird talking about myself all this time. Will any of this footage make it to the screen? And if so, am I happy about it?

Whether I'm satisfied with my life's story or not, I've told it. It is what it is. The camera has watched and listened patiently like a good partner should. Staring at the camera, I wish so much that it could talk.

"Why don't you say what you've been through?" I urge it. This camera has seen its share of crazy happenings, no doubt, having worked on *Alone* for years. I bet it's seen injuries, witnessed shelters burn down, been present while people sobbed and tapped out... maybe it's even been vomited on. It must have witnessed joys, sorrows, triumphs, and losses. But it never says anything, and so I don't pry or ask too many questions.

Eventually stirring from my reverie, I go outside and cut several armloads of firewood. Finally it's evening and I can prepare my fish to fry.

Using the tip of my knife blade, I pry a chunk of cold lard out of its birchbark container. Dropping the chunk in, I swing my pot over my fire. While I wait for the lard to melt, I prepare my fish, cutting it into small strips that will fry easily. I've learned a lot in my attempts to fry this stuff, and yesterday I produced a near-perfect crispy, golden fry.

My shelter is as pleasant as can be inside, with the fireplace glowing and popping. The mud-covered wall behind the fire reflects heat so nicely, better than I ever hoped. The smoke is drafting through the chimney for once, pulling a few sparks along with it now and then. The alder hook that my pot hangs from is so blackened that it looks like a piece of wrought iron. My pot, backlit by the flames, looks witchy and romantic. I love it.

I make sure the camera is on and has fresh batteries. I'm hoping it will capture some of the fantastic atmosphere I'm enjoying.

Once the lard is heated, I drop in the chunks of fish. They sizzle and pop, and I keep a close eye to make sure that they don't burn. Flipping the chunks over once, I see that I've achieved zero sticking - the bottom of the pot is clean.

In just moments the fish seems done and I take the pot off the fire, setting each chunk out on a birchbark plate. It smells so good that I don't wait for it to cool, burning my mouth on the first bite.

"Holy smokes! This stuff is perfect!" I hold a piece out for the camera to see. It's stunningly golden and crispy, almost like it has a flour breading. When I tap it, the crust sounds light and airy. It dawns on me that frying it so thoroughly might reduce the nutritional value somewhat, but it's so incredibly delicious that I hardly care. I've achieved what I dreamed of when I rendered the moose lard. I'm the champion.

"I can cook!" Beside myself with unreasonable happiness, I shout the phrase over and over.

"I can cook! Look at this stuff! I can freakin' cook!"

I'm finally doing more than just boiling something edible, and it's a breakthrough moment. I'm making *real food*. I realize that my simple fish-frying set up isn't exactly gourmet, and it's only one small skill, not an ocean of culinary wizardry. But it's something to be happy about. I'm good at this one thing, and for me it's a big step. With each piece of my delicate, golden, crispy pike, I'm feeling more smug and sophisticated. A more well-rounded survivalist.

My only real concern is that viewers will think I have it too good, that I'm living too high and comfortable. It would be embarrassing to ever leave this place while I'm faring so well. I don't plan to leave any time soon, but I actually become so concerned about my posh setting that I turn the camera off and finish my meal in silence, ashamed of the luxury I'm enjoying.

I am in fact really comfortable right now, more so than I could have hoped for. The only improvement I need is bigger meals. With a belly almost half-full of fried fish, it's like my hunger monster has just come to life. It's all I can do not to cook another fish immediately.

After supper, my fire dies down and starts smoking badly again, too badly to keep a fire inside all night. Once the flames disappear and there's only coals left, the smoke really starts chugging. This swampy wood is just not going to burn cleanly. It's why I would never have chosen to winter in exactly this location. I'd have moved over to the hills where I could get higher, dryer stuff to burn.

Throwing the last chunks of smoldering wood into the snow outside, I film my evening update and then slide into my sleeping bag.

Chapter 15

Freeze-up

*   *   *

"And God saw everything that He had made, and behold,
it was very good. -Genesis 1:31

Nature. The world around me that embodies life and harmony. I'm immersed in it. Not only immersed in it, at this moment I'm a real part of this ecosystem. I'm one of the creatures who manifest the rhythm of the wild, taking from and giving to the system as it all goes round.

I get so much joy from seeing it all working. Every sight, the incredible and the infinitesimal, thrills me. Seeing my moose as it scraped and thrashed the willow bushes with its antlers, majestic in a rut-fueled display of power. Being the first human eye to view a pike, all speckled and brilliant as it emerges from the shimmering water. Following the soft impressions that the wolves leave as they tread the earth on their circuit of endless hunt. Watching ducks cruise around my marsh, squabbling noisily until they take flight and vanish. I'm tasting life, true life, wild and rampant. Life that is succeeding over death. It's good.

The vibrance and zest of the wild has soaked through to me and impressed me with an incalculable sense of wealth. And slowly that feeling of wealth has broken through to my soul, becoming not just a wealth of experience, but something of real value that I'm a part of.

When God set up this great engine of life called earth, He must have taken no less joy in it all than I feel right now. The overwhelming pleasure I experience at being part of this circle of life must be just a shadow of what He's feeling.

Life is from God. If I'm a part of this creation, no less real than a moose or bear, He certainly must get the same joy from me, watching me live and breathe, hunt, eat and sleep. Yes, that happiness God feels seeing His creation extends to me. Even me.

Day 42

I wake up this morning with the thought that my creature-self is valuable to God—not the work I do that generates a positive effect, not the words I say to convey something important. My very existence is worth something. It's an epiphany that amazes me. My being is good when God looks down and sees what He has made. I don't need to exert any effort to make that more true. I don't have to generate positive force in order for God to turn His head my way. The truth is that I exist, and in existing I glorify God. I'm a love letter to the Creator. And I guess everything life should be springs from that fact.

My background is what gives this epiphany such a huge impact on me. The mentality I grew up with was a performance-based one, a culture where you accomplish something amazing or you don't eat. From my first waking memory, I was conditioned to earn everything. Those who fail or even rest don't deserve to breathe.

Now I'm seeing how life itself glorifies God. And I'm alive, surviving, breathing, showing in my body that God loves life. Now

I'm discovering once again, He redeems life from being broken and dark.

Throughout my adult life, I've understood with my head that God loves me no matter how well I perform. But the truth of how I still view myself inwardly is becoming clear to me here in the silence of the arctic. I can see that I've been approaching life as if I still have to pay for the air I breathe and the space I take up by working so hard that I can deserve to exist. I don't particularly want to prove anything to other people. I got over that compulsion a long time ago. But in some way I've always tried to prove it to myself, and maybe to God.

Effort can be a good thing. We should push ourselves, train like warriors and work with all our might: a healthy and necessary part of survival. But effort can become more than just that. Driven-ness can become our identity, even our path to virtue. I can see now that all the vast energy I've sunk into positive work doesn't make me one inch taller or shorter when I look up at the face of God. Out here in the clarity of isolation, I can see that. I'm just a creature.

That's not the end of the story, of course. Glorifying our Creator by existing is only the beginning of the road. I think that peace and unity with God, truly accepting and knowing the Creator, is where joy is found. That relationship is the ultimate end of the journey, the high water mark of this life and the guiding light to the next.

This all might sound a bit fanciful to readers. And yes, I could easily choose to interpret things differently. I could attribute the peace I have found to just spending extended time in nature. Many people express that. I could say I'm getting plenty of fish because I'm good at catching them. I could say that I found my arrow on day twenty-seven by random chance, and retrieved the big fish that escaped with its stringer by pure, dumb luck. But then I would have to go back and say that my son's legs weren't healed miraculously either.

I'd have to claim it was random chance. I would have to say that God wasn't involved.

You understand that I can't do that. I can't reinterpret that sacred gift. If you've ever had your little son's life given back to you, you'd understand. It was God. And since God would do something like that for me, it's easy to see that His hand is active here.

When I arrived here on day one, I prayed a secret prayer that God would meet me. I was asking for more than just a glimpse of God through nature. I wanted something really, tangibly, *Him*. I truly think I'm experiencing that unity with God. He's giving me peace and showing me that I can rest. And what's different after today is that I'm not trying to earn it. I'm just asking for it and resting.

After contemplating that for a while, I decide again to allow myself to rest. Rest has already been my strategy, but all of my resolve to rest has been fruitless up to this point. I haven't been able to make myself do it. But the epiphany I receive today suddenly changes me. I'm not earning anything here. I'm not impressing God. I know the tiredness I've carried inside for the past few years has not come from a weary body, but from an exhausted soul. I've wanted and needed so badly for true rest to happen to my soul. And now I'm allowed to rest, to be free from earning and proving. So today I get my first taste of simply existing. It makes me truly content.

Fresh snow has fallen during the night—just another light dusting, but it never melts now. Every flake that comes down stays, and it's building into a nice snow cover.

No fresh tracks have crossed my land for days, so as I check my snares, I'm surprised when I see a ball of whitish-gray fur hunched at my first snare site. Suppressing my excitement, I get the camera set up to capture everything. Then I approach the hare and lift it up in awe. It's bigger than I expected.

"My first ever arctic hare!" I breathe, admiring the amazingly soft fur. It's the softest thing I've ever felt in my life. Almost unimaginably soft. "Thank you God for this beautiful creature!"

My next snare set-up has a second hare in it, captured perfectly by the neck. Though this hare is much smaller, clearly a baby from summer's last brood, I'm elated.

Hauling my catches proudly back to camp, I hang them on the front of my shelter and admire how they make my camp look - the roof boughs under a layer of snow, the logs of my front wall, my axe leaning there, my moose antlers and now these hares hanging from the gable pole. It could be one of those scenes from a Jack London book, or a black-and-white photo of the early explorers.

"This is my dream life!" I've said it so many times now, but it keeps on getting better.

Stocking up food in the fall is a mood that harks back to some of my fondest memories.

*   *   *

As a young boy when we were living off the land, fall would come and the rhythm of the seasons would set us all to work preserving food. My brother and I would fire up the huge water bath canner, which held seventy-eight quarts at one time. We would can enormous quantities of green beans, tomatoes, apples, and everything else. Six or eight of us would be chopping the apples, snapping beans, or blanching the tomatoes. Then the next crew, my sisters, would stuff jars and sterilize the lids. Then into the canner, where the oldest of us would stoke the fire and keep the water level just right. Two or three batches per day in the canner would eventually generate so many quarts that it dazzled the eye to behold it.

It was wonderful, those times. We were all working together and a sort of harmony would take over that was refreshing and happy. I always thought that those moments were close to the feeling a

270

native camp must have felt after a successful buffalo hunt—everyone working hard, everyone happy, pulling together for the common good and enjoying the bounty.

Better yet was sorghum time for us. Sorghum was the only sweetener we used, and we made a lot of it. It was another one of those projects where the entire family was focused on just that one thing to get it done.

Just before the frost hit, we would strip every leaf from the cane, then let it frost that first time to boost the sweetness of the sap hidden in the stalks. In the early morning, in that magical time of orange leaves and steaming breath, we would press and boil the sorghum. The all-day affair was fun and rewarding. Usually we'd be eating a big mess of squirrels during the boil, and we'd talk of hunting while we cooked the sorghum down to a beautiful amber color.

I remember hauling one of those loads in a wagon pulled by a horse called Rubber-nose. He was a barely-broken horse, likely to jump at anything because he was often abused by my dad. Rubber-nose spooked and took off with a load, and my little brother Jed was riding on top. From a distance, I saw his tiny body bouncing around, clinging to the load and screaming with all his might as the horse and wagon raced off. Through a ditch line they went at a full gallop, with the load flying in every direction and the wagon breaking apart into wooden splinters. I thought Jed was a goner, but eventually the horse charged through a barb wire fence and got so hung up that he had to stop. Rubber-nose was bleeding and torn, but Jed was none the worse for wear.

I think those memories, my good ones, are why I love the first frost so much. When frosty weather comes, I'm filled with hope and energy that cannot even be contained. It's like I'm a little box full of gun powder that explodes with nowhere for the energy to go, except on a hunt.

*   *   *

The hares I caught today bring me back to that feeling of putting up food, but they also mean that I can depend on more than fish and moose meat. I can keep right on getting fresh meals as the winter progresses.

Down at the river, my fish lines are so entrapped and tangled in ice that I consider pulling them all out. But I've caught another fish on the lucky line near my flay table. It swims in tight circles as I pull it in, so I'm not surprised to see that it's a burbot. But I am surprised by its size—it's every inch of three feet long. I'm so happy with it that I blather on and on to the camera about how cool of a fish it is and how superior burbot meat is over pike.

I've saved half a hare to eat for supper, but the meat looks so good that I throw the rest of the hare into the pot as well.

"Just this once I'll eat a whole hare," I explain to the camera, as if that silent, black-eyed companion is judging my lack of self control. "It'll be fine."

I don't take any chances of leaving this hare tough and chewy, boiling it until the bone pulls right out cleanly when I grab its arm.

The meat tastes so good. I'm been living on fish and jerky for so long that this morsel of fresh mammal really hits the spot. The skull and organs are in the pot as well, and I dig into them with delight.

I've never been big on eating lungs, liver, and brain. Heart is okay, but those other organs just aren't my thing. This time however, the brain and organs seem even better than the meat to me. They're simply delicious and I suck the brains out, eat the eyeballs, tongue and ears, then lick my fingers to get the last bit of flavor. The lungs are the best part of all, being slightly reminiscent of potatoes.

I've always found it weird to eat heads. Chewing on some-things teeth with my teeth, eating it's tongue with my tongue...it's difficult to wrap my mind around. Picking at a skull while I'm staring at its vacant eye sockets usually makes me feel like I should explain something to the creature, or at least blindfold it. But this time my mind doesn't object at all.

After supper, I boil a pot of Labrador tea and drink as much as I can hold before bed time. I'm not using my quiver canteen anymore because water freezes inside it. So I take a special effort to tank up right before bed. It means I'll have to get up to pee several times, but it's worth it to stay well hydrated.

Day 43

Three skills determine if a person can kill food well. Those three things are hunting, fishing and trapping. Gathering herbs is a thing all its own. But hunting, fishing, and trapping are the trifecta of meat skills.

So far I've showed that I can hunt and fish, but I've only made the smallest attempts at trapping. I've been waiting on the snow.

This morning I grab all of my tools and head out into the early morning light to make my snare lines. The snow is here now, and it's soft enough to show every track that crosses it.

I've been reluctant to carry the big camera out on the trail for a long time. But I bring it with me today, hoping to get some quality footage of setting out snares. I should prove that I'm not just a one-trick pony. I can do the whole trifecta.

Carrying the big camera while trying to duck and weave through the brush is a real nightmare, with snow falling from branches and going down my neck in the back. The tripod is the main problem. To save time, I usually leave the legs extended between set-ups. Trying to maneuver with it between the trees, with my bow in the other hand and filming myself with two GoPros is an impossible chore.

Striking out along the river shore to the east, I follow the bank upstream checking inside the trees every few yards to see if I can cut some fresh hare sign. Then I find a moose trail that heads away from the river at the edge of my territory. Following it to the south, I pass through a number of small meadows and willow breaks.

All along the way, I've kept a sharp eye out, and I have yet to turn up a single hare track. With mounting apprehension, I wonder if there are any hares at all.

Eventually I'm way out on the east side of my meadow, near the area I dug moss from. Here I find a little band of larger trees. There are a few spruce and even a birch here and there, and among these trees I find two sets of hare tracks.

The tracks are not together. There's a set going and a set coming back, so they may have been made by the same animal. Hardly a hare run, but I'm excited nonetheless, and I take time to set up a handful of snares at chokepoints along the trail.

Once I've set up as many snares as I can justify for the amount of tracks, I head further south.

I discover no more hare tracks, but I do find something extremely valuable to me: a couple of birch trees with big sections of flaky bark, perfect sheets of nature's paper for crafting and writing. Peeling off as much bark as I can, I save the big pieces for paper and stuff lots of little flakes into my pockets to use as fire tinder.

Tiny clumps of dry grass also pop up here and there in this section of land. The little clumps are wet and muddy, but once I dry them out, they catch fire better than anything else.

The snow will be deep soon. Any day now, finding tinder will become impossible. So I spend hours searching out the little clumps of grass and stuffing all that I can into my jacket. I have a good-sized armload when I finally head back toward camp.

I stuff the grass I gathered into the rafters of my shelter where it can dry. It will make a supply that keeps me going for a couple of months. Then I head down to the river where I decide that I'll definitely pull the fish lines today. The flowing ice is shredding them.

I can't even throw the lines far enough to reach past the ice. This is the end of my open-water fishing.

It's a miracle that I've been able to fish for this long. I figured I'd get only three weeks of open water.

"Thank you for every fish, God!" I say as I start breaking the ice from around my lines, pulling them and hanging them on the poles where they'll be visible once I need them again.

"You've given me more than I asked for. It's kept me alive!"

In the beginning I asked for a fish per day while the water remained open. I've averaged way more than one per day. I have seventeen fish stored in my food cache where they're frozen and safe. Two of those fish are about four feet long, and all together the number of meals they amount to is huge. Thinking about it, I realize more and more that God has been watching out for me.

I pull up one of the last line to find a small burbot hooked deep in the throat.

"Dude, check this out!" I yell happily at the camera, holding up the squirming, tadpole-like creature. It's only about sixteen inches long, and being thin for most of it's length, it's a one-meal fish. But it marks yet another day when I don't have to draw from my food cache. It's my thirteenth fish since I asked God for ten more. I can't help but express some gratitude.

"Bless the Lord, oh my soul,
And all that is within me, bless his holy name.
Bless the Lord, oh my soul,
And forget not all his benefits."

I've memorized a lot of psalms in my life. That's mostly a gift from my mother, who forced me to learn them all when I was young. I didn't like it then, but now I'm just loving the fact that I have these psalms in my brain. They feed my soul in a way I'd never anticipated.

Every time I launch into a quotation, I feel connected somehow, enjoying a sense that my sphere of isolation has a small hole where heaven pokes through and touches me. Though I've felt connected to God for a long time and I've experienced Him answering me before, I've never felt the connection I'm enjoying these days. It's a big deal to me, feeling so certain that when I talk to God, He hears me.

My lines are all out of the water now. Fishing each morning and evening has book-ended my activities consistently since day one. I won't even know what to do without this part of my routine.

Pulling my lines feels like a true transition of seasons, the final end of fall. There's nothing out ahead but whiteness, more snow and cold. I'm like a ship that has lost all sight of land, and the daunting expanse of a trackless sea lies ahead. The trackless sea is winter.

Chapter 16

Winter

* * *

"There's a fine line between dreams and nightmares. Sometimes you must taste the one to experience the other." -Excerpt from my diary.

Day 44

An icy wind breathes on the land, dumping another three to four inches of fresh powder on me overnight. I can't make a snowball out of this stuff. It's so powdery and dry that it slips right through my fingers.

I'm glad that the snow is dry. When the temperature remains well below freezing it can make survival easier in a lot of ways. For starters, firewood and kindling stay dry even when they're piled high with snow. I can just shake the snow off and light the wood up. Secondly, I know my fresh fish won't spoil now. They're frozen as solid as rocks.

The third thing that's easier about cold is that travel gets much more convenient once you can walk across the surface of lakes and rivers. My section of river isn't frozen yet and the lake is still a little slushy. But I know that in a day or two I'll be able to get out on it.

The only thing inconvenient about today's snow is that it guarantees I've caught no hares. My snares will be snowed in and my main job today is to visit them all the move them higher so that hares don't run over top of them.

I head out with my bow and camera, breaking fresh trail the whole way. The work consumes a lot of energy, but I feel a renewed strength today.

For a long time I've been enjoying myself, but without the energy to really get wild and rambunctious. But it feels different today. An invigorating blast of oxygen-rich northern wind refreshes the land. Across the expanse of Moose Meadow, I can see the wind kicking up spindrift, carrying clouds of silver crystals. The sight not only is beautiful but also sets a stage for a more extreme survival story. It's like *Alone* is finally real. This is the stuff I dreamed of.

"Daddy! Let's play Savage Hunters of the North Wastelands!" In my mind's ear, I can hear my kids, Levi and Elliot, begging me to play-act our favorite game. Each of us grabs a weapon, a tomahawk or bow, and we go out into the woods.

It begins very simply: "Okay, guys, our village needs us to find food. Let's go up this hill and look for tracks." But then imagination always carries us away as we hunt.

"Look out for that charging mammoth! Elliot, throw your hatchet! Levi, shoot another arrow! He's charging again!" Their weapons miss, and the mammoth pins me down with his tusks. Struggling to get free, we all fire again, our hatchets and arrows sticking into whatever dead stump represents the imaginary beast. Then we finish it off and eat it.

We trek from one adventure to the next, pretending to make fires, eat, sleep, and waking up to hunt again. We track down fantastic beasts, battle saber-tooth cats, and save people from flooded rivers and mudslides.

The game can go on for a whole afternoon. It's one of the things my kids love most about being at our place in America, as opposed to some city overseas. We have weapons here, and we can go out and imagine all sorts of adventures. We call it "Savage Hunters of the North Wastelands." This game seems like the best way for little boys to learn to love the outdoors, to be careful with weapons and to just have fun. I'll miss it when my boys are too old to play it.

Right now in the snowy arctic, I feel like the special game I play with my kids has been fully realized. I hope that they know how much they are a part of it.

I set up the camera in the snow and walk out ahead of it, hoping that the winter landscape looks as epic as it feels. The air is sweet, rich with oxygen, and I draw deep lungfuls of it.

"Now this is the arctic!" I yell. "This is *Alone*! This is what I signed up for!"

Feeling a kind of rabid joy, I raise my bow and roar as long and loud as I can.

"Haaaaa! I love this! I LOVE this!"

Bellowing louder and louder, I shake my bow at the sky.

"I'm a wolf! I'm a bear! I am a north man!"

The gusting wind pelts my face with snow crystals, makes all my blood rise up, and I feel like I'm indestructible. I feel so awesome that I try a high kick, and it almost knocks me down.

"Whoa! I don't have the energy for that stuff!" So much for being indestructible. I'm pretty weak now.

With my near tumble, the moment is over and I retrieve the camera. Plowing through snow drifts, I make it back to camp and spend the rest of the day chopping firewood and staring out over Moose Meadow.

Day 45

"I didn't sleep much." I'm standing in my front yard filming my morning update. I've just emerged from my shelter, bundled up for the cold but still feeling chilly. The snow drapes everything in my background. My voice is crackly from tiredness. "The wolves howled all night, and I just couldn't sleep through the noise. So I went outside and tried to find the wolves for a while. Didn't find anything."

I suddenly notice my image in the camera and I try to fix my hair. It's sticking up everywhere and just springs back up when I run my hand through it.

"It's gray again today. Just never-ending grayness. I don't even believe the sun exists any more."

After a high point yesterday, my emotions have plunged into a stagnant swamp. I feels like it's been a month since I saw the sun, but two weeks would probably be a realistic guess.

"Anyways, I'm gonna get my bow and run my snare line. Then I guess I'll start a fire."

I sound bland and deadbeat. But there's just nothing to stir me from my lethargy. I've started sleeping less and less and the dreary grayness suffocates the life out of me.

My snare lines are empty, but I set more snares over the same old trackway anyhow. Then I make sure to gather more tinder and Labrador tea before trudging back to camp.

I've been drinking a full pot of tea every evening. I brew it strongly, usually tossing in a big handful complete with leaves and stems. I often leave it to brew all night. Occasionally I wonder if so much tea is harmful in some way. But then I stop wondering and just drink more.

Necessary activities pretty much end at camp once the firewood is cut. So I get out some of the big flakes of birchbark I gathered for drawing on and make some charcoal pencils. The pencils are just slender, dry spruce branches with burnt ends.

The closer I get to drawing on the birch bark, the value of the bark makes me hesitant to begin. This bark is my only sheet of paper. What if I mess up? What if I think of something more valuable to draw or write later?

The pressure is too much so I put the bark away and cook supper. My fish is tasty and the tea satisfying, packed with flavor. Wrapping up my evening rituals by tying a knot in my calendar string, I head to bed.

Being full of warm tea right before bed has its disadvantages, and before long I'm outside again to pee. The moon is barely visible through the cloud cover, and I wonder if the aurora is going on up there somewhere.

Once outside, I start losing heat quickly and my sleeping bag is slow to warm back up. So forgetting about the aurora, I hurry back inside.

Day 46

The river is acting really strange. Without any rainfall or melt, the water has risen three feet overnight. I can't even reach my flay table and only the tips of my fishing rods are sticking up out of the water. Hour by hour it rises and I'm afraid that I'll have no beach left to walk along. There seems to be no rhyme or reason.

"How is the water level doing this?" I ask the camera. I'm standing where my path ends at the river with my pot in my hand, trying to get some water to boil.

"Is the wind backing the water up? Is an ice jam downstream somewhere diverting water my way?" I don't have any answers.

The ice that had been forming and breaking along the shore is collecting into rafts of broken chunks. The constant action of the water churns the ice into crystals, piling them along the shore but not allowing them to freeze into a cohesive sheet. It's like shaved ice, the biggest slushy I've ever seen. Getting liquid water in my pot is impossible. Fishing remains out of the question in these conditions.

Day 47

My days are becoming anchored by the routine of long walks through the snow of my snare line. The activity has replaced my fishing but isn't nearly as productive.

The river is still a mess of rising water and roiling rafts of ice chunks. My fish poles are now unreachable to me. Only their very tops protrude from above the surface. I can't walk out to them to salvage my hooks, which I can barely see sticking where I left them in the tops of the poles. The ice is a semi-frozen slurry. I sink into the mass of flowing crystals whenever I try to walk on it.

I'm worried that the ice will rip the lines off of my fish poles when it solidifies. If so, I'll lose the hooks. But there's nothing I can do about it for now.

Day 48

A savage wind rises, coming straight out of the north. All day long it grows in strength, blasting through my thin band of trees and chilling me. It shakes the snow off of the tree limbs, spraying the sparkling dust like glitter from a cannon. Band after band of the thick clouds that have been obscuring the sky for so long are disappearing, being blasted off to the south by the wind. By evening, big streaks of blue sky are visible.

While I'm out in the snow checking my snare line, I begin hearing a sound that baffles me. It starts off as a low buzzing sound but grows throughout the day, getting closer, louder and more distinct. It's the sound of chanting.

At first I try to shrug it off. No one would be around here, not for miles in any direction. The land is so snow-locked that no human would ever come out this way without a snow machine or aircraft. But I become less sure that I'm alone as the day passes. The chanting gets closer and louder until I find myself looking around for people. I'm not alarmed, just baffled. It sounds like six or eight elderly people singing and muttering.

The sound becomes really distinct, and all throughout the day I dart out to look across the lake, hoping to spot whoever or whatever the sounds are coming from. Then it sounds like it's coming from behind, so I run back through my alder trees to stare upriver and northward toward the cliffs.

"Listen. Listen to that," I tell the camera. I feel crazy, but it's so real.

I expect people to appear, but nobody shows up. Still the sound continues, sometimes waxing stronger and stronger until I'm just sure a group of people are right in my very patch of trees, and sometimes dying away almost to nothingness.

"It's the wind. It's got to be just the wind," I declare confidently to the camera, but I still keep my eyes alert.

The wind becomes so powerful that the stronger gusts sometimes obscure the chanting, and I tell myself over and over again that the noise is a natural phenomenon. I've been in canyons that mutter when the wind blows through them. I've been in the Taklamakan Desert where wind makes sand crystals vibrate together and sing. Like those contexts, this chanting sound must be coming from some effect the wind is having on the spruce trees or river, or something.

The only thing I can do is ignore the strange phenomena and hope that it either goes away or an explanation presents itself. So I busy myself cutting more wood and battening down the hatches of my shelter in case this intense wind storm gets worse.

Toward evening, I'm hiding from the wind inside my shelter as I cook half a pike. I'm entranced by the food I'm about to enjoy, and I take every precaution to fry it exactly right. This special time of day is becoming more than just a meal. It's closer to a religion. I enjoy each bite of supper immensely, and I tell God so as I clean up and boil tea.

Lying in my sleeping bag later, I'm trying to drift off to sleep. But sleep won't come. The wind is building even stronger outside— strong enough to becoming a real concern. The big spruce trees behind my shelter are groaning as their branches are cracking and falling. I worry that a tree will fall on me, but I have no control and no ability to stop it. I just lie still and ignore it all.

Along with the wind, I can still hear the chanting going on somewhere not far away. I convince myself all over again that it's just the wind setting up some resonation with the spruce groves behind my camp.

Inside my shelter, my mind is buzzing with things I should do and decisions that would make life better. None of it has to do with the Arctic though. It's all about home, family, and that everyday life I left behind.

My thoughts range from cooking, which I've spent lots of time dreaming about, to decisions about vehicles and jobs.

The ideas and plans roll on and on, until I'm suddenly struck by the thought that I want a third child. The feeling comes out of nowhere, and I never expected such a notion. I've got two boys and I love them to the top, but I haven't wanted any more kids.

My wife has often talked about having another baby, but I've been afraid of having more kids than I can spend quality time with. I'm very afraid of that.

Instead of being a passing fancy, the idea that I want a baby takes root in me. The desire feels really right, but I tell myself that maybe it's just loneliness talking. Maybe I'm out of sorts from missing home, and therefore strange feelings of domestic need are welling up within me.

I decide to at least entertain the idea, to let it steep for a while like the Labrador tea I chug every night. But I'm almost sure it will go away.

All night long, the wind howls more furiously. The trees shake and my shelter rocks, but somehow I end up falling asleep.

Day 49

The snow has been blasted into deep drifts along the bank of the river, up to my hips as I break a trail down to the ice. Overnight, the river has frozen all along the shore. Yesterday's churned ice has solidified into a thick, solid layer. I chop a hole near the shore and find it five inches thick, but twenty feet away there is still open water. So I don't know how far I can venture out onto the frozen parts.

"I think I should just set more snares," I tell the camera as I stare out over the river wishing I could fish. "I've got to find more hares."

And so all day I trudge further and further afield, setting snares everywhere on the infrequent hare tracks I come across. I have yet to find a place where a hare ran twice. There are no established runs.

I'm pushing further upriver when I enter the willows to find the first decent hare sign: a little patch of woods that's crisscrossed by hare tracks. My excitement swells as I set snares all around the area, but then I hear an electronic beep from the GPS, and my heart sinks to my boots. I suspect what the message says even before I read it.

"You have crossed outside your territory. Please turn around."

"You've got to me kidding me!" I fume, as angry as I can be. Catching these hares is essential to my very survival, and I suddenly question my resolve to keep the rules and observe the boundaries. Should I take all these snares down? I spent so much energy setting them up, and this is the only good hare sign I've come across.

Kneeling down in the snow to think, I go back in my mind to a discussion I had in a remote village in Central Asia a few years ago.

*   *   *

I was sitting on a crude wooden bench with the leader of an isolated tribe. We were becoming fast friends, and each day we sat and talked for an hour or two about existential issues. He would solve domestic problems, make peace between neighbors, and counsel folks in need. Sitting beside him as a guest aid worker, I was humbled to see his process for solving problems. He had also been the one to suggest that I start building children's playgrounds and benches for the elderly in the town.

One day, he called me to discuss something, and he seemed extra serious. I guessed that it was because I had walked in on him while he was arranging a weapons deal the previous evening.

"Timber, there are two kinds of hooligans," he began. He was using the word "hooligan" to basically mean an outlaw, anyone who doesn't abide by the rules. I had been expecting this conversation to come up soon. The tribe I was living among was breaking a lot of rules, but mostly out of necessity. Their own central government severely persecuted them and wrote many outlandish laws, making it illegal for them to thrive and succeed in any way. Sooner or later, I had known that this chief would approach me about where I personally draw the lines on keeping such laws.

"There are two kinds of hooligans," he asserted again, and I nodded to show I was listening. "The first kind does bad things." He waited a minute for his words to sink in. He wanted everything he said to feel very weighty, like golden drops of wisdom from beyond space and time. His gravity cracked me up, but I listened with a thoughtful frown of deep sincerity.

"This kind of man beats up women, robs people. He steals things and does bad."

Another minute went by in silence but I didn't interrupt. It was the way of these people to speak slowly when talking about something of great importance. Then he leaned toward me conspiratorially, and his voice took on an otherworldly intensity.

"But there is a second kind of hooligan. This second kind does things that are *illegal,* but *good!*"

I knew that this was his way of feeling me out, probing to see how I'd react when I saw what he'd been doing to supply his people with income and food. He lived in a situation where a set of rules stood between his people and their very survival. No question—he should break the rules to keep his people from starvation, and he simply wanted to know if I was going to judge him for it or turn him in.

Without a second thought, I let him know that it wasn't my business to judge him for it. I'd keep his secret. Survival is a higher law.

*   *   *

Now, sitting in the arctic snow with fresh hare tracks all around me, I'm in a situation where my own survival is at stake, and a set of rules stands between me and my potential food. The rules state that I can't go outside my territory to search for other animals, and I have to observe the limits of game bagging. I can't try to kill a second moose, for example, which I'd love to do.

If I look at it from a certain viewpoint, my survival supersedes any other rule that can be made. I could break a rule here and there and calm my conscience down by saying it was necessary, that I'm adhering to the most basic law of all, the law of survival. But that's not the story I want to write with my life. I have something better to tell than that I simply "survived." Survival is not the highest good that a person can achieve.

287

I decide for the hundredth time that I want to be fair to the other skilled and honorable people who are competing here. And win or lose, I want to be proud of every action I take. So I tear all the snares down, leaving the hares to the owls and pine marten.

In the evening I spend a while staring out across the meadow. The wind out there is ripping like a hurricane. It has swept the ice nearly free of snow and and piled it up against the willows on the east side of the lakes. The swirling clouds of spindrift sparkle in the late afternoon sunbeams. For the first time in weeks, the sun has poked through; it looks like the sky will be clear for a while. The chanting sound continues in the background.

"Probably just the wind."

I feel like I'm crossing milestones every day now, and I'm truly thankful to be staying healthy and alive. I'm also thankful that the past has all but ceased to bother me. I've been resting deeply and more satisfyingly than ever in my life. No doubt in my mind, I've been tasting God.

Walking far out into the meadow, I raise my hands up and spend a minute staring at the sky, presenting myself to God.

"Thank you that I can be here. Thank you that you're here too. Thank you that I'm alive and well. I'm amazed by the life you've given me." I listen silently for a long time.

"God, I'm your creature in the Arctic. And I'm happy."

I don't want to end the conversation, to go inside my dark shelter and shut down. So I venture out onto the lake ice, experimentally pushing farther and testing its strength. A song is in my head, and no one is here to hear or see me. Not even my camera is rolling. Only God. And so I sing.

A thousand generations falling down in worship
Sing the song of ages to the Lamb

The ice echoes. Beginning quietly, I feel drawn into a special moment. A moment without time or space. Only lake ice before me covers a sea of dark water. Only sky above me presents endless, open sky. And God is there somewhere listening to this single, insignificant creature. A solitary creature lost in the wilderness.

> *Your name is the highest*
> *Your name is the greatest*
> *Your name stands above it all*

I can't remember some words, so I skip.

> *All creation cries, "Holy!"*
> *You are lifted high, Holy!*
> *Holy forever!*

My voice is inadequate, too small and weak for the great words. So I reach deep and sing with all the strength I have in my body. Chorus after chorus I sing, bending double to force more air from my lungs.

> *All creation cries, "Holy!"*
> *You are lifted high, Holy!*
> *Holy forever!*

Alone in the white expanse of snow, I repeat the chorus until my voice cracks and I can't shout anymore. The snow stands still, the wind stops. I'm thrilling from these moments, richer than anything I've ever known.

As the sound of the words echoes away into the waste of the arctic snow, I wonder if God is as moved by the experience as I am. I wonder what it would take for God to send a sign from heaven, to fill the sky with music matching the words I mean so deeply.

I can't answer any of the questions, so I go to bed.

The moon is halfway across the sky when I exit my shelter to pee. The night is so cold that the snow squeaks underfoot. My breath freezes as I exhale. This is the first clear night in ages and the absence of cloud cover has pushed the temperature off a cliff. The air is tingly.

I'm staring up at the brilliant canopy of stars when a faint, golden glow comes to life right up there beside the moon. It grows and morphs, sending out shooting tendrils of light.

"The aurora! I'm going to be treated to a northern light show at last!"

Racing to get my camera and gloves, I march out into the meadow. The snow is deep and I struggle a bit to get far enough from the trees that I have an unimpeded view of the sky.

By this time there's a highway of yellow light from the northern horizon to the southern. It twists and turns, always morphing into fantastic shapes. Sometimes it looks like pillars, other times like swirls, and I can never quite notice how it changed from one form to the other.

I try to imagine what ancient man must have thought, witnessing such an otherworldly spectacle. What would *I* think of it if I had absolutely no scientific input to set the stage for this experience?

I can imagine that I'd think it's spiritual, maybe a breath from God. Maybe this is the sign I wanted. Either way, it's awe-inspiring. But I don't stay and watch for long. The cold is savage, biting deeper than ever. I'm freezing after just twenty minutes, so I return to bed, leaving the lights to march their swirly pathway in the heavens.

Chapter 17

The Mental Game

*   *   *

"It is not the critic who counts; not the man who points out how the strong
man stumbles or where the doer of deeds could have done them better."
-Theodore Roosevelt

None of the activities that kept me alive in early season are
viable now. I can no longer roam as far or eat as carelessly. Everything has changed as winter grips the Arctic.

The grizzlies are no longer a danger, having gone into hibernation. But I find myself feeling sorry that I haven't seen the bear
that spent fall hovering around my camp. I really wanted to see it. But
as instinct drives me to a state of semi-hibernation in my shelter, I
realize that I am the grizzly on this land. My strategy and habits reflect the lifestyle of the bruins almost perfectly. I am the bear.

Day 50

Travel is much more convenient after ice-up. I can tell that
skimming across the snow with dogsleds and snow shoes would be
so much easier than hacking through those impossible willow and
alder breaks. This land would have never been explored if it weren't

for winter. I feel as light and easy as a bird as I glide across the surface of the icy lake. It's by far the easiest traveling I've done since I arrived.

The lake ice isn't smooth and glassy. It's all rumpled and textured, having melted a bit on the top and then refrozen during the incredible wind storm two days ago. The wind piled up waves of loose water and froze them in place. The ice-scape is weird and beautiful, but I keep tripping over the bumps as I cross the wide end of the lake.

Ice-up is great for beaver trapping, granting access to those watery places that were out of reach in early season. You can walk right up to their lodges or the entrances of their bank tunnels. If the ice is clear, you'll see trails of bubbles trapped under the ice. Those bubbles give away the beavers' runs, revealing the best places to set traps or snares.

"It's pretty far back here," I tell the camera when I reach the end of the lakes. "No wonder I didn't come here much in early season." I remember slogging through this area on day two and then being absolutely exhausted from the effort of wading through the swamp and brush. Now it's easy enough to reach.

As I survey the ice, I'm disappointed to find nothing that resembles beaver work. No lodge protrudes from the ice, no dam and no channel are suitable for under-ice beaver activity. So I shift my thoughts to ice-fishing.

I spend a long time out on the lakes chopping holes experimentally to find a deep place where fish might be. But one after the other, the holes reveal shallow swamp beneath the ice. In some places, the ice covers only inches of water; furthermore, twice I cut holes to find no water at all. The ice sits right on the muddy bottom.

Discouraged, I'm heading back to my shelter when suddenly I stand stock still and listen. The chanting has started up again. This time there is no wind to blame it on. Not even a breeze moves across the landscape to resonate with trees.

Shaking my head, I try to sense if my faculties are compromised in some way. But I feel fine, and the chanting is there.

"What *is* this?" I can't figure it out.

As soon as my evening fish is eaten, I rush to the river and dip up a pot of water to boil for tea. If I can bring it to a boil without it boiling over, the water stays coated with a delicious skim of fish-flavored oil, and I always drink that with awe and gratitude. It's like experiencing the fried fish all over again.

Pulling my warm gaiter over my neck, I zip up my sleeping bag and pull the strings until only my nose sticks out. Tonight is the coldest night so far. As I try to drift off, I'm still accompanied by the chanting sound. It's not close, but not far away either.

Day 51

"If I were just here for the adventure of it, I'd leave today." That's the first thing I say once I set up the camera outside my shelter this morning.

It's cold. Icy, tingling, stabbing cold like yesterday. I think I can smell the temperature of the ice.

"It's early morning, and it's light, but the sun won't come up for a while. I'm making it, but I'm cold."

Changing the camera and mic batteries bare-handed freezes my fingers.

"I wish I could know what temperature it is," I tell the camera as I wrap up my update and start collecting wood. The temperature is the single most difficult piece of information to do without. I need to know how cold it is so that I can project just how bad it will get and evaluate how I'm handing the cold. If it's only 10°F this morning and I'm feeling it this much, -20° or -30° is going to be terrible. But if it's already -10°F, then I have nothing to worry about. I'll be fine. Not knowing is really stressing me out.

Day 52

"Boom!"

A crack of distant thunder is the first thing I hear. I'm waking up slowly in the predawn, and outside a massive explosion has just gone off.

"Crack!" Another huge shot, and then an echo.

I would say it sounds like a rifle shot, but that wouldn't do it justice. It sounds more like artillery, like Russian 203mm guns a few miles distant.

I mentally work out what it could be and decide that it's ice cracking. I'm surprised and happy that I didn't jump or react very badly. My nerves must be doing well.

These days I often find myself looking for a hole to jump in when anything shatters or explodes. I've experienced my fair share of explosions, often marking a close call with death, and my nerves have suffered for it.

*   *   *

The first close call I remember was a car bomb that nearly took out the building where my family lived. My wife and I were working together on our first big job overseas, and things were going along peacefully for us. We had set up for a long-term humanitarian project and even rented an apartment and made it home.

The building we lived in was eight floors tall, and our apartment was on the top floor. I was sitting inside with my wife late one night, watching a movie together, when an explosion shook the building. A massive fireball that seemed as bright as the sun shot upward past our window.

Rushing to take a look outside, I saw the husk of a burning car with black smoke belching from its shattered remnants. The driver was still alive and burning as he flailed about.

It was sobering to realize that the car had been almost directly below our window, but hadn't made it quite to our wall. Had it not stopped, I don't know what damage it would have done. My wife and I might have been squished under a pile of rubble.

On subsequent projects, we've experienced plenty of times when small arms fire would happen during the night. But more recently, on my mission in Ukraine, Russian cruise missiles and artillery were the big risk factor, and those are things you don't want to mess around with at all.

*   *   *

So now, in a wilderness that has been silent until this morning, I listen to the booms and wonder how I feel so peaceful about them. I'm not bothered at all.

Another sound shatters the morning air; I can't spell it, but it sounds like a whale groaning mixed with little fire crackers. This confirms my guess that the "explosions" are coming from the ice.

Emerging sleepily from my shelter, I hurry down to the river to see what's going on. I find that the water level under the ice has dropped and the ice is falling in on itself. It can't support its own weight, so it's tearing and cracking in great rents, splitting apart and collapsing onto the surface of the water.

"Boom, boom!" A double crash echos from a distant lake. It sounds so much like artillery.

One collapse starts with a boom right behind my shelter and I can hear the crack lengthen as it rips downriver. The sound is otherworldly. It's like thunder and whales again, but with a longevity to it as the end of the crack travels at speeds probably greater than the speed of sound. I listen in awe until the echoes die away. In my best guess, I'd say that the crack traveled for three or four miles.

I return to camp and chop some firewood, then fill my pocket with jerky and leave to run my snares. All the while the booming and groaning speed up, filling the Arctic with thunder and searing wails.

I have a bunch of snares set in an alder thicket right beside the river. It's on the farthest eastern border of my territory. I've checked it for days without seeing fresh hare sign, so I don't expect much as I enter the trees.

This particularly thick patch of alder is a difficult section to get through. The trees are so thick that I have to push them aside, weaving and ducking. Piles of snow always fall down my back here because I forget to put my hood on.

I reach the very last snare, and there sits the biggest hare I've ever seen, snared by the neck but perfectly alive. It sees me turn toward it and starts jumping around, struggling to get away.

A big hare can break my copper snare wire if it's given long to struggle. I'm afraid it will escape right in front of my eyes so I throw down my bow, grab a stick and pop the hare. It flops down stunned, but I want to finish it as quickly as possible so I step on its head and pull its legs. It's head unexpectedly pops off and I find myself holding a headless hare, still flopping and squirting blood all over me. I put it down until it ceases to struggle, but when I retrieve it I can hear a rhythmic "whooshing" sound and I realize it's the animal's heartbeat. Without thinking I hold the hare right up to the camera

"Listen," I whisper. "Check this out."

Whoosh, whoosh, whoosh. The heartbeat stays steady for about twenty seconds, then slows down.

Whoosh. Whoosh...whoosh. Pause. *Whoosh.*

Feeling an animal's heartbeat stop doesn't bother me. I've felt it happen many hundreds of times. But I realize that it may not feel as familiar to viewers, and I want to show them that I value the life I've just taken, that I'm not a calloused monster. So I sit down in the snow and take a minute. I try to imagine my youngest son sitting in front of me. He's wondering why he feels sad that an animal is dying and why his dad is happy. I need to explain this to him.

"This is a pretty big deal. Life is important and special. It's special because God made it, and He loves life. He loves seeing His creatures hop around and live. But He also gives some creatures as food to others. It's nature. It's how the earth works."

I sit there for a minute admiring the hare, thinking about just how many creatures I've taken in order to survive out here. A quick mental tally tells me I've killed almost eighty animals, including fish. It strikes me that it's a high number, a lot of deaths so that my life can be successful.

Though I don't think that animal lives are the same as humans', they're still valuable, and I want my boy to understand that. I don't want him to be like I was as a kid, killing wholesale and without respect. In my imagination he's sitting with me, and in fact he might watch this very moment on TV.

"The best thing we can do when we take life is to be thankful, and be worthy," I tell him seriously.

I keep the camera rolling as I pray that I will lead a worthy life. Then another thought strikes me, and I consider whether I'll know when I've killed enough to win.

"God, only you know how long I should be out here. When I kill just enough animals to reach that point, stop me from killing any more. I don't want to kill one unnecessarily. I don't want to waste a single creature."

Day 53

"Look at this mark," I say to myself as I check my snares today. I note a strange depression in the snow. The ground looks as if I took a hare in my hands and pressed it down into the snow like a stamp. On two sides of the spot, the snow is scuffed up by the wing-beat marks of a big bird. In the bottom of the depression, where I can see the outline of the hare's face, there's one little drop of blood. Clearly an owl landed on this hare and took off with it.

I'm hoping there are enough hares for me and the owl, but as I check the rest of my snare line and don't turn up one fresh track, I begin to fear that the only hare around has been stolen from me.

The ice is cracking more than yesterday. Scarcely a minute passes when the thunder of collapsing ice isn't rolling across the landscape. All day long and all night as I lie in bed, great peals of rending ice split the air.

Day 54

Inspiration strikes me about the moose antler I found a while ago. I've decided to make a guitar out of it, and this morning finds me on the hunt for a perfect piece of wood to use as the neck.

"I'm gonna make something ghastly-looking," I tell the camera as I rummage through a bank of driftwood on the edge of moose meadow. "I need a piece that looks really gnarly."

Knocking snow off of the pile and inspecting piece after piece, I settle on a driftwood tree the diameter of my wrist with a root wad branching from the base. I know that the guitar isn't going to have the best resonation qualities, but at least I can make it look cool. It's all about the aesthetic.

Attaching the neck to the guitar requires holes to be drilled in the antler. I'm using the awl in my Leatherman to drill the holes. It had been easy until the awl broke on me while I was affixing a moose-hide gasket around my shelter door. Now drilling through the thick antler is difficult work. I'm sweating by the time I get four holes done.

Sawing a v-shape in the antler where the neck of the guitar should attach, I thread paracord through the holes and lash the wooden neck on.

While I work, I mentally run through my inventory of supplies and try to forecast what will make a better guitar string. Will a couple strands of twisted copper snare wire resonate best? What about steel wire? Two stands twisted together, or four?

I try the copper first, twisting six strands of snare wire into a tightly wound string. I had intended to adjust the pitch of the string with a lever attached to the neck. But once I get the lever set up, I find that the copper string is too strong to adjust. I can only access a three-note musical range.

Starting over, I try a two-strand copper string, a one-strand steel string and even monofilament fishing line. I find that the monofilament is the most dynamic of the bunch, and that's exactly what I need to get the widest range of notes out of a single string.

"Ha, let's try this," I say with a grin once I have my newest string ready. I've made a string from twisting six strands of twenty-pound monofilament together. I have high hopes, and I grin widely as I experimentally plunk a note or two.

"This is the perfect use for this mono. It was too weak to fish with, so I used paracord to catch all the pike. And since then my monofilament line has been useless. Now," I hit a couple more notes. "Now this mono is finally gonna be worth something!"

Instead of playing a bunch of songs right away, I decide to save it as something exciting to look forward to tomorrow. I'm learning that I always need something fun to make tomorrow worth facing.

"Stay tuned, tomorrow I'm gonna present something special. We're gonna have a concert."

Day 55

Instead of staging a concert, I feel motivated to go back out across the lake ice in search of something to kill. I hate the feeling of taking food out of my cache every day without bringing any in. The constant decrease in my food inventory is stressing me out, and so I lay aside the guitar in order to spend all day searching for new animal sign.

The cameras won't work in the cold unless I warm the batteries up first, so I carry them in my inner pockets. By the time I reach the middle of my snare line, they're usually warm enough to work.

My bow always goes with me. It's part of my body. But I haven't nocked an arrow in a week. No animals have stuck around this land.

"Okay, I'm here, God. Point me in the right direction."

For some reason unknown to me, I'm drawn to the little patch of birch on the eastern side of the lake. Obeying the signals I've come to trust, I trudge through the thick snow away from the lake to check it out.

Pushing my way through a dense band of willow, I find a number of birch trees I hand't seen before. These trees give me loose bark to peel away and use as paper, and I'm ridiculously excited about having more stuff to write on. But I'm even more excited to find several sets of fresh hare tracks. A number of trails crisscross the area, and although they aren't well established runs, it's more sign than I've seen anywhere so far.

The sky is almost dark, and I don't want to get caught out away from camp with night closing in. So I determine to bring snares the next day, heading home thankful for the prospect of more animals to kill and eat.

Day 56

I'm back at the birch grove early today with a coil of snare wire and my bow. The sun is shining, the snow gleaming white. Doing something constructive is great fun. Inside me I'm carrying the thrill of possibility as I set snare after snare on the fresh trails. Wherever I can see that a hare ran more than once, I place snares in sets of three. Using twigs and branches, I fence areas carefully to guide randomly roving hares into my snare openings.

I'm finishing up a snare set when a squirrel runs down a birch tree only four feet to my left and stares at me, wondering what kind of creature I am. As I slowly nock an arrow, I'm impressed by the certainty that this squirrel has never seen a human. It's incredibly special to be in such a place where animals have never seen man. It's a strong Paleolithic sense, a vestige of a world long lost.

I give the feeling a moment to sink in before I zap the squirrel with an arrow. It flies off the tree and catches in a bush with the blunt arrow sticking through its chest.

"Thank you God for this beautiful creature!" I say, placing the squirrel in my pocket to carry home.

Carrying meat to camp fills me again with the zest of knowing my life has come together, that I'm in harmony with my purpose. I have wished all my life that there could be some village where the hunting would fall on my shoulders. Even if I only had stone points or a rock to hunt with, that would be my dream life.

"Ah, childhood dreams." The best life I ever imagined is playing out right here, if only I could have my family here to provide for.

It seems we usually don't realize we're living our best life until after the fact, when we take a minute to look back and say, "Wow. Those were the days. Why didn't I think about it while it was happening?"

I hold a few times like that in my memory - times when it all came together. My purpose was clear and life seemed aligned like the stars, pointing me straight at what I'm created for.

*   *   *

One of the best examples was the Ukraine mission I've mentioned earlier. My friends and I were doing what we love to do, and so it was inevitable that we enjoyed ourselves while we rolled closer and closer to the front lines, our six vehicles jam packed with medical aid and capable men who knew what to do with it.

The joking started, I believe, about the time we passed a Ukrainian mobile artillery unit. They looked wary, keeping an eye on the sky, and it felt crazy to be driving past them while carrying no weapons.

"Hey, when will it suck worst to get wounded," someone asked with a grin. "Would you rather get shot when you're freezing cold, or when you have to pee?"

We started laughing and speculating about how we'd each rather take it. The jokes got worse and worse until we reached the silent zone not far from the front line. Though I didn't realize it at the time, that would become a core memory, and a good one. Just like a little later, we were all together in a bunker hiding from potential air strikes.

We had assembled to manage supplies and trade vehicles. Air raid alarms were going off, and we all went down into a cellar and waited, with nothing to do but chat or think.

Our team was joined in the cellar by another group of people passing toward the front, and one of the guys had swept the contents of a few minibars into a trash bag when his hotel was abandoned as the invasion first struck. Now he dumped the contents of the bag onto the concrete steps.

A British journalist guy was smoking a cigarette, and two of our guys were talking about the end of the world.

I just listened to the conversation until a voice broke through my reverie. "Hey, smoking's gonna kill you, man. Don't you think we've got enough health risks already?" The person pointed upward, indicating the air raid alarms.

The smoker casually drawled, "Roses are red, violets are blue. Smoking might kill me, but bombs *will* kill you."

Then suddenly the guy with the whiskey raised his mini bottle and shouted "We were here for the beginning of World War Three!"

We all laughed because the whole thing was ridicuous, and the release of tension was infectious. We were due to haul our loads of medical gear to the front lines the following day, and everyone had felt so tense. Now all the tension exploded into genuine laughter and fun.

Another guy had grabbed some whiskey and was downing it fast. I sat down beside him on the stairs; as he got drunk, he started rambling.

"I hate all the crap you Christians believe," he grunted as I sat near him. "I hate it. I hate all of it."

The fellow was an outspoken atheist, but that didn't matter to me at all. I liked him and we were friends. He went on talking, and as I sat listening to him, I began to understand that he was having a hard time. The red-eyed stare of terrible memories was on his face.

I felt moved to say something, but I didn't know what. Before I could think, words tumbled out of my mouth.

"I know what you're angry about. It happened to me too, and I hated God for it."

Immediately I checked myself, shocked that I would say that. But the look on his face was as if someone had jolted him with electricity. I didn't know this guy's story, but somehow I was certain that he had lost someone or something precious to him.

"I just want you to know it wasn't God who turned his back on you. It was Christians who let you down. They walked you to the end of a plank and pushed you off."

What am I doing? I asked myself. I didn't know what I was saying. I thought he would punch me in the throat, and I probably would have if the tables had been turned.

Instead, he started sobbing, great wracking sobs. The sobs were heartbreaking, and I sensed that it was really true—he had been destroyed, let down to the point of despair, and God hadn't been there. In all of the teaching and rules and church he had experienced, God hadn't been there. And so I told him my story, how I had thought of God as an angry father wanting to crush me but demanding my love. I told him how I had nearly committed suicide, and then I found the true love which transcended everything religion had thrown at me.

"I found love from Jesus outside of all that. It's real. God is outside of religion, just hoping you'll find life."

On and on we spoke, and he sobbed harder. Ignoring church and rules and Christians, we spoke of Jesus and life and light. I spent a while praying that God's love would break through the rubble of his experiences. For most of an hour while the air raid went on, he cried like a broken man. Years of hurt and anger came spilling out.

It was the strangest of situations. In the middle of a bunch of laughing Marines, nurses and journalists, there was a drunk in a bunker. And Jesus met us there, surprising us both. It reinforced a notion building in my heart: God can't be contained in a system. He must be found individually, by an honest human spirit crying for life.

That was one of the happiest moments of my life. I felt so in tune with my purpose, as if my whole life had pointed me to that one moment. It had all come together, and I belonged.

Usually those times have happened in the most dangerous or intense situations, and so I've begun asking myself the question, "Do I have a death wish? Do I like to push death?"

I do believe that we should push death a little during our lifetimes, if you're doing it for a good cause. Push it, make it respect you. So that when you turn and meet it one day, you can shake hands like friends and move on.

"But am I just addicted to adrenaline?" I ask myself time and time again.

I've come to the conclusion that it's not about the adrenaline or the wild ride. I just like to experience things that are real, when all pretense and custom are swept away, and the only thing left of us is the true human soul. That only happens in the most extreme situations.

*   *   *

I have rarely taken the time to realize during those moments that they'll be my best memories. But right now in the arctic, I take the time to grasp it: "There is no pretense or custom here. There is only what's real. I'm living my best days right now."

I feel it happening, and it's not lost on me.

Day 57

A big, beautiful hare waits for me this morning. It's caught in the snare I was setting as I shot the squirrel yesterday. Removing the wire from the hare's neck, I toss the animal toward the camera. Then I carefully reset the snare.

I'm thrilled with the hare, but the days are dragging out, feeling endless and tiring. Even though the light is rapidly diminishing, the daytime period still seems too long. It makes no sense that I feel this way. The sky is only light for about five or six hours.

Wondering how much time might still remain, I trudge though the snow of my snare line.

"How many days could this challenge still take?" I know it's still far from over. I expect it to go past sixty-five days at the very least. But it already feels like an eternity since I left base camp.

"How many more days can I last?" I've been asking myself the question a lot. I know I can go at least until my food runs out, and I still have enough food for another couple of months at least. But the thought of even one more month seems daunting right now.

I know I can handle it if I take it one day at at time. One of the biggest things I've learned here is that I can only face one day. I can't possess in one day enough fortitude and endurance to get through to the last day. I can't face *every* day, but I can face *any* day. So I'm constantly asking myself "How are you doing? Are you okay with whatever's going on today?" And each time I realize that I can handle today just fine.

Still, I decide that making a way to mark the time could help me. I need to come up with some meaningful way to represent time that I conquer going forwards day by day.

"Ha! I've got it! I'll make wooden people and vote one out each day!" The idea comes to me as I totter slowly through a deep snow drift, breaking trail. I'm envisioning some version of the game show *Survivor*, where eighteen people live on an island and vote each other off until only one is left standing. It just so happens that if I carve eighteen people and get rid of one per day, I'll end up at day seventy-five. The number seems auspicious, being the three-quarter mark to a hundred. So I decide that I'll make it all into a game. I'll start with eighteen people. I'll name them all, give them each a personality and then vote one person off each day, and that's how I'll mark the time as I count off days going forward.

Arriving back at my shelter, I cook half the hare and then I sit down to carve, happily losing myself in the project of making eighteen little wooden figures.

Taking an alder stick about the diameter of my thumb, I carve the end of the stick into a little, bald head with eyes, a chin and a neck. Then I use my saw to slice off the piece, leaving a little bit of un-carved branch at the base for a pedestal on which the bust will stand.

My figurines aren't very detailed, but I do give each one a little smile or frown, notched in and colored with charcoal. I even leave a beard of bark for a few of the figures.

There has to be a way of allowing the players to vote, and tallying which gets voted off. So I also make some dice. My dice have numbers on five sides, but one surface of each cube is dedicated to twists that are particular to *Survivor*. I've got an I that stand for 'Immunity Idol' on one die, and a B that stands for 'Blindside' on the other.

While I carve, I name the characters and imagine their personalities. I have a character for me of course, then there's Dave, Victor, Darrell, Michelle, Alexandra, Bob, Beard Dude, Tall Johnny, Short Johnny and several others who are difficult to name because I have't gotten to know them yet. I see right away that Dave is a reliable type of guy. Victor is dumb, Michelle is pretty, but Tall Johnny is the one that really worries me. He's smart and sneaky. Which ones will become good fellow players? Which ones will form alliances and stick together till the end?

"What am I getting into?" I wonder aloud. "What if I get voted out right off the bat?"

By the time evening rolls around, I'm so excited about playing the game that I put off supper. Setting up the cameras, I prepare for the first round of what I'll call *Trial by Fire*.

"Ok, we're all here, and we're about to kick off one of the most exciting adventures imaginable!" I say to the eighteen players standing in a circle on my log-end table.

I take a minute to explain the rules: how the dice will work and how votes are tallied. Then I divide the group into two tribes and the game begins.

"I'm Cynthia, and I'm soooo excited to be on this tribe!" I squeal, holding a thin, willowy player up to the camera for an interview.

"Everyone seems nice, and I think Victor is really hot."

"Yeah, I'm Victor, and I think I'm the ultimate survivor. I'm gonna do great on the tribe, and I have some of the girls in my pocket already."

Interviews over, the vote starts. Numbers are rolled and names written down. In the end, a nondescript player named Betty is voted out.

My spirits are so lifted by the game that I'm literally giggling and smiling. I feel a little ridiculous. But it is serving its purpose, getting me to live in the moment and feel excited about one tiny thing each day. I'll make it a part of my life until day seventy-five.

My supper of hare is deeply satisfying. I've boiled the front half of today's catch including its head, and since I'm feeling so good I decide to film an exhibition on how a hare's head should be eaten.

"First you take the lower jaws off," I explain, making sure the camera can see how I pry each bit loose. "Then you suck the meat off the jaw and use the spoon-shaped end to dip out the eyes and brain."

I get really serious as I dig in, enjoying every morsel and sucking every bone clean.

"And that's how it's done. That is the most thoroughly eaten hare ever."

One of my favorite parts about boiling a hare is that the broth is so tasty afterward. I drink and burp until it's gone and then get into my sleeping bag feeling happier than I have in days.

Day 58

Filming is becoming harder and harder. Dragging the big camera and tripod around in the deep snow is exhausting, so I take only the GoPros with me as I check my fish lines under the lake ice.

There seem to be no fish in the lake, and the GoPros aren't working well in the cold. Every time I turn them on, the batteries are dead again. So I have to take a lot of extra batteries with me. Warming them up in my pockets helps, but then they're in my pocket during those moments I'd like to film something.

I also wonder whether I'm getting enough usable footage. I'm not being very imaginative with the filming. I usually just set up a camera to get me walking away in the snow while I'm heading out to check snares. Then I get one or two shots of breaking trail and heading back to camp. I sometimes hold the camera in front of me to see my face while I check snares. All in all, the lack of imaginative footage is starting to stress me out. But messing with the ice-cold camera gear bare-handed just never seems worth the trouble.

I make myself wait until almost dark to get out my *Trial by Fire* game. I've been looking forward to it all day, and I feel ridiculous that such a frivolous thing is able to cheer me up. But that tells me that I've found a good thing. I'll keep it going.

"Once again, in the light of a flickering fire, we meet to decide who will go on in the game of *Trial by Fire*."

I film a big buildup this time, getting deep into the personalities and plans of each contestant. Inventing interviews for the little wooden figures is fun. The intrigue of secret alliances going on between the players really sucks me in. They've all made decisions and agreements throughout the day, and some of them surprise me.

The only difficult part is getting the camera to focus where I want it to. With the uneven lighting, the flickering fire and the generally dark atmosphere of my shelter, the camera's focus often drifts off to another spot or unfocuses entirely. I struggle to get the footage, but I'm having loads of fun.

With another player voted out, I cook my supper, boil my tea, and shut down for the long night.

Day 59

I'm out at the new snare line in the birch grove. My snares are all untouched, and no fresh tracks have appeared since I caught the first hare here. I have a multitude of snares set over every trail, with no more spaces to set them. So I spend a lot of time exploring further, hoping that hares have moved into some of the brushy willow thickets on the southern end of my territory.

Hares are not sneaky. They don't make any efforts to conceal their tracks or runs. If they are present, they leave loads of sign in the snow. But after scouring the woods for hours, I find nothing. The hares just aren't here, or they're being slaughtered by the numerous marten and owls faster than they can move in from the higher country.

Back at camp later in the afternoon, I decide to play my guitar a little. I'm getting better at using a single string to plunk out the base line of some songs. I've finished the song I've been writing for Cara and I'm trying to think of some way that I can film a cool music video with it. So I think of how to film it while I practice a few times.

We've got a lot of time to kill
Lie here with me and just be still
The moon that's in the sky so bright
Looks down on us tonight
Outside there is a frosty chill

The Mental Game

The arctic snow lies deep and still
The northern lights are overhead
Lie close to me in bed

I lean into the chorus, thumping the base as hard as I can.

Then I reach out from where I lay
We're miles apart, you're worlds away
So I will reach across this distance with my heart
We'll never be this far apart

While living free without a care
My lonely heart is hard to bear
Walk with me down each path of mine
Walk with me every time
It's worth it if you'll walk with me
Through happiness or tragedy
Walk with me down this path of mine
Walk with me every time

I hit the chorus again, then sing the whole song over and over. Music is just fun and refreshing. I keep playing until my fingers get cold and I need to start chopping wood.

By evening the cloud cover shifts, the sun throwing spears of sunlight through in brilliant golden-red shafts of color. The sunbeams light up the trees north of me and seem to set the arctic snow on fire. I didn't know white snow could glow so red.

For about fifteen minutes, everything is the color of flame. I stand there in awe the whole time, drinking in the rare sunlight and dazzled by the new sheen of beauty that color brings.

"Film this, you idiot!" I chide myself as I run to my shelter and grab the camera. But before I can reach the edge of the trees

311

again the light disappears. Just like a vapor, it vanishes, leaving the land once again just a dull, shadowy white.

While I'm staring after the vanishing sun beams, I notice something that has changed around me. I perceive a definite difference that I can't put my finger on for a while.

"What's going on? What's different?" I ask the camera. Then it comes to me.

Those booms and groans that had been so regular are missing. The ice isn't cracking any more. And without the ice cracking, there is nothing to experience. No activity, no event, no sound.

Total silence.

Chapter 18

Silence

*   *   *

And all I loved—I loved alone...
-Edgar Allan Poe, "Alone"

Stillness. Colorlessness. Utter lifelessness. I'm stuck in a sensory deprivation chamber. The snow is deep; it mutes all sound, and no animals are here to make sounds anymore. Nature isn't breathing here. Nothing is happening, and nothing exists.

I can hardly make a noise that outdoes the silence. My voice seems stifled and inept when I shout or sing. The snow dampens my voice, and only silence echoes back. The sounds in my head are loud, taking over everything. That terrible ringing in my ears drives me nuts.

The lack of anything to experience makes my loneliness grow. It's far more than just being here by myself. Every time I've been away from my family, even in war, I've had information to work with. The total lack of information of any kind, and now the lack of visual and auditory input, drives me to search my soul for strength. The isolation is intense.

The wind is most welcome whenever it blows. I used to fear the wind, dreading the blizzards and temperatures it brought. Now I long for it, because it is at least something to experience. Outside of the occasional wind storm, I'm trapped in a void with no edges.

Day 60

Today feels like a special milestone to me. Sixty days. I've lived well for two months alone in the arctic. I decide to mark the occasion by frying my remaining chunk of burbot, a special treat I've been saving.

But before I can settle down to a delicious supper party, I have to do everything I can do to pursue more food and see to it that I'll be warm. In addition to checking my snares and chopping firewood, I want to scout around and make sure I'm not missing any new animal movement.

I start out along the river, but aside from a double set of mink tracks, nothing new breaks the monotony. The ice beckons me to go out and fish. But defying all logic, it's still not safe to walk on. The surface of the river is a mushy mess. The deep snow cover is just too much insulation to allow freeze-up.

After a frustrating few hours of trying to reach deep water and failing, I return to camp with my clothes frozen solid, caked with ice from the splashing water as I chopped through.

After boiling a pot of spruce tea and bathing, I set my feast of burbot near the fire to thaw. Then I play *Trial by Fire* for half an hour. It's snowing heavily again as I start to cook supper. The burbot sizzles tantalizingly and my fire is cheery and warm.

All of a sudden I feel a compulsion to get up, climb over my fireplace, and glance up through my chimney hole. My odd compulsion reveals something amiss. Looking up, I see an exposed clump of moss chinking in my chimney is smoldering, a tiny red spark having caught in it. Leaping instantly to my feet with a blurted prayer to God for help, I snatch the smoldering moss out of its crack and see the moss behind it is smoking as well.

"Please God!" I breathe as I feverishly dig more smoking moss out of the crack. I have to run outside as well to check that the back wall isn't on fire.

A lot of moss chunks have fallen loose as I poked at them, and they lay on the ground smoldering. The smoking bits show just how close I've come to having a disaster. If my shelter were to burn down these days I could easily die.

At this point everything is safe, but I check the moss near my chimney hole about twenty more times before I go to sleep.

"Thank you Lord!" I mutter over and over again. I'm sure it was God who caused me to look up the chimney just at the right moment. I've been getting careless with my fires evidently, making them bigger and bigger because of the enjoyable light and warmth. I have to not only be more careful, but also fix the ceiling in some way that won't catch fire.

But what do I have to work with? The question that's plagued me since day one nags me while I lay in my sleeping bag. I have nothing that's not combustible to protect my ceiling against sparks. And it plagues me all night again while I toss and turn, trying to sleep.

Day 61

"Things aren't easy anymore." My camera is on its tripod and I'm clearing my front yard of a three-inch blanket of fresh snowfall. I work slowly, scraping the snow away with the side of my boot. "Staying warm, breaking trail on my snare lines, getting through the day. Especially getting through the nights. It's real now."

Today is the first day that living here seems hard. Not just challenging or lonely, but hard.

I have to fix my shelter ceiling so that it doesn't catch fire. It's the number one priority for today. I've puzzled on it all night, discouraged and sleepless. But at some point an idea came to me—the idea that I can repurpose my moose hide range hood and use it to shield the ceiling where the dry moss chinking is most vulnerable. I'll use the nails, if I can pull them from where they've been driven in. I'll nail the hide over the most exposed section of ceiling, and it will be the best protection I can devise. I'll just have to deal with the stray smoke inside my shelter again, not having the range hood in place anymore.

Struggling and sweating, I work for an hour or two and finally feel confident that I've protected the ceiling well. I successfully pulled the nails, straightened them and reused them to nail the moose hide up in the ceiling. I've used loose chunks of dirt from the edges of my fireplace to patch more holes. It looks pretty tight and I think every-thing will be ok. But I've gotten coated in soot and ash. My face, which I bathed just yesterday, is blackened and smudged.

"Oh well," I say after surveying myself in the camera. "I don't have the energy to bathe again today, so I let it go."

The fish poles I put under the ice yesterday have caught noth-ing and the bait is untouched. I tell myself that the hooks are just too close to shore, that whenever I can get to the middle of the channel I'll start catching fish again.

My snare line holds more discouragement for me. A marten has run almost the entire length of the line, following my foot prints from snare to snare. This virtually ensures that I won't get any hare for myself. The marten will polish off anything I catch.

After a difficult day, and having killed no extra food, I sit down and spread out the characters of my game, trying to lose my-self in the fun.

"Um, I'm feeling really good about my alliance," I say for Victor, using the bass voice I've developed for him. "I'm in really tight with the three girls, and I don't think they're ever gonna turn on me. It helps to have good looks."

Darrell complains about his alliance and says he feels like he's on the chopping block. Then it's my own turn and I talk about my plans to recruit Darrell into my circle of voters.

"It's the perfect time to strike. I'll get Darrell, and I already have Dave and Alexandra. If we stick together, we can get to the end."

Every time I talk about getting to the end I think about myself in this reality I'm living in the Arctic. It's a competition. One person will get to the end. I wonder what cross-over this silly game will have with my story on *Alone*. Will it mirror it in some way? I decide that it's interesting to see how it goes, to relinquish control of my character to the vagaries of chance, and see if my little wooden guy can pull through. I'll just roll the dice and see what happens. If my character gets voted off, I'll laugh and think it's funny. But my body will go on through this competition I'm in. Whenever my wooden character dies, I'll find another way to count down the days.

Spreading out the characters, I lose myself in the dice-rolling and vote-counting.

My spirits are soaring high afterward as I divide my piece of fish into small slices that will fry nicely and melt a big chunk of lard in my pot. Once the lard is popping I drop the fish in and place the lid on. My mouth is watering as I clean my hands with some snow. I just love this time of day.

After supper I decide to cut some more wood, stacking it high in case more snow falls. I finish cutting wood to the sound of chanting. I've been hearing it off and on for weeks now. But today as I go to bed it grows louder and closer until it's in the very center of my camp. I hear individual voices, and together they make a wall of sound that is definitely not coming from my imagination.

I pinch myself, put cold snow on my face, and do everything I can to tell if I'm tripping. I'm not. The sound comes almost right up to my shelter wall. A tension builds and my stomach starts to tighten.

"God, please back them off," I say under my breath. I don't turn the camera on. Although it would be good to have proof of the chanting, I'd rather not film myself praying this. "Please don't let that stuff get in this shelter."

Almost immediately the tension releases and the voices back away. They don't vanish but keep chanting all night instead. But there's no threat or danger. The chanting has become just another fact outside, like the snow and the trees.

Day 62

"Mice have overrun Fort Moose Head." I'm out in the fresh, morning snow of my yard filming an update.

"They have stormed the defenses, tunneled under the barricades and swarmed over the walls. I'm totally outnumbered and I'm making a final, desperate stand."

It's a true assessment of the situation. Last night I barely slept a wink due to the mice. They rampaged around in my shelter knocking things off my shelf and making an insane racket with the moose ribs I'm saving to make more fish hooks from.

Once when I actually did drift off to sleep, a mouse fell right on my face. He was trying to reach some jerky that I hang by a wire right outside my sleeping bag's face hole. I put it there so that I can conveniently grab a piece to chew on. But a mouse was dangling from it and fell right on my mouth, waking me up.

I've been killing mice all along. Sometimes I sit up at night popping them with my bow. It was a fun pastime until it got too cold to be out of my sleeping bag. My fingers and toes freeze while I sit there I the dark waiting for them to stick their heads out.

I've eliminated a good number, eating their bodies or using them as pike bait. But one particular mouse, who is a mastermind, has moved in. I've been doing my level best to assassinate him for over a week now. But he escapes every time, and each time he comes back smarter and more wary.

It all began when I missed him with my bow. As I shot, the arrow was fouled by a piece of kindling, allowing the mouse to get away. He evaded death twice, and just like that, an arch-rivalry was born.

I moved things from an area of floor so that my next shot would be clear, but he didn't come back until late at night. He learned that once my head goes inside my sleeping bag, I can't get out without giving ample warning while I unzip it and grab my weapon. So he takes full advantage of this fact.

In the dead of night when all else is still, this mouse chews on my moose rib bones beneath the fireplace and on flakes of birch bark that rattle like tin foil. His chewing is sometimes so loud that I can't sleep through it at all, try as I might.

I've spent lots of time each evening trying to kill the mouse. I shot at it four more times. Twice I should have gotten it but he felt the arrow coming and dodged.

Then I transitioned to propping up my table to use as a dead-fall. I've pulled the string to spring it on him three times but he can run away faster than the wood falls. It's ridiculous.

This morning I consider calling a truce and letting my little enemy live, out of respect for his cunning and speed. But I know he will keep me awake night after night. So tonight I'm crafting a cunning trap for the little devil, and I'm sitting up for as long as it takes to finish the job.

I've made two small boards and fastened their edges together so that they will close like a book. Then I made a spring out of a forked tree. Affixing the spring onto the wooden book, I prop it open with a moose-bone trigger and bait the inside with fish juice. This mouse loves fish juice.

And now I'm sitting in my sleeping bag, holding the end of a trigger string. An hour passes and then I see a shape. The enemy has arrived. I tense, but try not to move a muscle.

The mouse begins to explore the floor, hoping for scraps from my supper. He finds little y-bones from pike and chews at them. Every few seconds he runs behind cover and looks up at my sleeping bag, then creeps back out to sniff around.

Tension mounts as the mouse edges closer and closer to the fishy-smelling wooden trap. I squint my eyes almost closed and do my best not to project my overwhelming intent to kill.

Lethal intent is something that animals can occasionally sense. Anyone who has hunted much, at one time or another, has seen an animal reach the edge of your kill radius and stop, sensing something, turn the other way, and go back. Unless you've been betrayed by a bigger mistake like being upwind, that's just the animal sensing a presence of danger. They're detecting lethal intent.

It's no surprise that animals can sense that. Humans can too, especially soldiers and those attuned to dangerous environments. And so to be a hunter, lethal intent must be masked or eliminated. That's why I say that being at peace with God makes a person a better hunter. When one's heart is totally at peace, he emits no sense of threat or danger. Just peace. And animals, instinctively sensing that peace, are less likely to be alarmed. So I constantly practice peace when I'm about to kill an animal. It's like using their spirits against them, which seems unfair, but it's survival.

My fingers are starting to get really cold. I want to disappear into my sleeping bag and close my eyes. But I'm dedicated to this hunt.

After what seems like eternity, the mouse is finally right where I want him. He's licking the fish juice on the inside of my wooden trap.

In one smooth motion I jerk the string, pulling the trigger and closing the trap. I hear it snap shut on a soft, squeaky body.

"Ha! Got you!" I say, too tired to really triumph in my victory. "I win."

Day 63

"I'm hibernating. I'm conserving energy, staying warm." My face barely pokes out of the sleeping bag as I record a morning update. It took me at least twelve hours of laying still to get to the point I could finally fall asleep last night. Right now while I'm warm and drowsy, I'm staying in bed for as long as possible.

All of this time in the sleeping bag makes it especially hard to film enough footage to meet the daily quota. So this morning I just have the camera running, pointing at my bed. Every ten minutes or so I think of something to say, and I poke my face out and say it, then retreat back inside like a snail.

"I feel like hibernating is the right move. If I come out, I'll have to cut more firewood and eat more food."

Eventually the need to pee drives me outside, and in the twilight I get cold enough that I know I can't go back to bed. I have to light my fire and boil some tea.

I've decided that I want my fish to last longer, so I'm going to begin having just one hot meal of fried fish per day. That way I can make it parallel my jerky for as long as possible.

The moose jerky is giving me problems. It's good jerky even though it's pretty hard. But my teeth and gums are in bad shape. They're bleeding every day, so sore that I can hardly chew anything without moaning in pain.

My teeth have been problematic since 2012, when a flaky dentist worked my mouth over. I was in India at the time. I remember the incident well, but without any fondness.

*   *   *

I was teaching linguistic courses at a college when I got a badly infected tooth. I thought the problem would go away but the pain intensified until I couldn't speak. Since speaking was my job, I went to town to find a dentist. A good friend from Manipur took me on the back of his motorcycle, and we searched until we found a dentist who was being called the "best dentist in India."

"Oh, you are needing a root canal. I can do it," the dentist said after taking a quick look at my teeth.

Having grown up without ever seeing a dentist, I didn't know what to expect.

"This guy is the best dentist in India," I told myself. "He's got to know what he's doing." I could have taken his pallet-clad shipping container office as a bad omen, but maybe that's normal for a dentist office, right? How would I know?

"Okay," I said, "Then give me a root canal."

The fellow numbed my mouth marginally then went to work. It took a long time and there was a lot of drilling and grinding. Throughout the process, the numbing agent only partly took the edge off, and I felt most of his tools very keenly. But I told myself that this is what everyone faces when they go to the dentist's office. No wonder dentists are used to scare small children into obedience.

Squeezing the arms of the chair in a death grip, I hung on for dear life and tried not to scream. I felt like he was grinding away at teeth that weren't infected, and when he finally let me stand up and look in a mirror, I was horrified to find that he had done exactly that. Instead of shaping a new cap to fit my mouth, he had ground away at all the other teeth around it to make room. The whole time I was sitting there like a model patient, not complaining or putting up a fuss, he was destroying all the teeth around the infected one. My mouth has been shaped differently ever since that moment. It's why my grin looks lop-sided.

"What did you do that for?!" I tried to remain polite, but I was furious.

"Oh, it's good this way. It is fitting better. You have pain, so you need to have less pressure on the new tooth I made."

To be fair, he did technically do a root canal. But a big, missing section of my bottom teeth, plus sixty-eight US dollars, was a steep price to pay.

So ever since, I've had pain in my teeth, and I can't go to sleep without propping them just right so that I don't bite down on *that* tooth during the night. Many other teeth have gotten chipped, broken, and cracked as well. And now here I am, gnawing rock-hard jerky every day for breakfast. I try to stop every few days, to eat only fish and let my teeth rest. But each morning while I'm hibernating, awake and hungry in my sleeping bag, I grab a few pieces of jerky and by the time I get up my mouth is throbbing and my gums bleeding. I boil the jerky occasionally, and pound it with my axe, but excruciating pain is still the cost of my jerky diet.

*   *   *

The river has finally frozen just enough to walk on, so I grab my fishing equipment and head out to set lines. But the ice is layered. Below, a hard but thin layer sits on the water. The top surface is quite mushy and soft, barely able to support my weight. Between those layers lurks a zone of perfectly liquid water. I often sink through the first layer and end up getting my boots soaked. This situation is strange and incomprehensible to me. Why won't it freeze hard?

Feeling optimistic and happy, I chop holes to fish through. But the layer of fresh water between the ice splashes so badly with each chop that I'm soaked in less than a minute. The spray freezes to me instantly, making my overalls into a solid cake of ice. My face and whiskers are plastered and clumps of frozen slush dangle from the hair of my parka's hood. My axe is so caked that it looks like a huge chicken leg of ice.

"Grahhhh!" I really want to shout an expletive at the splashy ice, but I feel strongly that God wants me to give those words up for good. This makes it hard to think of a noise that properly reflects my aggravation. So I just growl.

After a couple hours' work, I have a few baited lines placed through the ice in the center of the river. The frozen pike stomach I've been saving as bait tends to float now, and that makes it freeze to the underside of the river ice. Eventually I get the bait thawed, and the lines sink to the bottom. This setup is the best I can do, and I hope against hope that I'll start catching fish again.

As evening approaches, something strange comes over me. I'm sitting on a log in camp thinking over my experience on the land. I think about what it might look like on camera, how viewers will perceive it all. I can only remember the mistakes I've made along the way. I can't remember the awesome feeling of killing the moose, only the back-breaking labor it took to save the meat and how weak I felt afterward.

"What kind of dummy kills a moose in warm weather?" I ask myself.

I also can't remember the amazing success I experienced catching fish. I can only think of how I could have done better by putting my weir in the river to get more fish, and by smoking more fish. I can't see the way I'm living well in spite of having poor materials to build things with. I only notice the smoke lingering in my shelter, the problems I've had with my fireplace.

Mistake after mistake bombards my memory, blackening the sky of my mind. And above it all is the roar of judgment from the invisible audience inside the camera. I've filmed almost everything, the mistakes and weaknesses along with the joys. But in the silence and stabbing cold of this day, the exposed failures and weakness I've put on camera lash me with the bitter whip of embarrassment and shame.

"I've mucked it. I've ruined my shot," I moan to the trees. It feels true. My story looks in this moment like an overwhelming train wreck, a path of error stretching out behind me. Sitting on my snow covered log, I brush tears away from my eyes and wish I could do it all over.

"This feeling isn't the truth," I chide myself, trying to take control. "It's fear. Fear and selfishness."

An element of fear persists in my heart. The great fear for me about *Alone* is not dying or getting sick. It's not suffering or being lonely. The fear every contestant feels is that of ending or ruining our experience. And that's the same factor that makes people fear death. It's not so much about pain. It's about ending our experience, and our experience not yet being complete and fulfilling, not yet ready to be ended.

"Have I ruined my story on *Alone* with mistakes?" A deep sense of self-preservation stirs within me when I consider that people the world over will see what I've done every day here. They will all know where I've erred and shown weakness. I have a rising compulsion to burn all the footage so that I can't be judged.

But I remind myself that I've already been judged by God. I've opened myself to his eye, and now no other judgment can harm me. People will see my mistakes and that's ok.

I want to react out of fear. But I have to choose something higher than the self-preservation instinct. And so I reach for that higher thing and as I do, the experience I portray on *Alone* loses its power over me. I'm a man again, not a perfect specimen of survival acumen. Just a man, not worth so much that my failures can be big enough to destroy me.

Day 64

The atmosphere is perfectly silent and still outside my shelter this morning. Not a breath of wind moves, not a single raven or even a jay stirs or makes a sound.

"It's so quiet this morning. It's downright eerie."

The silence is deeper, more complete than any I've ever experienced. While I give my morning update, my voice seems muted to my own ears.

A nighttime snow storm has piled fresh snow high on every branch of the trees, tall columns of white fluff balanced on even the thinnest tendril branches. It blocks my vision as I scan the area for signs of life. Absolutely nothing moves or whispers.

I've got bad tinnitus. I've abused my ears all my life by neglecting to wear ear protection when near shooting, explosions and loud equipment. My ears ring constantly, and now it's absolutely overwhelming. As I stand in the deep snow listening to the arctic silence, a circus of clanging and ringing builds in my head until it threatens to make me scream.

I decide that singing is the answer. I haven't played my guitar in a few days. I just haven't felt the mood. But today it really lifts me up as I stoke up a warm fire inside and play song after song.

I'm working on a song I wrote earlier. It's a song I call "If You Find My Body." I pick out the bass line on the guitar as I sing. The guitar is not loud, but it is at least some vestige of music. So I sing the song over and over while I think about how many of my life experiences are connected to the words.

> *If you find my body on the field of battle, I'll be walkin'*
> *Through fields of gold*
> *If you pick me up where I fall from my saddle, I'll be ridin'*
> *Where none grow old*
> *Oh-oh-oh.*

Silence

I'll live life free until disaster comes,
Until it comes for me,
And I'll be waitin'.

This song is a lot of fun. It has that element of soldier's humor that rejoices and revels in the ragged margin between life and death. I love that margin—it's full of the best life. I've been there a lot.

People tell me that I attract craziness. I don't know if I attract any more than the next man. But I do know that a cloud of the unexpected seems to hover around me. The number of times I've stared death in the face is far beyond the acceptable number for thirty-five years of life. Right now I'm thinking about a trip that probably contained the most rapid succession of near-death events I've ever faced.

*   *   *

I was driving down from the high Pamir Mountains, trying to get out before being snowed in. A meter of snow already covered the ground.

It's a bad idea to drive that road at night, being that it's narrow, full of avalanches and rockslides, and often hovering on the cliffside over the Panj River. People regularly die on that road, either from being crushed by a rockslide, or falling into the river.

A winter storm was pummeling the canyon, turning from snow to ice. As I drove through the night, a huge rock came tumbling off the cliff and hit the road just ahead of the vehicle. It would have smashed me like a bug, had I been a few yards further on.

The snow thinned as I descended, but freezing rain made four inches of ice, like a layer of glass. Time after time, I felt the tires break loose and slide toward the unguarded precipice.

The road at this point is barely more than a donkey track and so narrow and rocky that a sturdy 4x4 is barely enough to travers it. The cliff, which extend away above and below, is menacing. The road is absolutely unprotected by guard rails or even a stone ledge between a vehicle and the yawning chasm. Down below, the water of the Pan River rages with glacial melt water.

One wrong move and a car plunges down into certain death. I saw a Taliban vehicle, which happened to be a Ford Ranger stolen from the original Afghan border patrol, plunge into the river and when its husk washed ashore a few miles downstream, even the axles had been ripped off of the body of the truck by the powerful water.

Looking out my left window, I could see the edge of the road disappear under me, and only the yawning blackness of the river channel remained. I clinched my butt cheeks and prayed hard. The road provided nowhere to pull over, nowhere to wait until daylight. By stopping, I might get buried beneath an avalanche. I think the angels pushed my car back onto the road five different times that night.

When I finally descended to where the snow and ice turned to rain, a mudslide let loose, and in the rearview I could actually watch the first wave of rocks and mud splatter across the road right behind my vehicle.

It took eighteen hours to exit the canyon and leave the treacherous weather behind me—eighteen hours of adrenaline-soaked fear. That drive was memorable, scarring, the kind of stress that twists you into a sinewy old man.

*   *   *

The only way to live through that level of stress on a near-constant basis is to keep your shoulders loose and laugh. That's why I wrote this song, and so I sing a second verse.

If you find my body in a cold cold river, I'll be floatin'

Silence

On glassy seas
Even if there's nothin' but a bony sliver, I'll be restin'
Beneath the trees
Oh-oh-oh.

I'm having such a good time that I decide to go outside and film some videos of me playing the song. The sun peaks through the evening clouds as I film on the ice of the river. The southern sky is streaked with orange and purple. It's getting colder by the hour and soon my fingers are so cold I'm worried about frost bite. I've been playing bare-handed, and the tips of my fingers are blue and have no feeling.

It's been a lot of fun, but it's time to warm up and chop wood. I cut firewood for a long time before abandoning the fresh air of the outside world to burrow up inside my shelter and enjoy the evening.

Each evening, I select two small chunks of fried fish and roll them around in the hot lard until they're dripping in oil. Then I take them outside to let the oil immediately solidify. The resulting thick layer of cold lard on the fish gives them a doughnut-like quality and it's an amazing breakfast to wake up to.

Tonight, once it's as dark as pitch, I accidentally knock the tripod against my lard canister where my breakfast chunks are stashed. The birchbark can falls from its wire and pieces of lard and fish scatter on the floor and in my firewood pile. At the same moment, my flashlight dies.

I'm blind and worried about stepping on the precious food as I feel around. I can't find the pieces of fish, and I have probably lost half the lard from the can. If it stays on the floor overnight, mice will get every scrap of it.

Normally, missing breakfast isn't a big deal. But somehow I need these lost morsels so badly that I nearly panic. For half an hour,

I crawl around my shelter pleading with God to help me find my fish. I've almost given up when suddenly my flashlight turns back on and I can see everything. Chunks of lard are scattered about but easy to retrieve. My pieces of fish, however, are sitting on the edge of my bed behind me, safe from my trampling feet and knees. How did they get there? I don't know. I just thank God as I replace them in the bark container.

Day 65

A cacophony of shrill squawks and caws stirs me from my late morning sleep.

"What's all this about?" I wonder as I pry myself from the sleeping bag. The frigid air is shocking. I have to get into my parka quickly.

Outside my door, I'm greeting by a flutter of wings. The local gray jays are screeching awfully. They're stirring up a lot of activity, considering how silent things have been lately.

"What's wrong with you guys this time?" I ask them in a cold, croaking voice.

The more I watch them, I become sure they're trying to get my attention. They intended to wake me up.

The birds are harassing something up in the tree. They return to my shelter to screech at me and then race right back to the tree. It's quite a ruckus.

"An owl?" I wonder. But as I approach the tree I see that the creature they're tormenting is a pine marten. He's about twenty feet up, and every time he moves, the birds dart in to pick at his back and tail. They're badgering him so relentlessly that he seems at his wit's end. There are too many jays for him to fend off.

This is one of the martens who have been killing all my hares. I don't feel much sympathy for it. But it's the first time I've seen a marten up close, and it's way fluffier that I expected. The wide, red-dish-blonde face looks somewhat panda-like. Or does it look more like a teddy? It's so cute and fluffy that I'm thinking how fun it would be to catch it.

"Hey buddy. What do you think you're doing in my camp?"

The marten hisses and growls at me in response. He acts like he could chew me up if he wanted to. His black eyes shine with a magnificent gleam of defiance and superiority. He does't care that I'm bigger. Clearly this tiny creature isn't intimidated by humans. I admire him for that.

I'm not allowed to kill a pine marten, so I leave. As I walk back toward my shelter, the jays fly in front of me screeching and trying their best to herd me back to the tree. They're saying plainly that I'm supposed to do something about the invader. They feel like we depend on each other, and I should step up and do my part.

"And what do you guys do for me? Steal my food?" I shout in retort.

After drinking some tea, I take off into the snow to check my snares. Too much time has passed since I found fresh hare sign, but when I reach the most southerly extent of my trail, I find a set of new tracks in the snow. The tracks lead directly into my final snare, and a nice, plump hare waits there for me.

The hare is stiff and frozen, but I'm like a proud kid again as I carry it home on my belt. The weight of it swinging against my leg as I cross the lake ice feels good.

I haven't filmed anything exciting in days, so I set up my camera at my shelter facing the trail to my snare line. I'm planning to film myself coming in and showing off the hare. But as I approach my camp, an idea creeps into my mind.

Walking up to the camera I kiss it and hug it. The camera is supposed to be Ugg's woman.

"Mmm. Once again I have returned from a long hunt."

"Oh, Ugg!" I use a high pitched cave-woman voice, grabbing the camera and moving it in time with her words. "You're safe! I'm so glad to see you! And you have food!"

"Yes. Once again Ugg successful. I kill rabbit. We eat."

"Oh, Ugg, that's wonderful. You're amazing."

"Mmmm. Me tired. We go inside, eat. Then make baby."

My words alarm me. I've been thinking about having another baby so much, but I've kept it a close secret inside my head. My fear is that if my wife doesn't want to have another one and then she sees on the show that I wanted to, it will be hard for her. So I haven't mentioned a peep about it. This is the first time I've let the fact that I'm thinking about it slip from my lips. But I assume it will look like I'm just playing around. So I go along with it and duck inside my shelter.

"Woman, what good you are? Fire cold."

I have to build up the fire from scratch, but soon the front half of the hare is boiling away and my shelter smells like supper. It's glorious. Only a woman and child is missing from this scene, and that thought makes me think back to the day my first son was born.

*   *   *

We had just arrived home from the hospital. Levi was tiny and sleeping; Cara was tired and sore. I got them settled inside and then a sudden desire to kill meat overtook me.

Here I was with a woman and a brand new son sleeping in my house. The only thing left to make me a real man was to kill some food and drag it home. So I took a rifle and headed out into the woods.

We were in Texas at the time, and feral hogs were becoming more and more common. I headed down to a small creek and crept along it, nosing into every clump of dense woods I came to. Shortly, I found a fresh track and followed it to discover a band of hogs feeding on some spring roots. Two sows rooted through the sandy soil surrounded by an extended brood of half-grown offspring. None of them heard or smelled me, though I was just yards away.

Shooting two of them, I cut them up and lifted an arm load of back-strap and haunch. The bloody meat dripped on the trail and my rifle hung over my shoulder as I approached the house where my new family slept. The picture was fully complete. I was twenty-six, and felt as successful as a man can be.

Since that time, I've learned that the world we live in demands so much more than being able to father a baby, build a home, and kill meat. I wish that life *was* really that simple.

Day 66

Large tracks cover the snow right outside my shelter. Some animal came right up to my door, sniffed around, and headed to my food cache. They're unlike any tracks I've ever seen, but after a close study I determine that they're wolverine tracks. The gait and pattern match, but they're far bigger than I expected wolverine tracks to be.

Right away I fear for my food, and I follow the tracks to my cache. The wolverine climbed all over Fort Moose Meat, smelling the fish, jerky and lard stored inside. He chewed on the locking log and pried at stuff. But I'm thrilled to see that all his efforts were in vain. He failed to breach the cache.

"Thank God!" I mutter, studying the wolverine's movements. "He really tried to get in here. I'll bet he comes back every night till he finds a way in."

Following the tracks around camp, I see that the wolverine smelled my wooden canister of pike guts I'd been saving as bait. He dug it up, split the log open and ate everything. Then he rolled in the snow for a while.

All in all, I've been lucky. The marauder didn't do much damage. I have more pike guts inside my cache. But I make a mental note to stay extra alert and keep my cache wedged shut as tightly as possible.

My trail to the river and out across the ice is filled in with snow. Every day the snow drifts swamp my path and force me to break through fresh powder all over again. But today it all feels worth it when I lift the lid from one of my ice holes and find a fishing line pulled taught. It's hard to tell through my thick gloves whether there's a fish on the end of the line or just a stick. But as I get it close to the surface I feel it tugging, and I know I've finally caught another fish!

It's been a long time since I pulled in a fish. It might be because the water is shallow and they've all left for deeper channels. Or it might be because they're just not interested in my bait now. I don't know. And so this catch is a truly welcome gift.

"I'm back in business!" I yell at the sky. "I can stay here all winter!"

Walking back to camp with my fish feels more exhausting than usual, and I find myself clinging onto a tree when lightheaded dizziness swamps my senses. It must be a lack of minerals in my body.

Throughout the day, the lightheaded feeling persists. I'm just laying down to sleep when the ground starts shaking. It moves gently at first, but the longer I lie still the more noticeable it becomes. The ground beneath my shelter, my bed beneath me, everything rolls and vibrates. It's not violent, just regular and irresistible, like swells of the ocean.

I've been in earthquakes many times. The mountains of Central Asia are particularly prone to quakes, but they're usually so deep that they do little surface damage. This feels exactly like a deep earthquake.

It should alarm me but it doesn't. Somehow I'm already conditioned to feeling it, like a sound that you haven't noticed until it pierces your consciousness and you realize that you've been annoyed for a long time. This feeling pierces my consciousness but as if it's already been going on for days.

"This can't be real," I tell myself. "I don't think there's a real earthquake going on."

Deciding to do a little test, I prop an arrow against my door frame. If there's a real vibration, this will visually prove it.

After a minute of staring at the arrow, nothing has happened. The shaking is still strong and distinct, but nothing in my shelter moves or vibrates. Even the tendrils of grass fire tinder dangling from my rafters are perfectly still.

"Why is it doing this?" I'm baffled. There's clearly no earthquake happening here. "Is the Labrador tea doing something to my brain?"

The more I think about it, I become suspicious that it could be true. Tea is the only thing I'm ingesting that could affect me. I've been drinking copious amounts of it. Mentally I feel sharp and clear, but this earthquake isn't going away.

"It's got to be the tea," I tell myself. What else could it be, other than a lack of salts and minerals in my body? "I'm going to lay off the tea for a few days and see what happens."

And so I lie down and try to make peace with the quaking sensation. It will either go away or not, but it isn't hurting anything. It feels almost nice.

I've been asleep for what feels like fifteen minutes when I'm awakened by the thump of one log against another. It sounds like my food cache is being ripped apart, and my head fills with images of a wolverine digging into my jerky. That thought brings me bolt upright, sitting up so quickly that my forehead crashes into a roof log, sending sparks shooting through my brain. I'm dazed from the blow, but I can't afford to linger. I have to act fast. If I give it much warning, the wolverine will slink away.

Charging out my door, I grab the first weapon I can seize and race to the food cache. I've got my axe in a death grip and I'm ready to start swinging at something. But nothing stirs. Only the silent snow greets me.

Circling my food cache for a while, I don't see any signs of life or even tracks in the snow. I must have been dreaming. So I head back to bed, chilled and tired.

The tingling cold follows me inside and remains, almost as if it's in my bones. It's hard to warm my sleeping bag back up. I stay cold all throughout the night, struggling with my feet. For some reason I just can't get any circulation to reach my toes. They ache as if they've been smashed.

Day 67

"Last night was the worst." I'm out cutting firewood the moment dawn streaks the sky. The camera is sitting there recording my morning routine. But I don't have anything positive to say.

"It was definitely the worst. I didn't sleep at all. The cold was painful."

I struggled with my feet all night, getting only about an hour of sleep. My body stays warm usually, but for some reason the circulation has just disappeared from my toes. The fact that I can't keep my feet warm even inside my sleeping bag chafes at the edges of my mind. I know it's going to get even colder and that prospect makes me feel miserable.

I think through my options for warming my feet as my circulation disappears. One possible solution comes to mind, and it's something I've relied on before. When I was about seven years old, we went though a particularly cold winter without a house to keep warm in. We were living in a barn at the time, so it was drafty to say the least. One wall was made out of cardboard. So when it dropped down below zero that winter, we were in real trouble. Wind and snow blew through gaps, and water froze in the sink.

To keep the little kids, including myself, from freezing we put bricks and rocks in the oven of the wood stove until they were hot. Then we wrapped them in towels and took them to bed with us. It kept us warm for a few hours.

That memory simulates my thinking today. Can I do that? I have five small rocks on my gill net, the only rocks I found in the early season. I could heat the fist-sized one and sleep with it. But my sleeping bag is made from light, synthetic layers. It will melt. It's no quilt like we had back in that barn. I come to the conclusion that the likelihood of melting a hole in my sleeping bag with the hot stones is really high. The risk keeps me from trying it. If I melt a hole in my bag, I'm really screwed.

"How am I going to keep my toes from getting frostbite?"

Once I build up my morning fire I get slightly warmer, but after just five minutes out on my snare line, my feet are frozen and numb again.

Some unfathomable weight is pressing down on my spirit. I'm not thriving today. I'm gritting my teeth to get through.

A growing wind is blowing in from the northwest again, and by mid-morning it's kicking up snow spray and forming deep drifts. It whips at me as I check my fish lines on the river ice. The spray of water when I chop through the ice freezes to me instantly. I've got icicles all over my face. I have to take my hands out of my gloves to operate the cameras; when I do, my fingers chill instantly and painfully.

Slogging through my snare lines without much energy, I remain empty-handed. The whole time my mind is self-destructing, sinking itself into a depressing funk. My feet hurt from cold. I wish I wasn't here at this moment. Nothing is around to catch or snare today. Nothing is moving around out here. Only me.

"God, help me get through. Help me get through," I chant the phrase as I trudge through the snow drifts along the river. "Just help me not to freeze tonight. Keep my feet from freezing."

I turn off the camera I'm carrying, not wanting to film the sick, sad way I pray to God. The entire way along my snare line I beg for blood to circulate through my feet better, for more warmth. One verse rises to the top of my mental quagmire, from Psalm 25:

> *"Unto thee, oh Lord, do I lift up my soul.*
> *Oh my God, I trust in thee.*
> *Let me not be ashamed."*

Having returned early because I didn't set any new snares, I'm dreading the dead time I must endure until the light fades and I go inside to cook and go to sleep. But I know that getting into my sleeping bag won't bring me an escape. I'll lie there for nineteen hours. At least twelve of those will be sleepless hours. Maybe I'll catch five hours of sleep if I'm really lucky.

I start thinking about the other contestant who must still be out here with me on the land. What's he doing? Is he suffering too? Are his feet cold? Or is he warm and well fed?

In my mind, the other contestant is sitting in a well-lit cabin feasting on slices of fresh moose or bear. He's got a pot of bubbling fat going over the fire, and he's talking to the camera about how comfortable he is, how he can do this forever. Maybe two or even three contestants are all enjoying that kind of stuff right now.

One of the things that's so challenging about *Alone* is that you're competing against people you can't see. I think about that and wish I could see the other man just once. If I could put my eyes on that man, if I could see how he's doing, I'd know I can do one more thing than he can. I can kill one more animal than him. I can stay alive in one degree colder than he can. I'd know for sure that I had him. But I can't see him. The competition is invisible. I can only see myself, and what I see today is suffering.

The afternoon, usually short and fleeting, seems to drag by and I'm relieved when I judge that the night is near enough and I can sit inside and enjoy an hour of preparing and cooking food. The warmth and brightness of my fire lifts my spirits a bit and gives me just enough energy to start playing my *Trial by Fire* game. Getting out the dice and the eight remaining players, I do my best to become imaginative and I start playing.

My fire is burning brightly; in its cheery glow, I set up each contestant and film their interviews.

"Welcome to another exciting episode of *Trial by Fire!*"

I grab my own character and hold it up to the camera.

"Tall Johnny is gunning for me. He's doing everything he can to turn my alliance against me. He turned Darrell against me already. I've got to pull out all the stops tonight, but I have a bad feeling."

"Um, I'm pretty sure Timber is gonna be going home tonight." Tall Johnny looks smug and cocky. "I flipped Darrell and of course Michelle is going to vote exactly how I tell her to. We've both got similar goals, and tonight the goal is to get rid of Timber once and for all."

Interviews over, I roll the dice. Each player gets their chance to vote and I mark down their numbers. Alexandra and I vote for Tall Johnny of course, but my number comes up three times. I'm on the chopping block.

Stepping my character forward, I prepare to roll my defense move. It seems like a crushing defeat is inevitable.

My emotions are invested now. I'm about to get voted out by characters I created and carved from wood. Where will that leave me? Will I be able to continue the game for the other players after such a loss? Or will I have to reimagine another system of counting down the days?

The dice hit the table and I cheer when I see that I've rolled double fives. That means that I have a strong alliance and they've played an advantage that takes away one vote against me. Now me and Michelle are tied and the vote between us has to be recast.

My heart drops as I see one of my alliance members turn against me. The vote puts me right back on the chopping block and I know my chances are all but gone. I prepare to roll my last defense move.

"Blindside!" I shout so loudly that the wolves can probably hear me outside. I've rolled a B, and now the player with the second-most votes will go home. It's a huge reversal! I've done the impossible! Tall Johnny looks totally deflated, and losing Michelle upends his strategy completely.

It's an incredibly exciting episode, and I'm transformed suddenly into a positive person. I'm embarrassed that I could be down so low and not have to power to lift my own spirits back up until such a paltry thing as this silly game lifted me.

I eat the remainder of yesterday's fish. It fries perfectly in the moose lard and I enjoy it to the full.

Pike are full of bones. Each flay has rows of little toothpick-sized bones that have to come out before the meat can be chewed and swallowed. It's a big aggravation but I've become excellent at picking the bones just right so that I get them all. I'm also thankful these days that it forces me to eat slowly instead of gobbling my meal down like the hungry beast I am.

Halfway through my meal, as I'm crumbling a piece of flay to pick the bones out, I realize that the broken pieces soak up a lot of oil if I leave them in the bottom of my pot for a while. I grab a spoon and dip up the fish crumbles, slurping great amounts of oil up with the meat. It tastes heavenly, but it feels even better on some instinctual level. I can actually feel my body telling me "Hey, this is what I want. I need this oil." So I slurp up as much oil as I dare.

After supper and tea I come back to reality and see that the problem of freezing at night is still very real. My feet still have no circulation.

I ask God again to keep me from freezing, and then I make sure that my feet are perfectly dry and toasty warm from the fire. Then I stick them into my boot liners and like a flash, I'm in my sleeping bag. I zip it up all the way, pull the drawstrings tight and hunker down. As the hours drag by until I can fall asleep, I focus on relaxing my shoulders and thighs so that maximum circulation can get through.

Day 68

I'm afraid to check on my body systems this morning, not wanting to face frostbitten toes. But as I slowly wiggle my hands and feet, I realize that I'm not just okay—I'm warm and toasty. My sleeping bag is a comfortable temperature. My feet don't hurt. Everything is good!

"Wow, God! I'm alive and fine!" Surprised by how warm I am, I wonder what made the difference.

"The oil!" I snap my fingers in realization. "My body burned all that oil I drank last night, and I was able to keep warm that way!"

I slept like a log last night, maybe six or seven hours of uninterrupted sleep. It's better than I've slept in weeks, and I now feel light and upbeat. It's a big turnaround from my lowest point yesterday. Another crisis has been overcome. I feel like I've broken though a wall. Nothing out ahead can really be that terrible after coming this far. With a smile and a light heart I switch the camera batteries and set it up to start filming my activities.

Yesterday's wind storm obliterated my trail, and I have to wade through hip-deep banks of snow to reach the river. The lack of fish on my lines doesn't sink my spirits.

I decide to pull my snares from one particularly unproductive area. For weeks I've trudged through the snow to this remote spot where one or two sets of hare tracks had shown up. I've burned countless calories tending those snares for nearly a month and gotten nothing to show for it. There have been no fresh tracks there since the pine marten and owls killed everything. So I head that way and cut down each snare, happy that I won't have to expend the energy to reach this particular corner of my territory any more.

The sound of chanting accompanies me again, swelling and dwindling. I'm not bothered by it, but I wish I could put my finger on what's causing it. At any rate, it's a sound to keep me company in an otherwise still and colorless world.

The colorlessness is something that surprises me. I hadn't expected how thoroughly all vestige of color would disappear. The land contains only white and gray. Not even the starkness of true black contrasts with the snow.

Today the colorlessness and silence doesn't bother me. I've overcome them and I cheerfully trudge around my landscape checking snares, looking for fresh tracks and feeling thrilled again to be here.

Once I reach the edge of my meadow, I stop. An inner voice speaks to me and says "Take this moment to understand."

I only have to cross the meadow to reach my camp, but I pause for a long while to absorb what's really happening in my life right now. I understand suddenly that even though parts of this *Alone* life are hard, this adventure will become the definition of freedom and pure living in my mind. With each and every moment that I breathe here, I'm writing down golden pages of memory that I'll love forever. And it's beautiful. Before me the snowscape gleams in soft light. The sun is too low to say that it's in the sky, but it's touching the sky's edge. Blue sky remains visible in the south.

I stand in the snow for a long time, trying to solidify the reality of my position in the world. I'm on the very northern edge of the American continent. Wilderness extends a thousand miles or more in every direction, locked in snow and ice. In the middle of the sky dome lies my land, savage and clean, untouched by civilization. And in the middle of my land is a single set of human tracks, the only mark of man. Those tracks end where my boots are. Inside my boots stands a human.

Who is this human? When I arrived on this land I wan't sure. I barely knew who Timber was any more.

"Do I know now?" I think about that for a minute.

Is the man standing in these tracks a hunter? Yes. A wild man? Definitely. A good man? I hope so. A perfect man or flawless survivalist? Not by a long shot.

But what I do know is that this man is one who has learned how to live. I've understood that I'm created to be exactly the strange creature I am, and that God looks on what He made and says, "Behold, it is very good." I'm a man who can face the past and the future because God has redeemed the mess my life is. I've been made new, created all over again. It's almost like the day I first put my faith in Jesus. And I've experienced Him. I know that, firmly and unflinchingly.

I'm keenly aware that I'm not perfect and my story isn't perfect. But it's a good story because of what God has turned it into. And my journey on *Alone* is nothing less than that. I accept that it's not just about me. It's about my wife, my kids. It's about humanity inside me, and all of the humanity behind the camera who want to experience this. I'm doing something we will all be proud of. I'm not just getting through life to reach the end and get out of the next person's way. I'm building a bridge of some sort for my offspring. I'm marking a trail into the unknown. I'm becoming an ancestor.

Becoming an ancestor? That thought smacks me like a falling tree, and suddenly I know without a doubt that I really do want another kid. I've been thinking about it since day forty-eight, but I've been worried that it was because I missed home, missed my wife. Now I know that being a father to another child is what my life should be. Admitting this to myself, I feel an avalanche of happiness pile on me. My heart has swelled with the capacity to be there for one more kid. Just like the Grinch.

I cross my meadow toward camp with a heart as light and happy as it's ever been, feeling that each new track I make in the snow is leading me towards life. In my shelter, I make a smooth, wooden piece and carve a name on it. It's a girl's name, and that's what I start asking God for.

Somehow today has been the best and happiest day of my life in the arctic. I don't know how it turned out that way. I've reached a place of spiritual peace that I've never touched before. The only anxious cloud in my otherwise perfect sky is whether or not I can make it to the very end. I want to win.

I'm trying to stop drinking Labrador tea, but tonight I drink a pot of it anyways. I have the suspicion it's making me lightheaded, but it's hard to pass up. In a world of isolation and nothingness, tea is a ludicrously attractive flavor experience.

The earthquake comes back when I lie down, but I just let it rock me to sleep.

Day 69

After an uneventful day of checking snares, I'm taking off my parka and boots, preparing to climb into bed when I experience my most serious gear failure yet. My right boot liner falls apart.

My cold weather boots have a removable liner. I learned on a mountaineering trip years ago that removable liners are the trick I need, the strategy that keeps my feet well during extreme cold. In this cold, the boot liners are the only things keeping my feet from frost bite.

As I pull my feet out of my boots tonight, trying to keep the liners on, a thread snags on something and pulls. At first I can't find where the thread is coming from. But when I finally see what's coming unsewn, my heart skips a beat. The bottom of my boot liner has come off.

I look it over with something akin to panic. The whole bottom of the foot area has just come loose. The stitching has fallen out and my foot is sticking right out the bottom. The liners will be useless this way.

Immediately I go into emergency mode. I have to do something, but my make-shift sewing needle in my Leatherman can't go through the fabric and pull thread through.

Then I get a spark of inspiration. I have really soft snare wire, stuff I've been saving for a special project. Will the wire be stiff enough to be pushed through the boot liner, but malleable enough to cinch down like thread?

"This had better work," I tell the camera as I rummage through my supplies to find the wire. After a little testing, I'm thrilled to find that the wire is absolutely perfect for the job. I cut a good length of it and sharpen the end of the wire with my file until it's like a needle. Then I stitch the boot back together.

The project takes an hour or so and my sock feet are freezing by the time I get it finished, but I'm thrilled with the final product. It's impossible to tell that it's been repaired and I have no doubt that it's as good as new. Such a relief!

Some time in the night I again wake up thinking I've heard my food cache being torn apart. Again I charge out into the darkness brandishing my axe, searching everywhere for a marauding wolverine. But nothing is there. My food cache is undisturbed.

Chapter 19

Darkness

*   *   *

"If you can force your heart and nerve and sinew
to serve your turn long after they are gone,
And so hold on when there is nothing in you
except the will that says to them: "Hold on!"
-from "If" by Rudyard Kipling

In life, suffering is a given. Suffering well is a skill. Being at peace in the mind when the body loses control, keeping the spirit quiet and even happy when things are extremely disagreeable—those are the skills of the warrior.

From about Day 51 to 67 I did not do very well at suffering. But as the day count slides into the seventies, I feel like I've overcome the fear of freezing. I don't fear winter.

The sun is almost completely gone. Its full body never comes above the tips of the trees. The land is cloaked in darkness for twenty hours each day.

I spend too much time lying down. My kidneys hurt and I feel bruised where my hip bones stick out. The hours are truly endless.

Thoughts are the only bright path forward. I spend a lot of time thinking up mental challenges, inventing ideas and test driving plans. My brain is my only playhouse, the one way I can do something more than eat, sleep, and exist. For endless hours in my sleeping bag I guide my thoughts from challenge to challenge. I've designed the house I want to build for my family some day. I've planned all sorts of ventures regarding the humanitarian projects I've left undone. It all amounts to plans I believe will change my life. But I'm afraid of forgetting the things I plan. I only wish for some way to record it all.

The only way I can alleviate the data collecting in my brain is to jot down notes on the crowded birchbark scraps I have stacked on my shelf. I use these bark pages sparingly, making notes in shorthand and writing only those ideas that seem fully formed and most important. I'd give my left arm for a notebook and pencil.

Day 70

A faint sound wakes me up. I've been sleeping so lightly that I'm up and looking out my shelter door at the slightest noise. It could be food. I peer outside into the weird twilight and see four little piglets dart past my camp. My mouth waters and instantly I'm filled with an uncontrollable desire to eat that first little piglet. Then an idea strikes me. If there are little piglets, there must be a mama pig nearby. Sure enough, she's there by the big log that I chopped down so it wouldn't fall on my shelter. A black and white mottled mama pig. She's headed down toward the river with her piglets in tow.

I seize my bow and I'm so hungry, saliva literally dribbles from my mouth. I *have* to kill this pig! Think about how much meat I'll have! My mind races to stack all of that pork, some of which will be bacon, some sausage, and of course a big ham, in my food cache. It won't even freeze there. It will stay so very greasy and delicious.

I nock an arrow to my bow string as the sow stops full broadside. I'll kill her first and then pick off all four piglets. The shot is only ten yards. Or is it a hundred? Hard to tell. I think it's ten. But can my bow shoot that far? I can't remember.

Suddenly there's movement to my left. From the corner of my eye I see a cheeseburger dart under a log. I swing around and draw my bow, ready to take the shot. I can't be sure, but I think it was a Baconator. My movement spooks the pigs and they start to get away. I glance back toward them but something tells me that the cheeseburger is going to slip away if I give it a chance. Which one should I shoot at? I'm so torn!

Suddenly the dream dissolves and my eyes open. I see nothing until I switch on my headlamp, which hangs on a nail near my head. The resin-stained logs of my shelter above me come into focus. The only thing left of my dream is the persistent hunger that just never goes away now. My back hurts. My bladder really hurts. It's been 19 hours since I zipped up this sleeping bag and prayed that it would keep my feet from frostbite, and it's still dark.

The outside world is covered in hoarfrost this morning. The entire forest looks like a wonderland, dazzlingly coated in sparkles that are almost too shiny to be real. Especially where the north-facing bank of the river shades the land, the frost is feathery and falls down inside my hood in the back every time I bump into a tree or branch.

I take a while to film and admire the enormous frost flakes, which cling to everything like delicate feathers of glass. Then I begin my normal routines.

My routines are like a deep channel I've worn into the land. I feel like surrendering to these routines could blind me, and therefore kill me. But I don't know how to break them.

First thing every day, I wake up. Try not to move. I finally feel warm inside my bag. That feeling should be enjoyed and savored. I have to pee, and that is the alarm clock I live by.

348

Get my parka on and use the toilet. Get the cameras rolling. Brush the night's snow off the equipment box and get fresh batteries for everything.

Once I have the cameras ready and the microphone clipped in under my sweater, I film a morning update. Talk about how well I slept or didn't sleep and what I'm thinking today. Scrape the snow away from my yard and cut one big chunk of spruce from a dead tree. This gives me the piece of wood that will hold my fire all day.

Need a fire. Grab a handful of dead grass from my supply of tinder. Strike my ferro rod about ten times until the grass starts to blaze. Pile some spruce twigs on it and then add bigger alder wood. Sit down for half an hour of rest and warm tea. Drink warm tea. It's so great. My finger are warm now.

Stare at the flames for a while. This seems important. Eat a small piece or two of jerky or dried fish.

Now it's time to check the fish lines. Chop each hole open with my axe and re-bait the lines. Next it's on to snares.

Carry my bow and go slowly, keeping my eye open for game. Claw through dense willow and wade through deep snow. On and on. Lots of energy lost. Tired.

Return to camp. Poke the fire into a blaze. Stare at the flames again. Eat a piece of jerky. Play guitar or carve something. Chop some wood. Stare at some snow.

Go out into my meadow if the sun is out. Don't go far. Snow is too deep. Stare at the sun. Stare at the sky. Stare at some more snow. Sit on a log.

Chop more wood. Don't need wood. Chop more wood anyways. Stare at some trees. Walk around. Whistle a little. Talk to a gray jay. Look for grouse. Is that a grouse? No.

The light is gone. Get a fish. Cut the frozen scales off. Put wood in the fire, get it going. Thaw the fish. Slice fish. Wait for supper.

See a pencil. Get it. Put the tip of the pencil in the fire and blow out the flame. Write something. Stare at the fire. Read all the notes on all the birch bark.

Play my wooden game. Smile. Laugh. Put the remaining pieces away. Change the camera batteries. Stare at the fire.

Eat fish. Mmmmmm. Delicious. Say thank you to God about a thousand times. Slurp oil. Boil tea. Feel good.

Drink tea. Throw sticks at the fire. Stare at flames. Think.

Get tired of sitting by fire. My back is sore. Record a day's end interview and tie another knot in the calendar string. Pray for my wife and kids.

Unroll the sleeping bag. Go outside. Pee. Knock the snow off my boots again and seal up the door.

Warm up the feet one more time. Race to get inside the sleeping bag. Get comfortable. Think. Pray. Try to go to sleep. Wallow for hours. Sleep.

Day 71

A new challenge confronts me when I return from checking fish lines this morning.
The gray jays have decided to enter my shelter and steal stuff.

As I approach from my river trail, I see one of the birds flap out through my door way and drop a chunk of lard from his beak. They must be extra hungry, or just used to me now.

"Hey!" Get out of there!" I yell and throw a stick at the bird, retrieving the bit of lard and replacing it in its birchbark container. I can see that he's been sitting in my hanging lard tub, scratching and pecking at the lard, prying pieces loose. "Now this is a real problem."

I'm mad. Extremely mad. This is way worse than stealing fish eggs from my outdoor cooking area. This is an invasion of my home, a threat inside the one space I can rely on to keep me well. But I can't shoot these jays. It's maddening. If they would only respect this one space of mine!

I sit in my shelter throughout the afternoon, using it as a blind. Every time a jay lands in front, I shoot an arrow at the snow beneath the bird's feet. I hope this warning will be enough.

The earthquake sensation is so strong once I lie down that it makes it hard to sleep. The whole universe pulses and throbs. It feels like ocean swells inside me, heaving me about. I can't feel anything else. Eventually I sleep.

It's been some hours when I become aware. I don't know if I'm awake, asleep or dreaming. But the throbbing and quaking has grown into a storm that I'm caught in—like being sucked into a tornado of swirling light that pulls me both up and down at once. Suddenly the tornado pries me out of my body, and I'm pulled further and further from my sleeping form. I notice that my body is not breathing. I can both see it not breathing, and I can feel that I'm not drawing breaths. Part of me feels panicky like I've run out of oxygen, but an equally real half of me feels perfectly fine without oxygen. The swirly current of light is relaxing and nice, so I just go with it, letting it absorb me.

Suddenly something alerts me that if I go with this flow too far, I won't be able to reach my body again. I look back and see my body lying there, already out of reach. The part of me that needs oxygen panics, and I start swimming against the current, fighting and clawing to reach myself.

I'm making headway, getting closer, but my body doesn't recognize me. It's still and breathless. So I reach as far as I can and smack my body in the face. I hit it over and over again. It stirs.

I'm instantly inside my head, looking through my eyes, then I'm outside again, smacking myself in the face.

Finally I stick inside my body and in an instant I'm fully awake, gasping for air. I really hadn't been breathing. Somehow, I can tell that it's been an awfully long time since I took a breath.

"Wow God! Wow God!" I blubber over and over. "Oh, wow God! Thanks for waking me up!"

I'm totally freaked out and afraid to go back to sleep, but towards morning I fall asleep again and rest peacefully for a short time.

I wake up thinking about what happened, still unsure of the cause but considering that it might be the quantities of tea I'm still drinking. It alarms me. I don't want last night's experience to be repeated. I'm really going to stop drinking the Labrador tea. Seriously. I've run out of it anyways.

Day 72

"I still feel light-headed," I confess to the camera as I film my morning update. "I'm really light-headed."

I have to stop often as I work so that I don't fall over. I'm worried that if it gets worse, I could pass out. Then I might fall face-first into a snow drift and freeze. But for now I know that I'm not going to pass out. I can still feel the solid baseline of strength I need to not let that happen. But deciding what to do this morning seems especially hard. My brain is tired.

"Ok, I'm going to let muscle memory take over," I explain to the camera. "I'm going to let my body chop wood."

I've chopped wood all my life. Mountains and mountains of it. So when I release my body to chop wood I know that I won't have to think at all. My zombified corpse will walk around and drag trees in and chop wood, and I won't have to make any decisions. Maybe the activity will help me regain power over the light-headed sensation.

And that's exactly what happens. I stay dizzy for a while, but by the time I have a big pile of chopped alder wood and a few big spruce chunks, I feel pretty much myself again. I can think more clearly and I'm fine.

The thing that really surprises me about the Alone production system is that there really aren't people hovering nearby to disrupt the integrity of the experience. I had half-expected to find secret systems that don't get filmed for the show. I imagined that there would surely prove to be monitors, medics, or decision-makers nearby, watching and making sure the risks are all managed. I didn't want that to be true, I just expected it because of the liability-rabid world we live in.

But refreshingly, I found upon arrival that it's not that way at all. We signed releases and received a satellite phone and GPS to call with in case of an emergency. The crew is always ready to rush out, but given the extremity of the show's location and elements, there is always the possibility of technological error. Right now it's so cold that the satellite phone won't even charge as it should unless it's propped beside the fire. And secondly, if a contestant were to do something such as fall through the ice, chop his femoral artery with an axe or be mauled by a bear, the response time necessary in extreme situations like that is so short, there is no guarantee a constructive response could be activated in time.

This authentic aspect of the show makes me really happy. I like it. But it means I need to be careful about things like last night. I can't carelessly overdose on something.

"Is it really the tea bush?" I ask myself again and again. I don't remember anything about the bush being toxic in large amounts. But I know that if overdosing on it is possible, I'm the one to prove it. I've been cramming as much of the bush as will fit into my pot. I brew it black, let it steep overnight, and down it by the quart.

"Well, that all stops," I promise. And I can keep my promise this time, because there isn't any more tea in my shelter. I could go out to the southern edge of my land and dig through the deep snow and pick more, but I won't. I'm good.

The reality that I might have had a close call makes me think deeply while I throw sticks into my fire. Something almost happened, something that could have stopped me from winning. It could happen again in any number of ways. I could fall through the rotten river ice and freeze. I could get so lightheaded that I can't stand up. My shelter could burn down and leave me with nothing in a frozen night.

"What will I do or be if anything happens that stops me from winning?" I ask myself. "Will I be able to cope? Will I be destroyed?"

I wrestle with this thought throughout the day, running my snare lines, checking fish lines and cutting more wood. The thought pains me, and I stress out about the very possible outcome. Can I face it? And what if I reach a place where I myself decide not to continue? I don't see anything that could make that happen, but what if? Could I reconcile such a thing?

I decide to take that question of whether I'll win or not and forget about it. I have already become so happy and satisfied deep in my soul that I believe I can handle any outcome. Winning or losing becomes just another lump of fear that I hand over to God.

On my birchbark notes, I write this evening that real peace comes from a satisfied soul. Mine is completely satisfied. This step of growth is worth every minute of stress and loneliness I've endured here and in the previous years. I wish every person could share it with me right now. But would I ever have come to this without being isolated in nature for so long? And is my realization the same thing everyone references when they talk about nature making them feel closer to God? Just why does the wild do this for people? I feel like I know the answer.

Nature is life, imagined and put into existence by God. We touch it and we know that the life within us is connected. And it's more than consciousness. The life force pulsing within nature is a brush of God's breath, and we instinctively respond to it. We yearn for it. And the deeper we experience it, we come to find that there's even more there, an inexhaustible supply of life. And after just one small taste we can't be satisfied with less. We begin yearning to dive headlong into that endless reservoir of being. That's the reason some of us want to abandon modern life, head into the wild and never look back. We just want to live in that connection forever.

But just connecting with nature can't ever truly satisfy that bottomless pit of hunger for life. Only God has enough life to fill that, and it's right there for the asking. It takes humility to ask, however. It takes an admission that I and my thoughts are not enough to fill my eternal need for life. Today I am truly filled with life. Satisfaction.

I go to bed afraid of drifting away again. The world quakes and pulses. So I try to maintain a strong grip on consciousness, staving off any urge to let go and drift with the flow. Eventually, I sleep.

Day 73

Today I try to spend some time with the camera switched off. I'm in my shelter cooking, and I want some private moments. But I quickly find that I don't want to have any moments that are completely unshared. So I turn the camera back on and let it watch as I do nothing.

"Bang!" A loud explosion suddenly erupts from my fireplace. The sound is about on par with a 9mm pistol shot; it blasts sparks, embers, and small chunks of burning wood all over my shelter. My face gets pelted by flaming fragments.

Coals are all over me, melting pinholes in my coat and pants. More coals are sprinkled all through my firewood and kindling. Shaking them off, I stomp the embers out on the floor. Digging through my tinder supply, I find that one or two coals have landed there. It would be so easy to burn my shelter down this way.

When I'm sure that there are no more stray coals threatening my shelter, I take time to notice a big burn on the back of my hand. A large area of my skin is scorched and it's coated with a hard, black layer like melted plastic.

"Nice," I mutter, poking at the black layer that has cooled and hardened. Beneath it my skin is fried. "Spruce sap."

Every big chunk of spruce I burn has little pockets of sap trapped in the wood here and there between growth rings. When the fire burns down to them, the sap heats up and expands. If the pressure has nowhere to go, it will blow up. Usually it's just a pop, but sometimes it's a pretty loud bang. It always sends up a shower of sparks.

This blast was much larger than usual, more like a grenade than a pop. It blew the whole back off the chunk of wood, knocking a piece of mud out of my fireplace and spraying me with molten resin.

Out on my snare line, I see a flock on nine ptarmigan. The birds are so immaculately white that they're invisible unless the sun casts their shadow on the snow. I try for an hour to stalk them, but they won't let me get anywhere close enough for a shot. When I get closer than fifty yards, they flush. Eventually they fly off for good, and I watch as they disappear over the southern trees.

The lightheadedness diminishes as I lie in bed. The world no longer throbs and ripples. I feel much more secure as I let my brain drift throughout the night.

Day 74

Something has been bothering me since I woke up this morning. It's a tiny, nagging aggravation that I can't put my finger on.

Throughout my morning chores, a feeling chews away at me that I'm missing something.

Eventually I track the feeling down and realize that through-out the night I couldn't remember the Russian word for mustard. I know it starts with the syllable "gor." It's gor-something. I try a few combinations.

"Gor-*nitsa*? Gor-d*itsa*?" Nothing sounds right. "*Gorkulece*?" No, now I'm mixing the word for oatmeal into it. I give up, but keep a strong hope that the word will come back. I can't move on until it does.

I spent most of the night having Russian dialogues in my head. Eventually I must have fallen asleep and I found myself build-ing a hamburger in my dreams. I was explaining to a Russian friend how to make the perfect burger and when it came time for the mus-tard, I couldn't remember the word. The loss of the word from my brain has really gotten under my skin.

When I suddenly hear a helicopter approaching, I feel a giddy happiness. I haven't seen another human in so long.

Quickly rolling out of bed and dressing, I prepare for the medical check. Outside I'm greeted by a blizzard of chopper-blasted ice crystals.

Stripping down so that the medic can do his routine health checks is no fun - not in this weather. It doesn't help that I can see the crew wearing electrically heated gloves and boots.

"How are you feeling in general?" The medic asks me.

"I'm cold and I feel weak, but I'm good. I don't hurt any-where except my back when I'm lying down."

The medic is taking notes as I speak, but he looks confused.

"What? Could you speak English please?"

I realize that I've responded to him in Russian. Going through the info again in English, I hope that they don't get the idea that my brain is compromised or anything. It's not. (Well, no more than usual, anyways.)

The crew does their best to make the process quick and painless, but by the time I put my warm layers back on, my toes and fingers are numb. As the helicopter flies off, leaving me in a swirling blizzard of spindrift, I find myself swearing at the cold. I have to get warmed up.

My body feels really tired but my brain is in overdrive as I finish up supper and get ready for bed. I try to sleep but the paths of thought I go down are so clear and so rewarding that I can't abandon them. Step by step, sheets of confusion unfold plainly in my mind, as I find answers to the hardest questions I've held inside.

Coming onto the show, my biggest hope was that I'd find what's next for my life. My future had seemed so dark, so tangled in a cobweb of conflicting needs and problems. I hoped for an epiphany to either re-direct my goals or give me a new way to approach them. Do I want to keep working in those war-torn places that have beaten up my family so badly? My wife and I both love the aid work. It's been the best part of our lives, but it has taken its toll. We've all suffered from it. Should I change what I do entirely? Should I say goodbye to the life that we've dedicated so much investment and toil in? What is the goal I can live toward, the thing that can keep me alive with belief and conviction?

I've wanted more than anything to find a reawakening, a renewed passion for being alive and pursing something worthy. Looking back now, I can see that my thinking has been like a man wallowing through a thick swamp. My mind was so cluttered, so charged with unprocessed data that I could barely even think about what I was thinking about. My life played out in a way that reflected that clutter. I was like the subject of Seneca's quote: "If a man knows not to which port he sails, no wind is favorable."

The process of purging my brain with months of silence has been painful but so good that I wouldn't trade it for anything. In the pitch darkness of the arctic tonight, the horizon of my life has never looked more bright. I see a dream out there ahead, and it's a good one.

I decide many things, some of which I can't write about. But ultimately I see our family living happily, serving needy people in war-torn places again—the work we love the most. But doing so without carrying the weight we've carried, free from the pressure of earning anything or *having* to succeed. The truth that I'm a creature made by God, and it's not wrong to survive even though other's don't—that's a big realization that I've absorbed now. I can survive. I can make it through death, and my survival is not cheating. I haven't wrongly taken something by living. I haven't been unfair when I lived and my neighbors didn't, my brother didn't. I haven't held back life that I could have given to others. I can work, eat, rest, and sleep, and that's exactly what God designed me to do. I can enjoy it without guilt or shame. And I can face all these things again, and if I live it won't be wrong. It will mean simply that God has given me another day, just like each day I'm given here in the Arctic, alive, safe, well, and happy. I want that life, and I want to share it with people who need it.

Epiphany after epiphany hits me, showing me the way forward in life, making plain the confusion that has loomed ahead. This is what I've been waiting for. My soul is unburdened, free to zoom out into the future and explore all sorts of living—knowing that in all of it, I'll exist with God, and I'll be free and good.

Hour after hour of darkness I endure physically, but thrive mentally. It's as if all the quiet of the past seventy-four days was only an appetizer, and this peace is the main course.

I'm so keyed up that I don't sleep a single wink during my nineteen hours in the sleeping bag. And I'm more glad than words can express that I wasn't forced to leave earlier and miss all this.

The Arctic has taught me something new about God. Being quiet and still tunes our hearts to hear his thoughts. We must be silent if we are to hear the still small voice he chooses to use. God speaks in silence.

Day 75

I'm exhausted from lack of sleep as I get up and start chopping wood for the day. But the stimulating mental process has been worth it. As I sit warming up by my morning fire, my heart is bursting with zest for life.

The fire cracks and pops. My pot steams as the water approaches a boil. The situation is extremely pleasant.

Finding a piece of birch bark that's not already full of writing, I sharpen a pencil and put down the words that came to me in the darkness. I write that God spoke it to me.

"Do whatever is in your heart, for I am with you."

Today will mark the final episode of my game, *Trial by Fire*. My little wooden players are down to just three: me, Alexandra, and Darrell. There is no strategy to this game. It's complete chance, based on the roll of hand carved, misshapen dice. And given that I've never meddled with the outcome of the dice, it amazes me that I'm still in the game. My little character has seen his share of close calls, but the girl I call Alexandra has remained a loyal and reliable alliance member, and here we are at the final three.

I named this player Alexandra because that's my wife's middle name. It's a little tribute I'm paying to a wonderful and supportive wife.

After filming interviews with the last three pieces, I get out nine former characters and let them all vote. Alexandra wins by a vote. My character came *"this close!"*

While I sit in the firelight, I find myself contemplating life through the lens of the game. The winning player, Alexandra, sits on the wooden stump table, smiling a little smile at me. My second place character is overshadowed in the flickering firelight. Suddenly I find myself wondering if the outcome of these random dice rolls fore-shadows anything about *Alone*.

"Certainly not," I tell myself. It's nonsense. "This does't mean anything."

But the small wooden piece that represents Alexandra keeps smiling at me, turning my thoughts homeward to my wife. I hope that she is truly the winner of *Alone*, no matter how it turns out.

"How might my wife be the winner here?" I muse. Of course, the money would help her live more comfortably. But that's never been her desire. I remember what she asked me, what she urged me to do when I departed for the Arctic.

"Go get drunk on the wilderness. Let go of the stress, and be well."

"She will be the winner if I have changed," I realize quietly. If I can bring home the peace that I've found here and embody that, Cara Alexandra will have won.

The game piece smiles, and the firelight flickers, and I begin to understand.

Day 76

I spend a lot of time toward evening scribbling notes on birchbark. I'm so content and happy as I write ideas down, but soon-er or later I will have to go and live these ideas.

Thinking and planning turn into a balancing act now, giving the mind leash to explore ideas, but keeping it reined in when those ideas start to make me miserable. At times I look at my notes and want so badly to just go and start into the ideas on those lists, to live that life with my wife and kids, to be intentional and meaningful. During those moments the isolation and absolute void of the Arctic seems overwhelming.

So I do everything in my power to guide my mind. If it wants material to work on, I give it room to run, but when I start getting miserable from inability to tackle the ideas, I shut it down and go cut wood.

Day 77

Sitting with my feet propped up in front of the fireplace, I rotate each foot periodically so that my boots don't burn. It's a mindlessly entertaining activity that keeps me happy for a few hours as I throw wood into the flames.

All at once, I feel aggravated by my fireplace. The platform my fire sits on is too high now, being that I've thrown out the thresh from my floor. I've been getting by just fine with it up to now, but all at once I'm super mad at having to prop my feet up so high. So in a burst of energy, I grab my axe and completely destroy the lower part of my fireplace.

It's hard work because the river silt I used as plaster is frozen into a six-inch thick monolith. But I chop away, setting aside the bigger chunks of frozen mud as I break them free.

Then I set up a basic fire ring using the big chunks of mud. The fire ring is at floor level now and I feel smugly happy as I stoke the fire up again. I don't have to prop up my feet to warm them now. It's awesome.

A savage wind kicks up after dark and rocks my shelter all night. The ridge timber creaks and groans where it's fixed to a live spruce at the back. The creaking timbers make me feel as if I'm lying in the belly of a ship. The sounds keep me company, and so I've come to enjoy them. But the stronger the wind grows, the more I become alert for danger. This wind could knock a tree down on me.

The temperature starts to drop. We were already at the bottom of the thermometer I've come to recognize here. But as the wind clears the sky of clouds, the temperature falls off another cliff, entering a new zone of uncharted territory.

Day 78

"A hare hopped right through my camp last night." I'm standing in the snow after having cleared my yard of last night's accumulation. A set of perfectly fresh hare tracks range all around my camp site. I think I might get a shot at it so I'm following its trail with my bow in hand, but I haven't spotted the creature yet.

"I'm going to set up some snares for this guy. It's the first track I've seen in two weeks."

Not only do hare tracks cross in camp, but a lynx passed through during the night. Its big, round pugmarks are plain and crisp where it checked out my food cache before continuing west through the willows. I decide to set a snare for it as well, hoping that the smell of meat in my cache will bring it back. This lynx would be such welcome fresh meat.

After setting snares I check my fish lines and the gill net that I've finally placed under the ice. Nothing has been caught, and the ice is getting mushier. Three or four inches of fresh water splashes as I walk across the river ice and it freezes instantly to my boots with each step. I'm quickly dragging around pounds of dead weight in ice on each leg.

Supper time is nearing. A half of a fish is in my hands, and I'm staring at it. The tail is still there along with the scales, but the fins are trimmed off. That's how I cleaned it to store in the cache over a month ago. I left the scales on and being frozen and impenetrable, they're protecting the meat from mice, which have finally found a way into Fort Moose Meat. They must have chewed a hole in the moose hide liner.

I take out my Leatherman and open the serrated blade, cutting off the scales in long slices. They come off the frozen skin in big continuous flakes, like cutting sweet corn from the cob.

I'm unrealistically happy to be preparing this fish to eat, humming, smiling, and thinking about how good it will taste all fried in lard. The skin is almost bare of scales, and the white meat underneath is tantalizing. It's frozen in the shape of a half curl. It's beautiful, precious. If I weren't dehydrated, I'd be drooling.

Suddenly it dawns on me just how much I want this piece of fish. I want it an unhealthy amount. I'm holding on to the meal as if I'd give my life to defend it.

Suddenly in my mind, the sight of my slobbering desire juxtaposes with the images of children who have no food. Families in Afghanistan, kids hiding in holes dug throughout the jungles of Burma. People whose lives have been destroyed by war, and just as desperate as I am tonight for one hot meal. People who have nothing.

I'm one who has seen many of those hungry families, and in some small way I represent them. Here I am with possibly millions of people watching me drool over a meal of fresh fish that I'll fry and devour.

All at once my meal plan gets turned upside down. I can't just sit here and eat without representing those children who will eat nothing today. At the very least, I have to represent them to God. I'm going to use this fish as a spectacle, an offering of sorts. Instead of eating the whole thing, I'm going to try to raise awareness from viewers and compassion from God.

Just the thought of this hurts. I don't want to lose the calories from this meal. What good will it do anyways? I can't email this fish to a starving kid through my prayer. It's just going to be wasted. But I know what I have to do.

Taking the fish, and still struggling in my spirit with hunger and desire, I grab the cameras and go out into the meadow. An upturned driftwood stump sits there, and it's a place where I like to rest and look at the sky.

Stomping the snow in a little area where I can stand and set up the camera, I make sure that my face isn't blackened and my nose isn't running—two things that happen a lot.

Placing the chunk of fish on the stump, I look at the camera and explain about the situation going on in places like Afghanistan, where religious zealots are causing starvation and death. I hate religion that does those things. I talk about Burma, where the world's longest running civil war is still dragging on and on.

"That war has been going on for, what, seventy-eight years I think?" I'm pretty sure the number is right. "And this is day seventy-eight of *Alone*." That connection dawns on me and feels poetic.

Then I raise my hands and pray. I pray that God will look down on those two countries that are so torn and ravaged by war. That He will listen to the cries of every kid who is calling for food, and that He will make sure every one of them has a hot meal. Anything. A potato, a lizard, anything. Just a hot meal, and one that comes straight from God's hand.

I'm a nobody. I'm not a very righteous person. I'm not a shining example of humanity. I'm not very religious. But since in some way God has showed that He sees and hears me, I'm happy to hurl the poorly-worded prayer at the sky and let go.

I understand that this paltry sign of a chunk of fish isn't going to stop the civil war in Burma or free Afghanistan from its chokehold of terror. But if even one kid gets a hot meal who would otherwise have gone hungry, it will be well worth the hunger I may feel tonight.

And then there's the audience that could be watching. If people were to feel motivated through this spectacle I'm presenting, more hands might be there to carry food someday, meeting the needs

I'm praying for in a very tangible way. That thought sparkles in my mind.

Walking away from the stump and leaving the fish there, I feel happier than I expected. The fish is a sign: a sign to the world that we can't ignore the oppressed, and a sign to God that there are still children out there who need His love to wipe away their fear and sufferings. But I realize later that more than any of those things, it's a sign for me. It has showed me what I truly want to live for. As I sit hungrily beside my fire, I feel something I've wanted so badly: conviction. I have conviction that there's a path for me, there's something worth living for even if it means hardship again. I've come full circle.

I'm happy just picturing myself sitting in a distant village among a gaggle of kids or in a camp full of refugees. I want to be where I feel useful, where people are suffering and I can help. This dream feels so right, and understanding dawns on me that I never wanted to leave that work anyways. I just needed a break.

As my fire dwindles and my pot of water nears a boil, I realize that I'm ready for life again. I believe I can do it better than before, balancing family life more sustainably and with the right mindset. I want to get on with it.

Chapter 20

The Deadly Cold

*   *   *

*"The pathway to what's most real is in the hardest things
that you can do." -Jordan Peterson*

The cold is razor-edged. After two days of intense wind, the
sky is perfectly clear again, and the open atmosphere releases any la-
tent warmth from the landscape. The stab of winter drives deeper
than I've ever felt it.

This temperature drop is the real deal. It's what I've been
waiting on. I have no idea what the actual degree reading is, but I
know for sure that it's far below zero. My breath freezes in my
whiskers instantly; just minutes outside covers my face with a thick
white mask of ice. Frostbite has nipped my feet in two tiny spots. I
have to be careful with every act and with every piece of gear. I need
to keep my life-support systems of fire and hydration in flawless
condition. But I'm happy. If I make it through this cold snap, I'll be
able to say that I've done *Alone*. I've survived the Arctic.

Day 79

The hare that hopped into my camp yesterday is dead. I've caught it in one of my newly-set snares, and I couldn't be happier.

"This is amazing! Food coming right through camp!" I unwind the snare and lift the hare. It's a big one.

"Now I won't see hare tracks again for a couple weeks, if past experience means anything. But today I will feast!"

I know it will be Thanksgiving soon, and I should be able to figure out the date, but my mind gets lost every time I try to think through the math. Thinking about my wife and kids celebrating Thanksgiving alone is a difficult thing to face. What will she be doing? Will she travel to see family or hide out at home with the boys and wish I was there? Will she be upset, having expected me to be home by this time? We hadn't even talked about Thanksgiving, so I have no idea where she will be. I know she'll be missing me though.

Although these thoughts nearly make me sick, I'd like to have some kind of feast around Thanksgiving time.

Today I remember my most meager Thanksgiving feast ever. I was working on a project in India, and our group was so busy that none of us remembered it was Thanksgiving Day until one of the women broke out a special bag with a few goodies. Inside was a stick of gum and a jolly rancher for each person. That Thanksgiving meal was truly meager, but it reminded us what the day was all about. The candy was something from home too, and we all felt so happy. It was a real Thanksgiving feeling, the small treats paying tribute to the pilgrims with their five kernels of corn.

I think our hearts are most thankful and happy during times when we have the least. I'm finding that to be true here on Alone, and I treasure it. But I'm also glad I have more than a stick of gum and a jolly rancher to eat. I'll have real meat for Thanksgiving.

I skin the hare and cut it in half, stashing its back end in my food cache and putting its front end along with its head and all of its

368

organs into my cooking pot for lunch. Moose jerky is good, but fresh meat is so much better.

One of those things I've wanted to do while alone is to spend an entire day praying, and only for my family. So I take the whole day to ask my most important requests for my wife and kids.

From the time I light my morning fire until I go to bed, I pray for the three people that make up my world: Cara, Levi and Elliot, and I even include the possible fourth family member—the new baby I've begun longing for.

I also pray for a path for our family to follow. After all of the stress and trials, I'm ready to move forward again.

"God, show me the way. Show me the trail you've marked down for us—a path that leads to good."

Without a doubt, I know that God is listening as my heart requests come pouring out.

Day 80

"Ok, it's actually dangerous now," I tell the camera as I record myself getting wood. The air is freakishly cold—so frigid that as I break a handful of sticks, the branches *ping* like bits of tempered glass.

"This is the real Arctic! Ignore all the times I've said that before."

Absolutely no margin for error exists for me in this weather. If anything at all goes wrong, I'll freeze to death.

"How did I last through the night?" I wonder silently as I collect kindling. I had been unable to stay warm in my sleeping bag before, and now that it's colder I could so easily lose my feet to frostbite.

"Thank God for moose lard!" I muse, knowing that drinking the oil is what's keeping me well. "I'm alive and well! Ha! I can do this!"

My elation only lasts for a minute though, as I remember that soon I'll be out of lard, and what will happen to my circulation when I'm eating just lean, dried moose meat? I don't know. When all else fails, I can sit up all night throwing logs on the fire. I'll do whatever it takes. But at least for today, I'm doing great.

Day eighty is a huge milestone for me, a point I wasn't sure I could reach. But as the day passes it feels just like any other day, except for a growing feeling deep within me that says this adventure won't last forever. It will be gone soon, and I'll be somewhere else in the world looking back and wishing I could see my land again.

"I'm really going to miss all this some day," I murmur to the trees and snow.

Knowing that I'll long for this place and for all the peace and meaning it has brought to me, I tune out the biting cold and try to enjoy the hardship of this soul-devouring isolation.

"How do I preserve this?" I begin asking. "What can I do to lock this inside myself so that it can't be lost?"

It's still early but the light is fading, and I wander far out into the meadow. The snow is so deep that I struggle, almost swimming to get through it. Eventually I find myself in the center of the lake. From here I can see every point of land that defines an adventure I've had. I spot a clump of willows protruding from the snow: the place where my moose stopped and I shot him. There is the willow break where he fell. A leaning spruce tree points to where the grizzly ate the moose bones, and where I took them back to make fish hooks. To my left are the willows where I keep finding shed antlers, the ones I made my guitar from. Ahead is where I caught a few hares when I needed the encouragement most.

I'm soaking it all in, preserving it, and I decide to do this every day until I leave, knowing that once I say goodbye I'll never see any of this again. Even though I'm hungry and I long to see my wife and kids, I'm satisfied in a way I have never felt. The pain and exhaustion are okay, because they are just the price of the magic moments.

There are magic moments in life, times that glow like embers in our memory. They are the moments we treasure more than gold, the ones that define whole periods of time, setting the tone for months or years as we look back in remembrance. Like a gilded cover for the dry pages of our book of memory, they are where the beauty is found.

But there surely is a price, a fee paid in suffering to reach those moments. Because the magic moments don't happen while we walk a tranquil path of ease. They only come with a cost, in a setting of suffering, pain, or endurance. The magic moments are just like gems hidden in a mountain of torturous stone. And the digging for them is the price.

Here in the Arctic, I have had to chip my way through layers of adamant stones, the difficulties of solitude and hardship. But it's well worth it because of the gems, the moments like this one.

For a long time I stand on the lake, then turning to leave I spot a long line of tracks in the deep snow. Two moose crossed my lake here within the past day. Like a wolf, I feel a deep urge to lock onto their tracks and follow relentlessly until I kill them. I wish that today, day eighty, was like a level where a second moose tag could be unlocked. If it were, I'd hunt again. But instead I head back to my shelter and build up a fire to eat and drink by.

The passing of day eighty leaves me filled with confidence. I'm living through the deadly cold.

Day 81

A conflict rages inside me today, about the single frozen fish I have saved. A dream has slowly formed in my mind: the dream of cooking for my wife if she meets me out here. I want to bring her into my shelter and sit with her while I fry a fish and then we'll eat it together. It will be a rite of passage into the future. She will see me cook, and she will be amazed. If I can just save one big chunk of fish and some lard, I'll make her the most delicious meal she's ever had. We'll fly back to civilization with full bellies.

That's the plan I've been harboring in my mind. But my stomach is arguing with my brain now, and it wants that piece of fish.

"Save it. Save it," I chant to myself as I work. "It will be so thrilling to eat it with Cara." But as soon as those words are out of my mouth, another conviction seizes me and I'm chanting "Eat it! Eat it! She probably wants me to eat it more that she wants to share a meal in my camp."

So I decide I'll eat the fish, but in the next moment my decision seems selfish so I decide not to eat it. I'll save it for Cara. She'll really love it. But then again, I can't meet her here if I starve, so I'll eat it. All day long I go back and forth, eventually eating the fish, and finding that I have a lot more lard left that I thought. It will last at least another week.

Day 82

Winning is within reach. I know that now. But something strange is happening to me, something I could never have foreseen. I seem to be splitting into two different people, with two different dreams for life.

The Timber who arrived in the arctic is so focused on winning this competition that nothing else matters. But a second voice has begun arguing inside me. The second voice is the one who is looking ahead, thinking about life beyond the show.

"What should my life look like after this?" The voice asks me. Today, for the first time, I face the voice and try to answer.

"Well, it's going to be great. If I win, I'll have all the money I need to do mission projects for a while. More importantly, I'll be taken seriously, as the person who stood the longest on *Alone*."

"And do you really need those things to be satisfied?" The voice replies.

"Yes I do," I answer earnestly, but even as I say the words I understand that I don't need anything. I've been fulfilled in the deepest way ever since God brought peace to my soul here. No reputation or prize can make me more exactly what I'm meant to be. Seeing God feed me every day has brought the best life I've ever known, and so I don't *have* to have the money either.

"So why are you going to win?" the new voice persists.

This question is easy to answer. "I'm going to win because I want to finish this thing completely. I don't want to ever look back over my shoulder and say, 'Man, what if I had kept going?'"

Inwardly, I have suffered so deeply from unfinished work and unreached goals. In every effort I've been involved with, I've given literally everything, dedicating my body, mind, and soul to see them done. Yet so many haven't worked out, haven't come to fruition. Those loose ends and unrealized dreams have become thorns that tear at my soul.

"I can't let this journey be that way. I can't let this end in regret."

Then the new voice asks something I've never dreamed of: "And what if you look back and say, 'Man, I wish I had thought this through. I regret winning this money'?"

"What?" I ask myself. "Regret winning?" This question seems preposterous. "Think of all I would gain!"

There is so much to gain by winning. But would it actually lead to the life I want?

I roll back through all of the plans I've made while lying in my sleeping bag, enduring the darkness day after day. Every dream I have dreamed sees me back in aid work, helping in war zones and doing it all with my family at my side. I want that life. I *have* to be doing that. And if I win, I'll gain the money to do it more easily.

"And if you win, what will you lose?" the new voice asks.

Like an axe to my head, the truth dawns on me, and I know what I'll lose if I win this show. I'll surely lose the ability to be just a person, just Timber, not only to my friends, but also to the poor and hurting people I like to be among. I'll be Timber the rich man, and if I become that, then nothing would be right for me.

The argument inside me goes on and on all day, the two voices pulling at me in different directions.

"This show is my legacy," says the first voice. "I'll never walk away from this."

"If you can't walk away from this, you'll screw up. You'll change the path of your life, and it won't lead you to your heart's desire."

"But I'll never find peace or happiness without winning."

Then the second voice calmly persists, "Follow me, and I will bring you real peace."

"But if I don't have this, I've got nothing."

"You already have everything."

As this infernal argument rages within me, I begin to recognize the voices for what they are. There is me, of course. I'm the man who came here desperate for some light on my path, for a fresh start. When I arrived, I had been broken down by death and trials. Broken Timber says, "If I don't win this show, I'm nothing."

The second voice is the person who has been called out from within me, renewed and whole. He is the voice of peace, freedom, and wellness. He's the man I've been so happy to become—the one who doesn't fear anyone's judgment, because God has already judged him, and found him enough. It's the voice of Timber the Satisfied.

As this argument splits me in two, the incredible peace I've found is vanishing. I need that peace to return so badly. I don't want to be conflicted. Which man am I supposed to be? Which path leads to peace? Which person should I become and hold onto forever?

It hurts as I realize that what I really want is the path of Broken Timber—staying and trying to win, no matter the cost I'll suffer later. But if I choose that path, will I be rejecting the peace and satisfaction that this journey has brought me? Will I never see Satisfied Timber again?

Imagining the loss of my soul's satisfaction scares me, and I make a quick resolution to end the debate. So I grab the satellite phone and walk to the meadow where it will establish a connection, and I start dialing. Making myself do this is like cutting off my own hands. The buttons burn me like fire as I touch them.

With a huge effort, I force my finger to hit the send button, but panic seizes me and I quickly hang up. The call didn't go through, and I breathe a long, heavy sigh of relief.

I can't make myself go through with the decision. Something just isn't right. Maybe I haven't thought everything through, or maybe I'm just not ready to take the path of the satisfied voice. I want to win so badly that being on the verge of giving it up felt like actually dying.

In a burst of frustrated energy, I seize my axe, snare wire, and multitool. Hurrying out on the trail, I search until at long last I find one set of hare tracks and I set up snare after snare. The further I go, I notice more fresh sign and find that winter weather is pushing animals into my territory from the higher ground to the north-east.

With fresh hope and a silent smile, I set out a long snare line, knowing that I'll have a good shot at adding fresh meat to my dried jerky by morning.

As I set snares and then chop a big supply of firewood, I feel that I'm breaking through a layer of resistance that has stood between me and complete victory over any desire to avoid further frostbite, cold, and suffering. Setting out a brand new snare line and knowing that I've pushed through a real arctic cold spell, I feel absolute victory within reach. But the victory seems hollow as I feel the voice of Satisfied Timber growing distant, taking a different path.

"Right now is the time to ignore everything except winning" —Broken Timber's voice is strong and loud. "I'll stay here at any cost. I will not listen to this argument."

Through force of will, I have silenced the voice of the satisfied person. I'm good to go. Nothing matters as much as winning. I will try to be the last man standing in the Arctic, because I *can*.

I know I can make it for as long as I want. I'll make skis that will help me travel further in the deep snow. I'll go over every inch of my territory looking for hares. And each day I'll fill my belly with jerky, even though my gums are sore and bleeding. I still have a lot of jerky.

Suddenly, the one hundred day mark seems not only doable, but almost done. There is no question that I can make it. No fear of freezing or starving is left in my heart. Nothing in me wants to escape this. I feel like I've transcended.

Cooking half a hare for supper, I enjoy a warm meal. The meat is tender and easy to chew, the broth so warm and nutrient-filled. But my soul has no peace.

Night 82

"Nothing is the same now," I admit to myself hours later as I hunker down in my sleeping bag, drawstring pulled tight and only my nose touching the cold air.

The day's internal argument has shown me that I've come to a fork in the road that cannot be ignored. The money really *could* change my life, both positively and negatively.

"Don't worry about it," I tell myself. "Just give the money away."

"The money isn't the problem," says Satisfied Timber. And I slowly come to see his point. The identity of "Timber the rich man" would remain with me, forever defining me to all those who can't even imagine how much half a million dollars is. Those are the people I love, and slowly that distance between me and them would kill me.

A choice lies before me now, where yesterday there was only *Alone*. Two paths diverge here; I have to pick one path to live with for the rest of my life. This is what the voice inside me has been saying: "Think this through. You really want to consider where your path will lead."

I never imagined this struggle, and it's overwhelming. With screams of frustration, I wallow in my sleeping bag. The night is so long.

Why, why, why am I so conflicted? Why can't I just believe that I can win *and* have the life I want to live, unaffected by the stigma of money?

The reality of the two voices goes on and on, and even though I wish with tears that these two halves of me could take one path, it's clear that they can't. Choosing which voice to follow is becoming the most excruciating decision I've ever faced.

I wish there was just one person to talk with. Being alone in such turmoil is beyond painful. Crying out to the only one I can reach, I pray, "God, help me! Make this choice for me!"

The Arctic has taught me that God speaks in silence, and after hours of weeping and struggling, I fall silent. Then I understand what God would say.

"You choose. I'll listen and love you through either choice. I have given you freedom in your soul. Now the decision is yours."

Thinking about God's voice cuts through my darkness, and a verse comes to mind: "Consider Jesus, who, for the joy that was set before him, endured the cross, not regarding the shame."

This verse is dear to me, and it has guided me to the right path before. I'll use it as my guide. And so I ask myself, "What joy was set before Jesus?"

I know the answer well. We mortals are the joy that he wanted more than life. The joy of calling us back from darkness, freeing us from fear and slavery, was enough to carry him through the endurance of pain, and through the shame of losing his life.

"What is the joy out there in front of me? What is the greatest prize *I* see ahead?"

The answer comes ringing back as clearly as a tolling bell. The satisfied voice tells me "The greatest joy is to do what's best for others, not for yourself."

Survival is all about doing what's best for ourselves. I have survived, and done it well. I have won my battles. But the ultimate joy of the human life is not survival…it's love.

Love, not winning, is where I'll find my greatest joy. If I believe that winning could hurt any relationship I care about, then the choice is simple. I know what I have to do. I know which voice I will follow.

The realization that I'm going to end my contest, that I won't win, feels like drowning in ice water. My heart skips and throbs, I can hardly catch my breath. I've been given the gift of choice, but the price I'll have to pay is letting go of my dream. I won't be the last man standing.

I ask God for one final proof: "God, if I'm making the right choice, give me peace. Give me sleep."

Sleep comes very difficult when you're nothing but bones and you lie for 18 or 19 hours straight in your sleeping bag trying to just stave off frost bite. But I suddenly fall asleep and must have slept for a couple of hours when I wake up with such peace as I have never known. I know the choice is easy: I would rather have the life God is drawing me toward than to win, and I'm ready to go live that life now. I have chosen a path.

Yes, I want to be known as the last man in the Arctic. But now I don't need any prop for my identity. My person is complete in God, secure in Jesus. I don't need any validation or applause from people to make me satisfied. I am already satisfied. I am Timber the Satisfied.

Chapter 21

Choosing a Path

*　　　*　　　*

Two roads diverged in a yellow wood
And sorry I could not travel both
And be one traveller, long I stood
And looked down one as far as I could
To where it bent in the undergrowth.
- Robert Frost, "The Road Not Taken"

Day 83

　　The world is still pitch dark when I make myself get out of the sleeping back and run my snare line. One by one, I find my newly-set snares, and in the darkness I take them all down. This process should hurt, but it doesn't.

　　"I am Timber the Satisfied," I say to myself, and I like the sound of it so much that it makes me smile. The peace of my whole journey comes back to my soul like warm coffee. "I am Timber the Satisfied."

　　In a few minutes I'm back in my shelter building a fire and heating some water to drink. Silently I work, unwilling to say anything to the camera. My thoughts are too private for discussion, but my smile is deep and real.

As my water boils, I chew pieces of dried fish. Several strips of fish are greasy with delicious oil, and although chewing brings horrible pain to my gums, the savory taste is worth the pain. For a long time I just sit and eat, taking occasional sips of steaming water. It feels very luxurious.

Eventually I break the silence. "Okay, I've made a big decision," I tell the camera. "One that's going to set the course of my life for better or worse."

I can't say more; there's nothing to say. But I know that anyone viewing this will understand that I'm leaving today.

Because the sky won't lighten until noon, I have to keep myself occupied. Another boiled pot of spruce tips, one more wash for my tangled hair. I let my moppy hair drip-dry in the warmth of my shelter and try to comb out the tangles with my fingers.

At last the sky begins to brighten; after poking my head out the door, I know that my time has come. Gathering the cameras, microphone, and satellite phone, I trudge down to the edge of the meadow. Operating the camera gear is so familiar that I don't even have to think about it as I set up the tripod and test the audio.

"Okay, this is the path I've chosen, and I want to say that I'm as happy as can be."

With a confident smile, I press send, and the phone connects right away. This time no burning sensation hurts my fingers, and no panic wells up within me. It just feels... *right*.

The phone rings and I say the words I thought I could never say: "I'm tapping out." The phrase should hurt me, but the peace I feel within me overcomes all the doubt. Seeing into the future, I know I'll watch this moment with my sons and I will not be ashamed. Nothing has defeated me, and I'm not leaving because I can't go on. I *can* go on—on and on.

I'll be proud as I tell my two boys why I am doing this, why I'm leaving just short of the finish line. Because I believe that I'm reaching for a higher prize. I'm seeing the finish line, but choosing a different path.

A blizzard of icy crystals envelopes me as the helicopter settles into the deep snow; its engine whines and the rotor blades spool down and come to a stop. The producer and camera crew disembark and tramp through the meadow to where I'm waiting for them in front of Fort Moose Head.

Greeting them with a smile, I give the speech I prepared during the morning hours. It's a pitiful attempt to explain my decision, careful not to mention the part where I don't want to be known as "Timber the rich guy." That, my biggest reason, is too private.

- - -

"Whoever else is out here and I could easily go past one-hundred days. The Arctic is not too much for me. I'm not being forced out by anything. I'm not beaten, or too hungry to go on. I've met every challenge and answered them all.

Now each day that passes begins to feel pointless. I don't want all this to get lost in pointlessness because it's too special for that. God has renewed my soul and spirit and I just feel a desire again to start living the life I love, going to crazy places to minister to the needy.

So I'm ready to go. I only hope that my journey has been fun to watch and that I've left a trail of love from God that someone will find hope in. If I have, that's prize money enough for me."

- - -

Directly afterward the producer asks a thousand questions that poke and pry at me from every angle, and the camera captures my struggle to stay true to the core of my tap-out reasons. In the end, it seems irrelevant to have even prepared a speech at all.

For another hour we film scenes of me packing up, saying goodbye to Fort Moose Head, and carrying my pack out into the meadow toward the helicopter.

The distraction of filming helps keep my mind off the fact that my journey on *Alone* has just ended. But as I sit in a bubble of noise-induced solitude aboard the helicopter, it all sinks in. I know that it is over.

After being isolated for so long, the feeling of the helicopter vibrating around me is over-stimulating. Mentally it puts me right back on that rumbling train ride as I left Ukraine with crowds of refugees. I'm again inside a mass of shuddering metal, staring out though a plexiglass window at a pristine landscape.

The chopper lifts and I'm surprised to find myself still smiling as I see the home I've built become a shrinking picture below me. My shelter is directly beneath us, and I can still see the antlers of my moose all draped in snow. The trees that conceal my food cache pass by below. There is the swath of ice marking my fishing ground. The path I made to the lake shrinks as we rise. I see those moose tracks I would have followed, and from this altitude they run like long, shadowy lines across the land and into the future.

"I would have followed those tracks to the end," I think. "But what does the future hold for me now?"

How can I leave this place that has meant life and peace to my soul? The home falling behind me is tearing part of my heart out with it as it shrinks. I will miss it all like a lost love, but I'm leaving. With my own hand, I've severed the silver cord to one of the greatest dream goals of my life. The emotional pull is too much, and the vista blurs as tears rise unbidden to my eyes. Staring up at the ceiling of the chopper, I weep silently.

"God, save me from regret. God, save me from regret."

After mouthing the words for a full minute, a smile returns to my face and I'm grinning through hot tears. It's okay. I did it. I did everything. And God was with me.

"Thank you, God!" I breathe with all the strength of my soul.

The frozen land slips by, just like the vision from the refugee train. But this time I see no war, no strife. No broken refugee families are here, carrying memories of death. All is peace. I'm happy—so happy and well. This life, all of this, is exactly what I had longed for.

I'm leaving this place of incredible peace, and in a way, I'll be the homeless refugee for the rest of my life. *But better than peace is a path, and I have found my path again.*

As the helicopter settles into base camp, I steel my mind to greet the real world—the world of humans. "I'll have to explain my decision to Cara over the phone," I begin telling myself. This will be the hard part.

A small crowd of crew waits in welcome, and the intense colors of their clothing dazzle my eyes. After such a long absence of color, the reds, blues, and oranges of their winter gear are so bright that I stagger a bit and have to look down at the snow.

"Hey, I've got a little surprise for you, Timber," I vaguely hear a producer say. I imagine that he's got a chocolate chip cookie or something. I decide it's not important, and I'm reaching out my hand to greet a crew member, when suddenly I see a familiar person is standing in front of me. It's a person I should recognize, with her smile that beams pure starlight, her eyes shining and her beautiful, blonde hair streaming out from under a cute hat.

I don't know if it takes a nano-second or a year for me to process the vision, but I suddenly recognize Cara! It's my wife! And she's right in front of me! The clash of reality with dream is so intense that I stagger and blink. "How is she here? What trick is this? Am I even awake?"

The crew never brings in a loved one until after the win. I haven't won, but here stands a literal piece of my soul, and so beautiful! She's beaming at me through tears and I think my heart might erupt like a volcano as we fall into each other's arms. She's here for real. I don't think we've ever clung to one another more desperately, like holding on for my very life's breath. And in this moment I know: God has taken a master stroke with His paint brush and swiped a beautiful image over the painful spot where I feel loss. His brush stroke says, "I see you. I love you. I will be with you forever."

This one act of bringing Cara to the Arctic fully confirms my heart in the choice I've made. As Cara and I talk about the life that has transpired while we've been apart, many things come up which I realize only God could have done.

Seeing my wife today reinforces a truth that has slowly revealed itself to me: survival is not the ultimate goal of life, or the high-water mark of the human experience. No matter how good you are at "survival," there comes a time when you ask yourself the question, "What am I surviving *for?*"

Shakespeare said, "The meaning of life is to find your gift. The purpose of life is to give it away." We need something to survive for, someone to share it with—because every trial is meaningless unless it is shared by someone, and all success is hollow until given away. I have been surviving pretty successfully. As the medic checks me over today and takes my vital signs, he's impressed by how healthy I am. It turns out that I've actually gained a few pounds during the past week: not an easy feat in the frozen wild lands.

Another crew member begins to tally my kills and catches, preparing the details for the Fish and Game department. I've caught fifty-two fish, killed a twelve-hundred pound moose, and taken numerous squirrels and hares.

I've been very successful. But all the success is empty without an object, and I understand now: the high-water mark of the human experience is love.

Day 84

"Bless the Lord, oh my soul. And all that is within me, bless his holy name."

In the darkness of my first morning at basecamp, I begin the day with the same psalm I've used for the past fifteen mornings to get myself out of bed.

Waking up in the warmth of a recovery tent is comfort like I've never felt before. The automatic heat and the light that comes on when I pull a string, all of it feels unreal and luxurious.

I've been unable to sleep because my brain wanted to check on my feet all night long, just to make sure they aren't getting frostbitten. My wife is still here in camp, and I wait all night for her to wake up and come to my recovery tent, almost beside myself to just stare at her face and hear her voice.

To pass time, I look up the Russian word for mustard, still bothered that I can't remember. It's *gorchitsa*. I was *so close*! And now I can put that irritating memory gap to rest.

The camp staff will be coming soon to check on me and bring a tiny breakfast. I'm supposed to eat only what they provide, hoping that I can avoid any sickness from over-eating. But I have a couple of big chunks of moose lard in my pack, and I compulsively start biting pieces off and letting them melt in my mouth.

You might think that I'd kick myself on day eighty-four, that I'd wake up and realize that I really *do* want the money. You may wonder if I constantly ask myself, "What if I had just waited another day?" You may think I'd wrestle with regret and wish I had made a different choice. But that hasn't happened. After a few months at home now as I write this, I understand that my conclusion would have remained the same no matter how many days I wrestled with the choice of leaving. So then, why should I and whoever else remains out here miss Christmas?

And I'm wealthy too. Though everything I have is intangible, I am very rich. In fact, I may be the richest man alive. The beautiful woman who calls herself mine and the two incredible boys she has given me are enough to make the wealthiest palace look like nothing to me. I've experienced actual love. On top of that, I've lived a life filled with adventure that I never could have dreamed of.

I've also gotten everything I needed from the arctic. Where a dead spot was growing in my soul, now only life springs up. Just as I wished back on that train to nowhere, when I sat among a crowd of refugees and saw the woodland passing by, I have rushed out into the forest and forgot the world that was. I lost myself and became one of the creatures who belong. Though my thirst for the wilderness isn't quenched, I've drunk as deeply as a human being can drink.

The greatest richness of all is the fact that God walks beside me. The Creator sees my deeds and hears the words I say. I can't describe how valuable that seems to me. It's more precious than gold.

Epilogue

*   *   *

"The price of anything is the amount of life you give in exchange for it." -Seneca

"How was your trip?"

I face this question often, usually after I've returned from some life-altering thing like a year-long stint in some conflict zone. It's a hard question to answer, as folks don't usually want a long reply. They're looking for a three or four-sentence summary, a concise and positive report like, "Yeah, it was great. I'm doing well, and I'm glad to be home."

My personal view is that whenever a trip is three months or longer, it stops being a trip and becomes a life. How can you answer the question "How was your trip?" when in your head you hear "How was your life?" So how *was* your life? Try to answer *that* in three or four sentences!

Alone became a life for me. After months in the Arctic, I had established a life of my own, completely crafted to the specifications of a dream—a dream I thought I may never realize.

Letting something like that fade into the distance as you walk away from it is more than difficult. Whenever an experience is so overwhelming or life-altering, it's impossible to let it slip silently into the past and march onward, keeping pace with time. It's like an amazing sunset that you keep staring at even after it vanishes. How can I make myself look forward when what I've left behind is so big, so beautiful, and so much a part of me now?

True beauty cannot be captured or related, only enjoyed. Like taking a picture of a sunset, the experience is too magnificent to appreciate unless you're right there.

What is so magnificent about the sunset? Is it the colors? Yes. Is it the vibrance of the light? Yes. Is it the backdrop of the surrounding sky? Yes. The magnificence is all of those, but so much more. The real beauty lies in something that cannot be explained. A sunset will never be perfectly captured, and that fact somehow makes it even more beautiful. You just have to be there.

Alone was like that for me: something too beautiful to relate. I've done my best by filming and writing, but it can't really be captured. And because it can't be captured, I worry that I'll forget.

I may forget little details, like the smell of alder-smoked meat, and I may lose the memories of what catching a pike felt like. But I'll never forget the ways that *Alone* changed me.

Alone did change me profoundly. I found that I have so much to learn, and I should be learning every day. I'm quieter now, and I love the sound of silence. Being more thankful and happier, those things are part of me now. I've learned to live in the moment and enjoy the small things, even cooking. Taking one day at a time is easier, and I'm more patient. I talk to God a lot now, and I love hunting and wilderness living more than ever before. My vestigial tail might have grown a couple of inches as I became a wildman. But I think most of all, I'm satisfied. I don't need any validation. I don't need any success. At my core, I'm simply satisfied that God walked with me.

Though it's too much to ask anyone to fully grasp the journey and how deeply it affects you, I'm lucky that my wife shared the whole thing. She drew the story of *Alone* out of me and cherished it, as she had shared it with me all along. She took on a lot of heavy burdens so that I could go and be wild, and she also likes the wild-man in me.

But for most conversations, it's okay to just scratch the surface and reply, "How was my trip? Hey, it was great. I loved it. I'd go back in an instant."

If you've made it to the end of this book, you've taken the time to see and understand the journey. And I hope that what interests you is not the quirkiness of my weird life or viewpoints, but the freedom I've found - the freedom that's helped me overcome lots of difficult and heartbreaking things.

Because freedom doesn't happen accidentally, I want to point you to the reality that set me free. It wasn't wild, carefree Arctic living: it was God. He is the great lover of freedom. He loves it so intensely that he doesn't intrude on our freedom or make our choices for us. He allows us to choose our own paths and set our own course. But if my life has taught me anything, it's that God always stands by wishing we'd choose the comprehensive freedom that only comes from him.

While we're running around doing our own things, we become slaves to things. We become slaves to fear: fear of being judged, fear of failure, or fear of regret. We find ourselves in bondage to survival, expectations, pain, and heartbreak. We serve the gods of remorse and regret for things we've done, people we've hurt.

We may try to free ourselves by simply refusing to care. But when life thins and breath fades, fear shows back up and we know that we're not free. Eternal freedom, freedom for the soul, is what I have found in God.

If you're stirred by the following words like I am, then let them speak freely to you:

"For God so loved the world, that he gave his only begotten son, that whosoever believes in him should not perish but have everlasting life."

"For God sent not his son into the world to condemn the world, but that the world through him might be saved."

"I am the way, the truth and the life. No man cometh to the father but by me."

"I am the resurrection and the life. He that believes in me, though he were dead, yet shall he live. And whosoever liveth and believeth in me shall never die. Believest thou this?"

"Therefore, being justified by faith, we have peace with God through our lord Jesus Christ."

"For he that comes to God must believe that he is, and that he is the rewarder of them that diligently seek him."

"For all who call upon the name of the Lord shall be saved."

"And let him that is athirst come. And whosoever will, let him drink of the fountain of the water of life freely."

These are some of the words that brought me out of real darkness, and believing them has saved and changed my life eternally. I hope that you see in them the light that I have found.

I also hope you've thoroughly enjoyed my journey through this book. The only thing left is for you to experience all the freedom and joy yourself. So go and find your freedom in all that's free. Drink from the well of eternal life found in Christ, and from the peace of the wilderness that God created. I hope that you will, as deeply and wholeheartedly as I got to!

And if you are one of my fellow contestants, then "Here's to us, the lucky few."

-Timber the Satisfied

Acknowledgements

I'd like to thank everyone who not only enabled me to compete on *Alone*, but has helped to shape me in life through their grace, love and friendship.

Most especially, I'd like to thank Cara, my wife and best friend, for taming my wild self just a little. Thank you for valuing the same things I do, and for setting a course with me through all the ups and downs of our wonderful and wild life. And thanks for keeping my fire burning at home while I was in the Arctic.

Thanks to Levi, my oldest son, for inspiring me to be stronger and kinder, and for single-handedly putting out the fire that burnt his shirt while I was gone on the show.

To Elliot, my youngest. Thank you for being so brave, and for cheering up your mother with hugs and kindness.

Thank you to my brother Jed, who came on short notice to help me get my gear together for the show.

I'd like to thank Adam Dufour, who has never failed to watch over the mess we leave behind in the states. You pick up the pieces and still eagerly wait to go fishing together every time I come home.

Thanks to Jacob and Rachel Dufour for a life-long friendship, and for helping me put this book together with cover design, edit suggestions and unwavering encouragement.

Thank you, Grayson and Julia, for working shoulder to shoulder with us and holding down the fort overseas. You share our values. You get beat up just like us, and heal back like gecko tails. You are our blood family.

Thank you to our friends Islom and Gulia for unwavering friendship, and for our home away from home.

Thanks to Barrie Greenfield, for visiting us in so many lonely places, and for sharing those incredible adventures in the Tak-lamakan Desert and Eastern Pamir. You're my long lost sister.

To Sky, my brother in arms, and a person I'd follow through fire and flood. Thanks for encouraging me to be open and honest about what has taken place in my life.

Marc Monte, thanks for having all the guys pray while I was gone, for being my biggest fan, and always having my back. You're there when I'm particularly stressed, and you've strengthened me more than tongue can tell.

Thank you Marnie and Jamie Bennett, for looking out for Cara while I was gone, and to Deitz and Lora Froehlich, for hosting a send-off party fit for a king.

And to the wonderful producers, safety team, survival experts, casting directors, editors, loggers, film crew, and the rest of the *Alone* production team: thank you for telling the stories well, and for presenting true glimpses of humanity to a jaded modern audience.

Most of all, thank you God for hearing my voice.

About the Author

Timber grew up off-grid, living in a remote patch of woods in southern Indiana. Raised with no modern conveniences, he learned survival skills in the most effective way possible - by living off the land. This taught him to have a resourceful spirit and resilient mind, along with a unique perspective on life.

In his professional life, Timber is a research linguist and humanitarian aid worker. His job has taken him all over the world and into all sorts of adventures in remote places and conflict zones. His fondest memories are of working in war zones to bring relief and help to civilians.

In his personal life, Timber is a survivalist, hunter, bush-crafter, songwriter, and all-around lover of life. But, most importantly, he's a husband, dad, and follower of Jesus.

Made in United States
Orlando, FL
26 November 2024

54513556R00246